WIPERS

Tim Carew, after what he describes as 'an
outstandingly undistinguished career' at
Marlborough, joined the Exeter City Police as
a cadet in 1938 and, two years later, enlisted in
the Royal Horse Guards. Subsequently he
became a corporal in the Parachute Regiment,
a lieutenant in the 3rd Gurkha Rifles and a
captain in the Devonshire Regiment. His
service took him to India, Burma (where he was
awarded the Military Cross), Java, Hong Kong,
Malaya, Eritrea and Egypt. He is the author of
several other books on military history.

'Tim Carew's book is really a history of the Old
Contemptibles – told in descriptive language
such as no regimental history that I have read
can approach. . . . An excellent memorial'
Books and Bookmen

'Vigorous . . . an almost rollicking zest'
Irish Press

'A powerful and moving picture of conditions
of soldiering and dying that were unknown in
the last war'
Sheffield Morning Telegraph

Wipers

Tim Carew

CORONET BOOKS
Hodder and Stoughton

First published in Great Britain 1974 by
Hamish Hamilton Limited

Photos: Imperial War Museum

Coronet Edition 1976

Printed and bound in Great Britain for
Coronet Books, Hodder and Stoughton, London
by Hazell Watson & Viney Ltd, Aylesbury, Bucks

SBN 0 340 19983 0

TO

THE IMMORTAL MEMORY

OF

THE MEN OF THE OLD ARMY

WHO SAVED ENGLAND

AUGUST–NOVEMBER 1914

PROLOGUE

THE Cavalry Club has changed but little in the past century because, as right-thinking cavalrymen will tell you austerely, there is nothing about it which needs to change.

Today, of course, the Club has a bar equipped with actual high, leather-topped stools: the Guards Club has installed a fruit machine, and if that can happen *anything* can happen, although the Cavalry Club has not yet acquired one. Behind this bar, dispensing the endless spate of dry sherry, gin and tonic, scotch and soda and, for the more extremist hangovers, 'horses' necks', is a tolerant club servant who has been there since 1924 and does not appreciate progress, although he puts a brave face on the contemplation of the 1970s – as indeed he has to. In his young days, cavalry officers did not sit swilling at the bar; they sat at ease in worn saddle-bag armchairs (many of the same ones are still there) and flapped a languid hand at a waiter—the pre-lunch or pre-dinner drink appeared on a silver salver and was acknowledged with the usual indecipherable signature, which a harassed steward strove to convert to currency at the end of the month.

Today there are mini-skirted waitresses in the dining-room, and a cornucopia of nylon thigh sometimes distracts youthful and not so youthful cavalrymen from the serious business of lunch. But in spite of all this wayward modernity the Cavalry Club remains traditional, serene, everlasting and remote— from the vantage point of its postal address, Number 126, Piccadilly, it is remote from the swirling traffic outside or the expense account luncheons in the Park Lane Hotel, and it commands a benign vista of Hyde Park.

In early December 1914, there strode through the patrician portals of the Cavalry Club a Lieutenant-Colonel, Commanding Officer of an ancient and illustrious British regiment of the Cavalry of the Line and at present on two weeks' home leave from Flanders.

He was in plain clothes, because uniform was rarely seen in

the Cavalry Club even in wartime. His suit was oldish but well cut—in 1914 the well-dressed gentleman wore clothes that were either old or new, but not in between; his collar was snowy white and very stiff, his tie a sombre grey embellished with a pearl pin; his black shoes bore the brilliant shine that only the older *genre* of soldier servant can produce without apparent effort; his 'hard hat' adorned a peg in the cloakroom. The Colonel entered the Cavalry Club in the same way as he had done scores of times since he was first gazetted as a pink-checked cornet, who rarely had to shave very seriously, in Queen Victoria's army in 1894. If the Cavalry Club had not changed appreciably in these twenty years, the Colonel had.

His hair and trim cavalry moustache were both plentifully streaked with grey; his eyes seemed very deep in their sockets and told of many recent nights without sleep. Although the Colonel had only recently celebrated his fortieth birthday (if a tot of issue rum out of an enamel mug can be termed a celebration), he looked ten years older.

He had had a busy morning: first, a call at the War Office, where he had been received with unexpected affability by a major-general. The Colonel, well acquainted with the mercurial temperaments of generals, had been pleasantly surprised, for this particular one had hinted guardedly—no guarantees, mind you—that it was quite on the cards that he might be given command of a brigade in the near future: not a regular cavalry brigade, of course—that would be too much to hope for at the comparatively immature age of forty, with the substantive rank of only major. But Kitchener's New Armies were being formed and they would need experienced fighting men in command. Well satisfied with his meeting with the Major-General, the Colonel, without qualms of conscience or feelings of shame, treated himself to a double whisky and soda in the Silver Cross tavern which stands just opposite Horse Guards. In normal circumstances the Colonel would have deplored such an action, which he associated with temporary officers in the South African War. But on this particular day circumstances did not seem to be entirely normal; after all, one was not considered for promotion to brigadier-general every day of the week.

Next a visit to his military tailor. The elderly attendant, who had known the Colonel as a young subaltern before the South African War, asked him almost coyly if the new tunic should be embellished with the red tabs of a brigadier-general. The Colonel almost said yes, but decided that such an action savoured of 'jumping the gun', and he would feel a double-dyed idiot if he were not confirmed in a brigade command and had to have them removed. He did, however, make one order which gave him an almost boyish feeling of pride: the three stained and fraying medal ribbons on his old mud-bespattered tunic were hardly recognisable as the crimson and blue of the Distinguished Service Order and the two South African War medals. The Colonel ordered a new set with one tiny addition: a small silver rosette, indicating that he had been awarded a bar to the D.S.O. which he had won as a subaltern in South Africa.

The Colonel felt well pleased with his morning. The Club seemed, as always, serene and everlasting and the pictures were just as he had remembered them for the past twenty years: Prince Rupert's last charge at Edgehill, the 21st Lancers (with the not inconsiderable addition of Winston Churchill) charging at Omdurman, the charge at Klip Drift; the 1st Marquess of Anglesey and the Duke of Wellington seemed to eye the Colonel with approval from their hallowed positions on the wall downstairs.

The Colonel lingered awhile as he contemplated yet another picture—that of Captain Oates, formerly of the 5th Royal Inniskilling Dragoon Guards, who had staggered out to die in the wastes of the Antarctic in 1912; the Colonel had known Oates well, and in the spacious pre-war years had ridden against him at polo. A fairish player, Oates, conceded the Colonel generously, even if he did have a tendency to swipe at the ball in front of an open goal when a gentle tap would have been adequate.

A good death, Oates's, thought the Colonel, who had seen many men die in the past three months: he had seen them die quickly and cleanly from a bullet through brain or heart; he had seen them die quietly and uncomplainingly from shrapnel wounds; he had seen and heard men die querulously and

blasphemously from fearful cavernous wounds in the abdomen
—on more than one sleepless night during his leave he had
heard their pain-extorted ravings again. Death had come in
many guises in the first three months of the Great War and the
Colonel had seen them all.

By 12.30 p.m. the Colonel was very ready for a drink and
went into the smoking-room; here, too, nothing had changed
—the same worn saddle-bag leather armchairs and the same
ancient servants : the steward, who bore a visibly shaking silver
salver holding the large gin and angostura that the occasion
demanded, was, by the Colonel's attentive reckoning, nearing
his century. But then, of course, the servants at the Cavalry
Club had always been old; the great-great-grandfather of the
oldest living servant, whose province was the washroom, had
allegedly blacked the Young Pretender's boots—and the
Colonel could well believe it.

There were many other old men besides the servants in the
Club on this day, the Colonel noticed as he sipped his drink
and smoked a cigar : they had all long since retired from
lancer, dragoon and hussar regiments, but they all knew 'a
chap at the War House' and were determined somehow or
other to get back into the service again. The 'chaps at the
War House' received the old gentlemen with the patience and
courtesy due to such august old warriors and cursed them
roundly after they had gone; they were snowed under with
work, trying to mould new armies to fight a war which, contrary to early expectations, was not only going to last for
months, but years.

The old gentlemen longed to ride into action again, with
lance and sabre to the sweet note of the trumpet; they had
charged Zulus in 1879, Egyptians in 1882, the Kaleifa's dervishes in 1898 and Boers in 1899. The oldest of them, a
veteran of the Indian Mutiny, had said in his letter to the War
Office 'although nearing 70 [he was in fact 81] I am still in
possession of many of my faculties and feel fully capable of
leading troops in the field'.

One of them had served with the Colonel in the late 1890s;
he had been a major when the Colonel had joined as a brand-
new cornet, and naturally could not think of him as anything

else. He immediately bombarded the Colonel with questions about the Regiment's recent activities in France.

In the Second World War, the Korean war and a dozen 'confrontations' since there have been war correspondents everywhere, fiercely dedicated to delivering breakfast-table shellshock to every home in Britain.

They have shared billets with staff officers, and on battered portable typewriters re-shaped stories which they had hammered out under fire. There have been correspondents who have never heard a shot fired in anger and do not intend to, who have picked their copy from a big board in the briefing room at Corps Headquarters, and other correspondents who have made up their stories from a fertile imagination under faked date lines. There have even been women war correspondents, wearing trousers and steel helmets, trying to look feminine and warlike at the same time.

But in the early days of the Great War there were no war correspondents in France. Censorship was rigid, and the public could only glean information from meagre communiqués and very far from meagre casualty lists.

The old gentleman, sitting in his leather chair as if he intended to gallop into the ground, bombarded the Colonel with questions; it goes without saying that he was only interested in *mounted* action and the Colonel could tell him depressingly little.

He did, however, tell of the first action of the war fought, appropriately enough, by the 4th (Royal Irish) Dragoon Guards—the type of action so dearly loved by the cavalryman of the older school: a wild, cheering, 'split-arse' gallop across open country, culminating in close and gory work with sabres.

He told of the gallant, futile, Balaklava-type charge of the 9th Lancers at Quiévrain, and of how Captain Tempest-Hicks of the 16th Lancers had formed his troop up as if on manœuvres at Aldershot and routed a full company of Jägers (German light infantry). The old gentleman bounced up and down on his chair and said 'good lads' at approximately two-minute intervals.

But he slowed down to a hand canter when the Colonel told him of horses which went ungroomed for weeks on end; of how the Royal Scots Greys dyed their horses with a solution of permanganate of potash; of horses handed over to horse-holders, and cavalrymen caught up by peremptory orders to bolster an ever-sagging line and fight as infantrymen armed with rifles and bayonets. On receipt of this last information the old gentleman shook his head sadly, as one who mourns the passing of an era. 'Dismounted action,' he said; 'that's bad, that's very bad.'

'It was bad in the Retreat,' said the Colonel, speaking almost to himself, 'it was bad on the Aisne. But neither of them were in the same country as the doing we got in the North.'

He was referring to the First Battle of Ypres.

CHAPTER ONE

A river can be a peaceful and gently-flowing stretch of water from which one can pluck trout of surpassing sweetness; on which one can meander gently in a punt or chug gently up and down in a cabin cruiser; one can swim in it, but preferably one can just sit and look at it—ideally from the vantage point of a pub in Henley-on-Thames or Pangbourne.

But a river can also be a sullen, sluggish and unfordable muddy stream of about 170 yards in breadth and nowhere shallower than 15 feet; when the weather gets worse it becomes a treacherous, swirling brown torrent which threatens to burst its banks at any moment.

Just such a river as this was the Aisne in September 1914.

Like two punch-drunk boxers who are reluctant to leave their corners for another bloody hammering, the British and German armies peered warily at each other from trenches on the north bank of the Aisne.

The weather was unspeakably vile: an icy wind, which sometimes increased to gale force, lashed and tore at the soldiers, who were reduced to a state of sodden misery. The rain rarely ceased for long; the water mingled with the chalk in the heights above the Aisne and produced a revolting milk-coloured slush in which British and German soldiers stood to fire, sat down to eat and lay down to sleep—or die.

In appearance there was no sharp dividing-line between Briton and German: they were perpetually soaked to the skin and chilled to the marrow of their being; their faces were caked with greyish clay which gave them a ghost-like appearance.

Both sides, in truth, were getting heartily fed up with a war which seemed to have reached a stultifying stalemate. The British were, in their own homely and Chaucerian phrase, 'fed up, fucked up and far from home'; the Germans wondered why it was taking so long to annihilate what the Kaiser referred to as 'this contemptible little army'.

Back in London little seemed to have changed: the streets were darker—there had, as yet, been no air raids but the possibility was always present—and there were more uniforms to be seen, but that was all. Declaration of war had come as a paralysing blow, but the city had soon recovered its 'business as usual' attitude: the theatres were as gay as ever, gayer if anything, and the restaurants more crowded. There was, as yet, no home leave for British officers from France, but many a home-based officer was mastering a new-fangled dance called the foxtrot and heroic marriage was proposed in many a dimly-lit nightclub.

There was, of course, nothing about the war in the newspapers as morose breakfasters petulantly observed every morning.

But occasionally a small paragraph *did* appear in a newspaper, and one of them read like this: 'On the afternoon of October 4 we gained a small local success. Enemy casualties are estimated at approximately 500; our casualties were one officer killed, two officers wounded; 25 other ranks killed and 70 wounded. . . .'

'Anything in the paper, dear?' asked a lady in Bayswater of her spouse, one of the afore-mentioned morose breakfasters.

'Nothing, as usual,' said her husband.

A senior German officer, mindful of the proximity and bad temper of the Kaiser and his own promotion prospects, launched his men into an attack which was typical of a hundred such attacks in the earlier stages of the Battle of the Aisne. Unfortunately for this German commander, the 2nd Battalion, the Grenadier Guards were in the path of this attack, and the German officer legitimately blamed the Grenadiers for his subsequent premature retirement.

The attack went in just before dawn—a mass of grey infantry in six closely packed ranks with reserves following. The Grenadiers were ready for them. They had been bogged down in their trenches for a week; they were frustrated and belligerent, and a frustrated and belligerent Grenadier spells trouble for someone.

The first two ranks appeared at 400 yards from the guardsmen in their trenches; one moment the faint rim of ground in front of them was bare and empty, the next it was alive with bobbing spiked helmets. With the studied nonchalance which characterises officers of the Brigade of Guards in moments of high drama, fire orders were given: 'At 200 let 'em have it. Aim low.'

The machine-gun and rifle fire of the Grenadiers ripped into the advancing Germans and in twenty yards half of the men in the first two ranks were down. But there was no check in this senseless and suicidal advance; they were stepping over the bodies of their fallen comrades, and with every ten yards covered the slaughter became more deadly: guardsmen who had all but reduced their officers and N.C.O.s to apoplexy on the rifle range in peacetime found that they could not miss—frequently, indeed, the same bullet was striking two and even three Germans.

Just fifty yards from the Grenadiers' trenches there was no wavering in the attack; those behind were literally clambering over the dead, and those who climbed were scythed down like grass in the path of a motor-mower and fell upon the writhing parapet of bodies.

The attack was beaten off, but only with fearful effort; the German dead lay where they had fallen and many of them were to remain there for the next three or four days, for any attempt to bury them would have resulted in certain death. And, when the battle was over, followed the inevitable disgusting aftermath: the rain-sodden bodies became swollen and bloated, and with their gradual decay came the smell—the vile, foetid odour of death; the sweet, sickly stench which is like no other smell on earth.

It was, in truth, little enough to read about in an English newspaper, if indeed it was ever printed. No wonder the morose breakfasters remarked that 'there was nothing in the paper as usual'.

But one ensign—he had but recently celebrated his twentieth birthday—and twenty-five guardsmen would never mount another guard at Buckingham Palace, resplendent in scarlet and bearskin. It may not have been much, but it wasn't 'nothing'. . . .

In the British Army through the centuries the allocation of Battle Honours has always been a tricky business: some are shown on the Queen's Colour and some only on the Regimental Colour. To complicate matters further, the Army List tells us that certain Battle Honours in heavy type are borne on the Queen's Colour, whereas others are borne only on the Regimental Colour.

The awards of Battle Honours have always been decided in close committee by elderly gentlemen who, with pursed lips and speaking in clipped voices, estimate whether their regiments have been sufficiently bloodily engaged to merit the inclusion of, say, 'Pekin 1900' on their Colours.

Some regiments become insufferably superior on the subject of Battle Honours: for instance, only six regiments — the Suffolks, Lancashire Fusiliers, Royal Welch Fusiliers, King's Own Scottish Borderers, Royal Hampshires and the King's Own Yorkshire Light Infantry — bear the Battle Honour 'Minden' and are known as the 'Minden Regiments', a distinction which permits them to wear roses in their hats on August 1 every year in commemoration of the Battle of Minden in 1759; only four regiments — the Seaforth Highlanders, the Queen's Own Cameron Highlanders, the Royal Warwicks and the Lincolns — are entitled to 'Atbara' (April 8, 1898); only the North Staffordshire Regiment have 'Hafir'; the Black Watch and South Staffords share 'Kirkeban 1885' exclusively between them; the Welch Regiment carries 'Detroit' on its Colour, and challenges the entitlement of any other regiment to it.

But once in a while the lips of the old gentlemen in committee tighten and their eyes narrow, for every regiment has a skeleton rattling gently and sometimes noisily in a cupboard; there is always something on the debit side which is one particular regiment's responsibility, and sometimes a Battle Honour has to be forfeited.

Thus, in North America the Black Watch fought magnificently against the Red Indians (North America 1763–64 was one of the 42nd Highlanders' most hard-won honours) but the Reading Fusiliers spent their time raping Indian women; at Lucknow the Duke of Cornwall's Light Infantry held the residency, while the Kensington Sharpshooters lay supine in their billets, drunk on looted rum; the East Surreys stood firm against thousands of fuzzy-wuzzies (Suakin 1885), but the Royal Ruislips fled at the first assault; the Argyll and Sutherland Highlanders marched across the Johore Causeway, ninety-strong, having fought their way down Malaya (Slim River), but the Wincanton Rifles legged it to Singapore without firing a single shot—and so on and so forth.

But there is one Battle Honour, proudly borne on the Queen's Colour of almost every Regiment of the British Army, which required no old gentlemen in committee to ponder over, for in this particular battle all battalions were reduced to one weak company at best and a single depleted platoon at worst.

That Battle Honour is 'Ypres'.

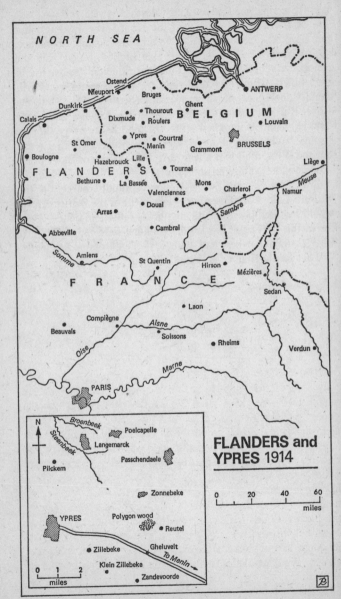

NORTH SEA

BELGIUM

Ostend
Nieuport
Bruges
Ghent
ANTWERP
Dunkirk
Calais
Dixmude
Thourout
Roulers
Louvain
St Omer
Ypres
Courtral
BRUSSELS
Boulogne
Menin
Grammont
Hazebrouck
Lille
Bethune
La Bassée
Tournai
Liège
FLANDERS
Meuse
Mons
Charleroi
Namur
Valenciennes
Arras
Douai
Sambre
Abbeville
Cambrai
Somme
Amiens
St Quentin
Hirson
Mézières
Sedan
FRANCE
Laon
Compiègne
Alsne
Beauvais
Soissons
Rheims
Verdun
Oise
Marne
PARIS

FLANDERS and YPRES 1914

0	20	40	60
miles

N

Broenbeek
Poelcapelle
Steenbeek
Langemarck
Passchendaele
Pilckem
Zonnebeke
YPRES
Polygon wood
Reutel
Zillebeke
Gheluvelt
To Menin
Klein Zillebeke
Zandevoorde

0	1	2
miles

18

CHAPTER TWO

The British Expeditionary Force which crossed the English Channel to France on August 12, 1914 resembled a cross-channel 'stag' outing rather than the best-trained and most efficient army that Great Britain had ever put into the field.

There was a holiday spirit about them, although they travelled in the appalling discomfort which inevitably characterised the seaborne transport of the British Army: they were packed like the proverbial sardines, and there were not even the most basic amenities on board. In conditions which would bring soldiers of today to a state of near mutiny they cheered and sang; from time to time, for no attributable reason, a soldier shouted at the English Channel, 'Are we down 'earted?', and a thousand voices roared, 'NO!'.

They had heard that the German Army had a General von Kluck, and this prompted them to sing to the tune of 'The Girl I Left Behind Me':

> 'Oh, we don't give a fuck,
> For old von Kluck
> An' all his fuckin' Army!'

In spite of their schoolboyish demeanour, they were not all young men—very far from it: freely interspersed among young and pink faces were those with a hint of double chin and thickening jowls; when they removed their stiff-peaked 'cheesecutter' caps one could discern heads which were getting thin on top, as gentlemen's hairdressers have it, and others which were unashamedly balding. Many upper lips were heavily moustached, and on the left breasts of a number of tunics could be seen ribbons of well-nigh forgotten wars— the Sudan, South Africa, the North-West Frontier of India.

Any British battalion proceeding overseas has always had its quota of 'old sweats': the tattooed veterans with forearms, chests, shoulder-blades and legs embellished with snakes, tigers, unclothed women, ships in full sail, Red Indians and altruistic declarations that death is preferable to dishonour; clasped hands, bleeding hearts and Jesus Christ on His Cross (a hardy annual, this one). These are the men who 'have got some service in' and have four-page-long conduct sheets to prove it.

Why were there so many older men on the transports which left Southampton for France between August 12 and 17? Thirty-five, of course, is not old, but to the nineteen- and twenty-year-olds, their recruits' training barely completed, they seemed positively antique, with their tall stories of Boers, Burmese, Chinese, Fuzzy-wuzzies, Pathans, pagodas, poisonous snakes, oranges growing on street corners in Palestine and camels which gave you a dose of the pox if they bit you. These stories, approximately one tenth of which were true, were retailed for the fearful enjoyment of young soldiers who had never travelled farther than the Isle of Wight, and many of them not even that far. Surely this was to be a *young* man's war?

The presence of so many of the more vintage soldiers in the ranks of the British Expeditionary Force is simply explained.

The B.E.F. was made up of two Army Corps: the 1st, commanded by General Sir Douglas Haig, and the 2nd under General Sir Horace Smith-Dorrien. In addition, there was General Edmund Allenby's Cavalry Division. In overall command was Field-Marshal Sir John French.

There were sixteen regiments of cavalry, forty-eight battalions of infantry, sixteen brigades of Royal Field Artillery, five batteries of Royal Horse Artillery, four heavy batteries of Royal Garrison Artillery, eight field companies of Royal Engineers, plus ancillary units, sometimes referred to as 'odds and sods'—Army Service Corps and Royal Army Medical Corps.

At first sight it seemed an impressive array of armed might, but a second and closer look revealed that the British Expeditionary Force, despite its strength on paper, had hardly anything at all. For it woefully lacked the one commodity that really counted in war—particularly in a war against Germany, who had been arming night and day while Great Britain slept—and that was soldiers.

No regiment of cavalry, battalion of infantry, battery of artillery, company of engineers or detachments of A.S.C. had its full complement of men; many of them, indeed, were as much as sixty per cent under strength. In order to combat this depressing lack of manpower the War Office had perforce to call out that variegated, griping, and peerless host—the Regular Army Reserve.

The Reservists poured into depots from Inverness to Bodmin, having been peremptorily summoned by letter and telegram. They came on bicycles, by train and on foot. There were men who had clearly prospered in civilian life if their spreading waistlines were anything to go by, and others who equally clearly had not—their faces were haggard and pinched, their suits threadbare and their boots down at heel. But the Army at least guaranteed three square meals a day, which was not always possible in that place which old soldiers allegedly yearned for—'civvy street'.

Of the Reservists it has been written, not entirely truthfully, that they went to war without fuss or recrimination. Among the 'seven year men', whose reserve liability extended for a further five years, there was fuss and recrimination in plenty: as a company sergeant-major of the Coldstream Guards neatly phrased it, 'they were ticking like clocks'.

Not unnaturally, the married men with children—something like sixty per cent of them—'ticked' the loudest: they could give their tearful wives no explanation except that 'it was back to the army again at the double and orders is orders'; they could tell them nothing about separation allowance and, as it sombrely turned out, there was pathetically little to tell.

But there was also a high percentage of bachelors, to whom civilian life had been rather less than kind, who got uproariously drunk as civilians for the last time and were delivered to their regimental depots by indulgent policemen—they went back to the army in a mood of raucous celebration.

In this manner some 30,000 men went to war. And almost as many women—married and single; young and old; pregnant and virgin; resigned and resentful—wept for them,

21

prayed for them or were glad to see the backs of them.

There were also boys on board the transports—pink-cheeked and beardless children, who gazed at the English Channel in pop-eyed wonderment; they were not allowed to smoke on boy's service (on a salary of one shilling a week they could not have afforded it anyway), but some of them puffed surreptitiously at cigarettes given to them by their indulgent seniors. These were the buglers, trumpeters and drummers, and their average age was sixteen years and six months—many of them, in fact, were younger than that, but they had lied barefacedly about their ages to recruiting sergeants, who didn't particularly care anyway. They were boys, whose present-day counterparts are wrestling with 'O' levels, but they would very shortly be men.

Later in 1914 there was a furious and countrywide outcry from the mothers of these boys, who wrote personal and frequently abusive letters to the War Office and besieged Members of Parliament with demands that their sons should not be sent to France. But that day was not yet; the thought that many of them would not celebrate their seventeenth or even their sixteenth birthdays never occurred to them for a moment —they *were* going to France, whatever their mothers had to say about it, and this was the beginning of the Great Adventure. . . .

When the B.E.F. disembarked in France it was accorded a welcome the like of which no army has ever experienced before or since. The rapturous reception at Le Havre, Boulogne and Rouen was fantastic even by French standards of demonstrative behaviour.

The population shouted and cheered and waved miniature Union Jacks. They showered chocolate, fruit and wine upon the soldiers. The women, with a refreshing disregard for rank, kissed everyone indiscriminately: a red-faced cavalry colonel was the recipient of a passionate embrace in Rouen's main square; a regimental sergeant-major of the Coldstream Guards, a fierce disciplinarian with waxed moustaches, was observed minus his cap badge and with a rose behind each ear. The Ladies of Boulogne speculated ribaldly as to what, if anything, the 2nd Argyll and Sutherland Highlanders wore under their kilts, and the pipe-major, in the act of fending off one young woman who seemed intent on finding out, had his glengarry snatched from his head by another. The children, not to be outdone, demanded souvenirs with piping insistence and reaped a rich harvest in cap badges, shoulder numerals and buttons. Everywhere wine flowed, as one young officer phrased it, 'like milk at a goats' picnic'.

Lord Kitchener had almost certainly anticipated welcomes such as these, and every soldier had this message pasted on page one of his paybook:

'In this new experience you may find temptations, both in wine and women. You must entirely resist both temptations, and while treating all women with perfect courtesy you should avoid any intimacy.'

In the heady atmosphere of Le Havre, Rouen and Boulogne it was very much more easily said than done.

In villages and small towns, as the B.E.F. marched or was conveyed by train to its positions on the left flank of the French Army, the scale of riotous hospitality never lessened: at every halt, cloths were laid on tables and succulent steaks appeared as if by magic: in Aldershot steak had never figured prominently in the private soldier's menu, and the men tucked in with voracious appetite. Wine had *never* appeared on any soldier's menu—they knew that the officers drank it in the mess and on nights out in London, but beer was the staple alcoholic solace of the other ranks. Yet here was wine of a remarkable potency, produced in huge jugs by comely and forward young women with pink cheeks and by less young women who should have known better; the young soldiers, ignorant of its effects, drank with initial caution but with gathering enthusiasm; the old soldiers, with the single damning word 'drunk' entered on several pages of conduct sheet, drank with delighted appreciation.

Sergeants, some of them somewhat less than strictly sober, strode among their men, preaching temperance with half-hearted dedication—in sergeants' messes of the pre-war period teetotallers had always been in short supply; officers, replete with gargantuan omelettes and *entrées* which would have relegated the Ecu de France to the level of a transport café, washed down with liberal draughts of wine and cognac, wondered vaguely if this scale of sybaritic living was good for discipline and properly conducive to the prosecution of modern warfare. They were brought back to reality in very short order by grim-faced colonels, majors and adjutants (who had also lunched extremely well) who reminded them that they were on active service and not an extended picnic.

The point was forcibly made, but it certainly looked like being a lovely war.

And then, suddenly, playtime was over and it was the moment to start fighting.

The British Expeditionary Force was in fine fettle when, on August 22, it reached the drab, industrial town of Mons. The men sang 'Tipperary' and at frequent intervals shouted, 'Are we down 'earted? NO!' 'Will we win, YES!' Even the most jaundiced reservist, yanked from a comfortable civilian life, caught the infection of invincibility and speedy victory: 'just let's see old von Kluck's Allemans off and we'll be home to the wife and kids for Christmas'.

Kaiser Wilhelm II took a less exalted view of the British Expeditionary Force, and from the headquarters of the German Army at Aix-la-Chapelle he issued the following explosive and annihilating order to General von Kluck:

'It is my Royal and Imperial Command that you concentrate your energies for the immediate present upon one single purpose, and that is, that you address all your skill and all the valour of my soldiers to exterminate the treacherous English and walk over General French's contemptible little army.'

Thus was born the proud title 'The Old Contemptibles'.

Before we rejoin the 'Contemptibles' in their waterlogged trenches on the Aisne, let us see what they had achieved since they landed in France.

They had proved themselves to be very far from contemptible, and in every encounter to date they had given the Germans a salutary beating. Much of the credit for this must go to the cavalry and the Royal Artillery, but it was the 'mad minute' fire of the infantry battalions which gave von Kluck most pause for second thoughts.

The principal instrument of execution in the Battle of Mons was the Lee-Enfield rifle: the rifleman of average competence could be sure of firing fifteen rounds from his rifle in a minute, and even the rustiest reservist managed to achieve this during his first week of refresher training on being recalled to the Colours; the most expert could achieve anything up to thirty. It was this competence with the rifle that led the Germans to believe that they were opposed by men armed with light automatic weapons and scores of machine-guns; in fact, there was no such thing as a light automatic weapon in the British Army at that time, and no infantry battalion boasted more than two machine-guns.

All Belgium was ablaze when the British Expeditionary Force arrived at Mons on Saturday, August 22: the city of Louvain was burning, the forts of Liège had been reduced to smoking rubble by huge siege guns and Brussels had fallen to von Kluck's army. Von Kluck had swept the pathetically small and ill-equipped Belgian army aside, and felt fully confident of doing the same to the British.

The B.E.F. was ready for von Kluck: all through the sweltering heat of the 22nd they had marched, and they spent most of that night digging trenches; by dawn on the 23rd General Sir Douglas Haig's 1st Corps and General Sir Horace Smith-Dorrien's 2nd Corps had sunk into the ground like moles. They were established on a twenty-mile front on the Mons-Binche-Charleroi road, on the left of the French Armies. 'Now, let 'em all come,' said the men of the B.E.F., 'for we don't give a fuck for old von Kluck. . . .'

'Christ, there's bloody millions of them . . .'—the incredulous speaker was Private Bert Denner of the 4th Battalion, the Royal Fusiliers, and it seemed that he spoke the literal truth.

For the German infantry—a veritable wall of field grey—were advancing head-on in column of fours; they made no attempt to take cover and advanced shoulder to shoulder, as unhurriedly as if on a ceremonial parade. The entire skyline seemed to be full of Germans in solid square blocks. The fusiliers blinked incredulously, pushed their safety catches forward with fingers that shook a little and cuddled their cheeks into their rifle butts. At 600 yards company commanders bawled 'open fire—rapid independent!' and two days and nights of continuous slaughter had started.

Attacks on other battalions were on the same suicidal pattern: at Obourg, the 4th Battalion, the Middlesex Regiment were attacked by six battalions in densely packed waves and gave them the same treatment as the Royal Fusiliers had meted out; at Jemappes the 1st Royal Scots Fusiliers shot them down in heaps, as did the 1st Royal Northumberland Fusiliers at Mariette and the 1st Lincolns at Frameries; the 1st Royal West Kents demolished no fewer than 3,000 of the illustrious Brandenburg Grenadiers; the East Surreys, Duke of Wellington's Regiment, Bedfords, King's Own Yorkshire Light Infantry and Royal Irish Regiment all chalked up a deadly tally of German corpses.

Throughout August 23 and 24 the B.E.F. were still killing Germans fast, but not quite fast enough; in the early attacks it had been as easy as hitting the side of a house, and even the most mediocre marksman could hardly miss. But the Germans were beginning to learn sense, and had abandoned the suicidal advances of men tightly bunched, shoulder to shoulder; the new tactics started with sustained and murderous artillery barrages, followed by infantry attacks into which had clearly gone careful planning—planning which had been totally absent before. It was one thing to take careful and deliberate aim with the reasonable certainty of killing, but it was quite another to emerge from the depths of a trench, dazed and partially deafened, to engage an enemy who were now advancing in open order in a succession of disciplined rushes.

By the morning of August 25 it was apparent that the position at Mons was rapidly becoming untenable; both flanks had become exposed, bridges had been lost, the French were retiring on the right from the line of the River Sambre. For Sir John French there was only one choice—to retire to a new defensive line from Le Cateau to Cambrai.

The word 'retreat' was not used in the British Army of 1914—they preferred the more dignified expression 'retirement'. For since when had British infantry, when had British artillery, when had British cavalry, been known to retreat? Not in a century. Not since Corunna. Not since Sir John Moore.

Although no officer or man of the B.E.F. yet knew it, this was the beginning of the Retreat from Mons.

Le Cateau—pronounced 'Lee Catoo' by the British soldiers —was the bloodiest and most decisive battle of the war so far. It had been called a defeat, but never in the presence of an Old Contemptible of General Smith-Dorrien's 2nd Corps, who will stoutly aver that it changed British history. And although Smith-Dorrien was broken for that day—August 26, 1914, the 568th anniversary of the Battle of Crécy—there was never a fighting soldier, and never a student soldier, but gave him honour for it.

At Le Cateau, Smith-Dorrien faced a dilemma of the most daunting description; it is doubtful whether, in the history of war, any commander has had to make such an awful decision. Smith-Dorrien had fought the Zulus in 1879, the dervishes in the Sudan in 1898 and the Boers in 1899: as subaltern, captain and commanding officer of the Sherwood Foresters, he had never once disobeyed an order. As a lieutenant-general in command of an Army Corps he did so for the first and last time.

Sir John French had ordered 'retreat', and retreat it had to be, but it came as a shocking surprise to the men of the 3rd and 5th Divisions, who had, so far, borne the brunt of the early fighting. Retreat, always a dirty word, became positively obscene: why should they retreat? Had they not given 'old One O'Clock' (the soldier's pseudonym for von Kluck) what for? Were they not superior to 'Brother Boche' in every way —in musketry, discipline, bayonet fighting and marching? Of course they bloody well were; even a German officer thought so, and he had this to say of the Battle of Mons: 'Our first battle is a heavy—an unheard of—defeat, and against the English, the English we laughed at': the Kaiser's phrase, 'this contemptible little army' was rapidly falling into disuse.

So what was all this bullshit about retreating? Platoon commanders and sergeants strove to keep their men's morale high by pointing out that they would not be retreating—they would just be advancing in another direction.

Nevertheless, retreat it was, and there must, stated Sir John French unequivocally, be no stopping on this retreat: Haig's 1st Corps and Smith-Dorrien's 2nd were ordered to continue the backward move, come what may. And Allenby's Cavalry Division was ordered to cover that retreat.

The B.E.F. did not like the idea of retreating, and said so with mournful insistence: the 2nd Corps, admittedly, had been retreating (but fighting as well) for five days and accepted the fact that a further retirement—they declined to use the hated word 'retreat'—was necessary with a certain stoicism.

But to Haig's 1st Corps the news of an imminent retirement came as the ultimate insult: they were fresh and spoiling for a fight; apart from two brief, bloody and entirely victorious actions fought by the 1st Royal Berkshires and the 3rd Coldstream Guards, they had not as yet been committed to hard action. The men of the 1st Corps were still roaring with undoubtable defiance 'Are we down 'earted? NO!', except in the hearing of men of Smith-Dorrien's 3rd and 5th Divisions, who had borne the brunt of all the fighting so far; they answered, 'you may not be down 'earted now, mate, but you bloody soon will be.'

On receipt of the news that the retreat was to be continued, Major-General Samuel Lomax, a belligerent Cameronian (the Cameronians were always one of the British Army's most belligerent regiments, in action or at peace in a garrison town), called a conference of the commanding officers of his battalions. There were clearly audible mutterings of dissent from his colonels, and to Lomax much of it sounded almost insubordinate. The colonels in the conference room did not know that General Lomax was in earshot; had they done so, they would have preserved a dignified and disciplined silence.

But the General was not yet in the room; there were no red-tabbed staff officers in sight, and the commanding officers were in full cry:

'Retreat? Why the devil should we?'

'My chaps'—the speaker was Major Paul Charrier, temporarily in command of the 2nd Munster Fusiliers, and never a soft-spoken officer—'haven't had a crack at the Boche yet, and if I tell 'em we've got to go back I'll have a damned mutiny on my hands.'

'For the 42nd it's absolutely unthinkable'—this contribution came from Lieutenant-Colonel Grant-Duff, commanding officer of the 1st Black Watch, who had never retreated from anyone or anything yet and did not propose to start now.

'My battalion,' declared the commanding officer of the 1st Scots Guards, Lieutenant-Colonel Lowther, 'has not practised such a manœuvre in peace; it is therefore unable to carry it out in war.'

General Lomax, who disliked the idea of retreating as much as any other officer present, smashed down on them relentlessly. 'The orders, gentlemen,' he announced, 'call for a further retirement. Are there any *more* questions?'

Clearly, there could not be: that, undeniably, was that, and the colonels promptly stopped muttering and went back to their battalions, to urge them ever rearwards.

Le Cateau is a pleasant little town set in countryside not unlike the Sussex uplands between Tonbridge and Hastings—broad, open pasture and meadow-land, cut by tiny valleys, rolling away southwards to the dip of St. Quentin. Through the town runs a single broad street and here, in the town hall offices, Sir John French set up his temporary headquarters.

At first the portents for victory seemed good enough: although both the 3rd and 5th Divisions were woefully tired on August 25th, Major-General Thomas Snow's 4th Division, fresh out from England, were detraining and they were a sight to gladden the heart of any hard-pressed commander. Among the new men was a strong Irish contingent—Royal Irish Fusiliers, Royal Dublin Fusiliers and Royal Inniskilling Fusiliers; there were the 2nd Seaforth Highlanders, Lancashire Fusiliers, King's Own, East Lancashires, Essex, Somerset Light Infantry. Also in the 4th Division were the 1st Battalion of the Rifle Brigade and the 1st Royal Warwicks, with the noteworthy addition of one Lieutenant Bernard Law Montgomery.

The impeccable appearance of the men of the 4th drew derisive comment from the weary and battered soldiers of the 3rd and 5th: their buttons and boots shone, and their cap badges had not, as yet, fallen prey to souvenir hunters. But the time was not far off when the 4th would be every bit as exhausted.

Into Le Cateau, then, on August 25, 1914, staggered the 3rd and 5th Divisions, commanded by Major-Generals Hamilton and Fergusson respectively: the men of both divisions were exhausted, and on arrival in the town they were scarcely capable of putting one foot in front of the other; when ordered to a halt they collapsed where they stood and slept, heedless of the rain which descended on them in a merciless torrent. A staff officer at 2nd Corps Headquarters, who had not slept for forty-eight hours himself, gave this melancholy judgement on these men: 'They're too damned tired to march another step, but provided they can lie down and still fire their rifles they'll fight all night.'

Covering Smith-Dorrien's men in the retreat from Mons was General Allenby's Cavalry Division in a mood of morose fatalism; they were fatalistic because cavalrymen always were; they were morose because only the 9th and 16th Lancers and the 4th (Royal Irish) Dragoon Guards had fought what could be termed real cavalry actions.

The Royal Scots Greys and the 18th Hussars had killed some five hundred Germans between them, but they had carried out this slaughter dismounted, fighting as infantrymen.

The 2nd Dragoon Guards (The Queen's Bays) were particularly disgruntled: on a glorious morning in early September they were near Nery; in the lines, whistling troopers, with their braces over their hips in the tradition of British cavalrymen, were grooming, watering and feeding their horses, cleaning rifles and saddlery. Other men, stripped to the waist, were washing and shaving in canvas buckets; in screened corners of fields some of the officers were removing mud from their persons in portable baths. Tea was being brewed and the encouraging odour of frying bacon testified to the imminence of breakfast. Although the prospect of still more retreating was sufficiently depressing, it was generally agreed in the Bays that life could be a great deal worse; indeed, it was very similar to manœuvres on Salisbury Plain which in peacetime had always resembled an amusing mounted picnic.

Then suddenly all hell was let loose as a salvo of shells fell into the Bays' position. The horses, who disliked retreating almost as much as their riders, stampeded into the middle distance. At first the rearward charge of the horses, with the dismounted troopers — many with lather still on their faces — had an ugly illusion of panic, although it was in fact no more than the swift reaction of the cavalryman to go after his horse; a cavalryman without a horse was, according to the unsubtle reasoning of the Cavalry, totally useless.

The horses were eventually secured and tethered, but there was much bitter swearing in the ranks of the Queen's Bays: in action for the first time, they had not even seen a German, let alone killed one.

This mood of *ennui* was equally prevalent in the Household Cavalry Regiment, forced by the uncouth circumstances of war to wear khaki; the 3rd Hussars, the 5th Dragoon Guards, the 5th, 12th and 16th Lancers; the 6th Dragoon Guards and the 20th Hussars.

These splendid cavalry regiments, all stiff with battle honours, had arrived in France bursting to give of their best. On receipt of the news that Great Britain was at war they had cheered lustily at Aldershot; they had cheered all the way across the English Channel. Now there seemed depressingly little to cheer about: hoping to find wide rolling downs, good galloping country, ideal for the headlong charge knee to knee with sabre and lance, they rode instead through endless small smoky villages, surrounded by coal mines, slag heaps, railway embankments and a profusion of barbed wire.

For the first fortnight of the war the cavalry were, in the words of the troopers, 'buggered about from arsehole to breakfast time': there was a cascade of confused orders and they were despatched hither and thither on largely abortive reconnaissance patrols; roads frequently became blocked as westward-moving cavalry bumped into eastward-moving infantry; ration limbers got lost; some of the reservists, still soft from civilian living, were beginning to feel the strain of active service and said so with dogged persistence.

Sometimes there were sulphurous exchanges between infantry and cavalry brigadier-generals when infantry bumped into cavalry, thereby causing a seemingly immovable road block. Tempers became frayed, and there was one particularly thunderous outburst from an infantry brigadier, who found the road near Mauberge blocked by a brigade of cavalry which made the road a veritable forest of lance points.

Among the many virtues of both brigadiers, patience had never been the most prominent and they opened rapid fire on one another to the undisguised joy of the soldiers in earshot. They had not met one another before, and in the fullness of time they both became major-generals; years later they were to dine together and recall the occasion with friendly nostalgia, but there was nothing friendly about this particular encounter.

'Get your men off this road at once, sir,' blared the infantry brigadier. 'You're stopping the advance of my brigade.'

The cavalry brigadier counter-attacked with vigour: the question of seniority was a delicate one, but to be addressed like that by a brigadier of the despised 'Feet' was something that no cavalry officer could listen to unmoved.

'And you, sir,' said the cavalryman, 'are blocking the march of *my* brigade. And please be careful how you speak to me.'

'I will *not* be careful how I speak to you, sir,' rejoined the brigadier of 'Feet', an officer of tremendous gallantry with a tendency to high blood pressure.

It went on like this for some time. As two privates of the East Surreys, fascinated eavesdroppers, said afterwards, it was as good as a bloody play.

For generals in war, the dividing line between success and failure is a very narrow one and luck plays a big part in any outstandingly successful campaign. If the luck falls one way it can mean a field-marshal's baton or the governorship of a colony—or could in the days when Great Britain had colonies to govern; if the other, retirement to the gentle breezes of Bournemouth until he dies.

A general is supposed to win battles, and if he wins them he gets the adulation of the civilian population. If he loses, complaints about bad luck, the weather, the terrain and inefficient subordinates will fall on deaf and unsympathetic ears.

The general who rallies a seemingly beaten army and presses on regardless to victory may find himself, on retirement, a director of numerous companies; he will administer such diverse concerns as breweries, insurance companies, the Jockey Club, the Betting Levy Board, the railways, the National Coal Board and television companies. He will be knighted (possibly twice) and may even become a Peer of the Realm. If he is an American, a Frenchman, an Egyptian, a Cuban or a Sandhurst-educated African he may finish up by ruling the country.

It goes without saying that he will write his memoirs and commit searing remarks about other generals to thirsty print. These memoirs may be serialised, translated and even filmed —indeed, his memoirs may earn him three years' army pay and allowances overnight. He will fight battles over again to a bemused audience of millions on television: war veterans will grunt guarded approval, while a less martial generation will sit it out politely because 'Match of the Day' is coming on the other channel.

None of these things came the way of Lieutenant-General Sir Horace Smith-Dorrien, Commander of the 2nd Corps. Admittedly, he became Governor of Gibraltar at the end of the war, but this was scarcely more than a consolation prize and was tantamount to being 'kicked upstairs'.

Smith-Dorrien had always been essentially a regimental soldier, and an unlucky one at that: never blessed with substantial private means, so essential to an army officer in the nineteenth century, he spent all his regimental life with the 95th—2nd Battalion, the Sherwood Foresters—which had never been known as a 'fashionable' regiment; in theory, at any rate, it was almost possible for a young officer of the Foresters to live on his pay.

Smith-Dorrien's bad luck, which was to dog him throughout his army career, started in the Zulu War of 1879 when he was recommended in the warmest terms for the Victoria Cross, but did not receive it. He very nearly died of typhoid fever and smashed his knee in a hunting accident in 1881 and was fortunate not to have the leg amputated. He served with distinction in the Tirah and Sudan campaigns and the South African War. In the early days of the twentieth century he seemed set fair for an illustrious career.

He was popular with the rank and file, who referred to him

(sometimes accidentally in his earshot) as ' 'Orace'; this popularity chiefly stemmed from his period in command at Aldershot where he instigated drastic reforms.

But primarily, his soldiers liked and respected Smith-Dorrien because, to use their own phrase, 'he'd got some service in' — considerably more, indeed, than Haig or French; as an infantryman, Smith-Dorrien had experienced *active* service in its most dangerous and uncomfortable sense, whereas French and Haig — gallant and dashing cavalrymen both — had buttressed the British Empire in more gentlemanly fashion (the severer critics of Haig, and they have been many during the past half-century, made much of the fact that in the 1898 campaign in the Sudan a camel loaded with claret accompanied him whithersoever he rode). In France so far Smith-Dorrien had been in constant range of gunfire (and frequently nearer than a corps commander should have been) while Haig and French prosecuted the war more comfortably.

Smith-Dorrien's thoughts were heavy indeed as he toured his command in Le Cateau on August 25. He was, in fact, perilously close to tears as he contrasted this tragically depleted and exhausted force with the splendid cheering formation which had landed in France only a short fortnight before. He saw men lying about in inert heaps, scarcely capable of advancing a yard; he saw the drooping heads and thick-coated flanks of the horses; he saw companies of infantry which had been reduced to two weak platoons, and squadrons of cavalry scarcely the strength of two troops, he saw batteries of field artillery reduced to a single gun. In short, he saw a force which was incapable of retreating any farther.

He said as much in strongly worded messages to G.H.Q., but Sir John French would have none of it; French, indeed, seemed obsessed with retreat and the orders were unchanged: the retreat must and would continue. The exact wording of the order was as follows: 'The 2nd Corps will NOT make a stand at Le Cateau, but will continue the retirement.'

' 'Orace will get us out of this one, mate,' said the old soldiers to their younger comrades, some of whom could see annihilation ahead, and were beginning to say so with mournful persistence; 'know wot 'e'll say to them blokes in G.H.Q.?

34

'E'll say, "we'll stop 'ere and we'll fight." '

None of these confident prophets were present at the orders group presided over by Smith-Dorrien on August 26, but that is exactly what 'Orace did say. He had under command Hamilton's 3rd Division, General Fergusson's 5th, the newly arrived 4th under General Snow and two brigades of Allenby's Cavalry Division.

To these officers Smith-Dorrien explained that he could not see his way clear to obey the order to continue the retreat; he feared that, with the men as tired as they were, further retirement might end in a rout. 'I considered that to show our teeth was the only way of stopping the enemy.'

Hamilton, Fergusson, Snow and Allenby agreed readily enough: none of them was in telephonic communication with G.H.Q., and they were happy enough that this was so. They were all imbued with the necessity of acting through the 'proper channels'. The proper channels, in this case, were clearly Smith-Dorrien's Headquarters at 2nd Army Corps.

General Smith-Dorrien was on the field of action; Sir John French was at G.H.Q., some twenty miles to the south. The man on the spot, realising that the only hope of stopping the enemy lay in a successful action, proceeded with his plans for battle. Smith-Dorrien abruptly closed the meeting with the words which were to hasten his return to England, an obscure campaign in East Africa and the governorship of Gibraltar. General 'Wully' Robertson, the indefatigable Quartermaster-General of the British Expeditionary Force, had started his military career as a private in the 16th Lancers and in moments of stress and deep emotion occasionally had trouble with his aspirates: his damning announcement—'you're for 'ome, 'Orace'—sounded the knell of Smith-Dorrien's ambitions for higher command in France.

It is possible that Smith-Dorrien had some inkling of what was in store for him, but if he had he gave no sign of it: the set of his prominent chin was as pugnacious as ever; his hand as he signed an operational order was perfectly steady.

Then he spoke the words which were to get him 'sent 'ome' and alter the course of history:

'Very well, gentlemen, we will fight.'

And fight they did—fought and died in their thousands: the battle of Le Cateau called for those qualities of unflinching courage and dogged self-sacrifice in which the old regular British Army was pre-eminent. The soldiers who died in this battle had all been told by recruiting sergeants *'dulce et decorum est'*, although the rest of the tag had usually gone unspoken because Latin had never figured largely in the education of senior N.C.O.s of the British Army; they were given the opportunity of dying for their country and they died uncomplainingly. They were all men of a great simplicity, having little skill with pen or voice—unlike some of the pacifists, intellectuals and loud-mouthed muckrakers who have tried to belittle them since—and they died for their simple faith which held it good that a man should offer his life for that thing some of us now make mock of, the honour of a regiment.

The Battle of Le Cateau, so far the bloodiest and most decisive battle of the war, has been called a defeat but never in the presence of the men who fought it. Smith-Dorrien's stand sparked off a long and bitter controversy which was a long time dying—indeed, in some military circles it is not dead yet: Le Cateau, say some of the pundits, should never have been fought at all; Smith-Dorrien flagrantly disobeyed orders and deserved all he got; Smith-Dorrien should have been court-martialled; Smith-Dorrien should have been given a peerage; Smith-Dorrien saved the rest of the B.E.F. from annihilation; Le Cateau was an unmitigated disaster; the battle was one of the most brilliant exploits of the B.E.F. during the retreat from Mons—more: it was one of the most splendid feats of the British Army during the whole of the Great War.

Whatever the rights and wrong of Le Cateau, whether assessed from the viewpoint of the men who were there or a chronicler who was not born until seven years later, it was a battle which had to be fought. Yet no man who fought at Le Cateau can describe it with any degree of accuracy; it can only be a confused and frantic memory of endless artillery shelling, endless infantry attacks carried out by the now familiar hordes of field grey, endless fatigue.

The decision to stand and fight at Le Cateau was as difficult a one to make as any in military history; the dilemma facing Smith-Dorrien as to when to break off the action was equally so. He had to make this decision without obtaining the sanction of General French because all telephone wires had been rent and scattered by shellfire. In the absence of any other means of communication, the order to retire was given verbally to units of the 3rd, 4th and 5th Divisions by furiously galloping staff officers from Smith-Dorrien's Corps Headquarters — no one, not even the 9th Lancers, who always gave the impression that they thought that no one but they could ride a horse with any degree of competence, criticised the horsemanship of 'staff wallas' after Le Cateau. The orders were both curt and simple; to the artillery, 'Cease firing, limber up and get out of it'; and to the infantry, 'The action is broken off. Retire immediately.'

It was easier said than done. Some of the staff officers succumbed to shrapnel or bullet on their desperate journeys; others, in the prevailing confusion, galloped headlong into German units and were taken prisoner.

The order to retire never reached a number of infantry battalions who, in the absence of orders to the contrary, fought on: in these desperate battles the 2nd Suffolks, 2nd Argyll and Sutherland Highlanders, 1st Gordon Highlanders, 2nd Manchesters and 2nd King's Own Yorkshire Light Infantry virtually ceased to exist.

At a crossroads Major-General Sir Charles Fergusson watched what was left of his 5th Division march past him. He was still mounted on the seventeen-hand charger which had accompanied him to France, but changes were sadly apparent in both horse and master: the charger no longer pranced, strutted, occasionally reared and sometimes had to be brought under control by cruel use of the curb; now the General had to use his spurs to coax it into a trot. Its coat was shaggy, like an aged hearth-rug, and there was scarcely a wafer of iron under its chipped hoofs because farriers and the tools of their trade were in short supply — like grooms, saddlers, batmen, bandsmen and signallers, 'shoeys' had had to take their place in the fighting line, for there had been no 'cushy' jobs for anyone in the battles of Mons and Le Cateau.

A major of his staff, also careworn, as was his horse, edged a little nearer to his general with the vague idea of engaging him in a little inconsequential conversation. But he quickly edged away again because he saw in one bare, glistening fraction of a second that General Fergusson was crying.

Generals must never cry, and certainly not in the presence of their staff officers. Fergusson's tears were the untrustworthy tears of a strong and brave soldier who had been strong and brave for nearly long enough; in these circumstances the staff major, whose own emotions were not strictly under control, realised that this must be a private affair.

Generals in both world wars have adopted a number of different techniques in talking to soldiers about to go into battle. The late Major-General Orde Wingate uncompromisingly told his Chindits before they went into Burma that many of them would die of wounds, starvation and sickness; Bill Slim interlarded his addresses with the salty kind of talk that he had heard as a private in the Royal Warwicks; General Eric Down, a distinguished airborne leader, deflated the ego of his men by telling them that there was nothing clever or brave about jumping out of aeroplanes; Mountbatten conquered soldiers of all races with his folksy charm and raised laughs which were spontaneous rather than dutiful; Montgomery, in richly assorted headgear, stood in front of a jeep and distributed free cigarettes with gay abandon.

The employment of such gimmicks in 1914 — the expression 'gimmick' was not yet part of the English language — would have caused the soldiers of the period to gape in open-mouthed and unbelieving astonishment: 'Generals dishing out fags? wot the 'ell next . . . ?'

Charles Fergusson, every inch a Grenadier of the older school, veteran of a score of bloody encounters in the Sudan and South Africa, knew what active service was all about, and spoke to the men in the sort of language which the soldier of 1914 expected to hear from generals: before the departure of the 5th Division for France he told them that there would be no easy victories in this war; that they would be called upon to withstand every sort of discomfort and boredom; that there would be no friendly picture-palace or pub just round the corner. Some of us—Fergusson was careful to say *us* and not *you*, for he had been severely wounded in the Sudanese campaign and was fully prepared to be so again—will get bloody noses.

The General permitted himself only one joke, for he considered that jokes should, and indeed must, be cracked by subalterns to their platoons in desperate situations but seldom by generals: bravery in battle, he told the men, would be rewarded by decorations, provided that all the DSOs and DCMs were not snaffled by the base-wallas for so courageously dishing out plum and apple jam.

A party of men came past General Fergusson, and he noted the white horse of Kent in the caps of those who still had badges: since their arrival in France the 1st Royal West Kents had inflicted enormous slaughter on the Germans—in particular they had shot the redoubtable Brandenburg Grenadiers down in heaps on the Mons-Condé canal—but the slaughter had clearly not been entirely one-sided.

The youthful subaltern at their head, just six months out of Sandhurst, stared hypnotised at the General's red tabs and gave the order 'March to attention' and then, 'Company, eyes right!' Somehow his hand came to the salute, and somehow the fours of exhausted shuffling men aligned; somehow shoulders straightened and heads turned to the right as they plodded past and by.

Fergusson first wanted to shout 'No compliments on active service!', but the words would not come. He wanted to call out 'Well done, West Kents!', but these words would not come either. Instead, he sat motionless in the saddle, his hand at his cap peak, saying over and over again under his breath, 'Well done, well done. . . .'

This, then, was 'B' Company of the 1st Royal West Kents, commanded by Second-Lieutenant George White, the sole unwounded officer. The company strength was one officer, one sergeant, two lance-corporals and twenty-four privates.

Other companies of like size staggered past Fergusson at that road junction: King's Own Scottish Borderers, East

Surreys, Duke of Cornwall's Light Infantry, Bedfords, Norfolks, Dorsets, Manchesters. They all had the same utterly exhausted appearance; in men who have just come out of battle it is their jaws that you notice first—they have been clenched for so long that afterwards chins droop, giving men an open-mouthed and almost idiotic appearance. General Fergusson only spoke once. To one of his staff officers he said: 'The Germans may be able to kill them, but by God they can't beat them. . . .'

CHAPTER THREE

The retreat, in all its misery, went on. They stumbled along in a sort of cosmic slow motion, like sleepwalkers; they were more like ghosts than living soldiers, unconscious of everything about them but still moving under the twin compulsions of discipline and regimental pride.

Let us take a look at one of the numerous roads which converge on Paris—a Roman road, deadly long and deadly straight. Down this road came an ever-moving, endless stream of khaki; close up one could see that the cheeks of these men were bloodless—grey under the bristles with the utter exhaustion of battle and marching, and their eyes glazing, as the eyes of the dead glaze, under the dusty lids.

Here came what was left of the 1st Battalion the Norfolk Regiment: here two fit men, here two more supporting a third with a shattered foot; a man without a cap with a blood-stained bandage across his forehead; six unwounded men, one of them doggedly playing 'Tipperary' on a mouth organ.

Here came a sergeant—a sergeant of the type which John Brophy created in his great novel *Immortal Sergeant*: he had been in the army for seventeen years; long service spent in India, Egypt and South Africa had burned his face to a deep mahogany colour—a face as brown as a kipper and as devoid of expression. On the left breast of his tunic were two stained and fraying South African War ribbons.

He was, like most of that *genre* of senior N.C.O.s, extensively tattooed: snakes and dragons writhed up his gnarled brown arms; the thick black hair on his chest all but obscured the ship in full sail put there in 1911 by a one-eyed tattoo artist in Cairo. He was unshakeable and indestructible; he used appalling language, exploring the uttermost depths of obscenity in his everyday conversation; he had a swallow like a thirsty horse and gallons of beer in the sergeants' mess made not an atom of difference to his speech, gait or immaculate bearing on early morning parade. Here was a Man.

He was carrying two rifles as well as his own, and exhorted his men on with hoarse endearments, telling them that he'd seen better soldiers than them in an Egyptian whore-shop. The men of his platoon—the officer had been killed earlier—loathed him for his frightful optimism and cursed him openly; the sergeant answered them back in the same language and promised them a liberal dose of detention when they got back.

'If we get back,' said a morose private.

'You'll get back,' the sergeant assured him, 'even if it's on your bloody hands and knees. So keep moving. . . .'

'Keep moving . . . keep moving'—these men seemed to be almost past suffering; starving—but past hunger and thirst. At every halt men fell down where they stood and on the resumption of the march had to be booted awake by sergeants who in their turn had been booted awake by officers.

For the younger soldiers, conditioned by long route marches on Salisbury Plain, it was not so bad as for the reservists; for these men, many of them nearing forty, the murderous marches were an agonising ordeal—indeed, prior to their recall to the Colours they had never expected to march again. Heavy packs dragged agonisingly at shoulders, and many were thrown away; boots felt as if they were filled with broken glass and feet became swollen and blistered; many reservists threw away boots as well as packs, and plodded on with their puttees bound round their bleeding feet.

In this manner the B.E.F. marched 136 miles as the crow flies, and more like 200 as the soldier marches.

So the B.E.F. went back—back to the very outskirts of Paris itself.

Generals Haig and Smith-Dorrien differed widely in their approach to the soldiers under their command. Haig inclined to be remote and Olympian; he was also intensely shy and prone to inarticulateness when talking to his inferiors in rank. In fact, he rarely spoke to a soldier at all, except to give orders to a servant or groom.

When the retreat finally came to an end, a visit to a unit by Haig was heralded by a week of feverish 'window dressing': frantic polishing of everything from studs on the soles of boots to dixies in cookhouses; frenzied scavenging fc empty cigarette packets and anything else that might offend the eye of a corps commander. When the visit finally happened and Haig appeared, accompanied by a proletariat of staff officers and with the inevitable escort of 17th Lancers, colonels who had led their men into the hells of Mons and Le Cateau were frozen into shivering immobility and felt the cold wind blowing at their promotion prospects.

The story is told of a private soldier who, on being told that the battalion would be visited by General Haig, said ' 'Aig? 'Oo the 'ell's 'e?'

Smith-Dorrien, on the other hand, frequently descended unannounced and unaccompanied, except for an A.D.C. and orderly. He paid just such a visit to the 1st East Surreys early on the morning of September 5.

No battalion of Smith-Dorrien's 2nd Corps had given a better account of itself than the East Surreys; no soldiers had shouted 'NO' to the rhetorical question 'Are we down 'earted?' with more explicit vehemence; no battalion had objected more volubly to the continuation of the retreat after they had unquestionably demonstrated their superiority to von Kluck's hordes. The East Surreys were predominantly a Cockney battalion—almost every man was representative of the permanent Londoner, virile, cunning, cheerful, cocky, brave. From the capital of Great Britain came the country's most resilient soldiers.

The 1st East Surreys, in common with every other infantry battalion of the 2nd Corps, were sadly depleted in numbers and could barely scrape together two full companies—about 250 men. But they had had two blissful nights of sleep, and by incredible ingenuity the Army Service Corps had procured fresh meat as a welcome change from the interminable diet of bully beef, biscuits and a nauseous confection known as 'Knock-me-down' stew.

They were washing and shaving in the open air; the sun shone and birds sang; an encouraging odour of frying bacon in a corner of the field in which they temporarily lived testified to the imminence of breakfast.

In his usual unobtrusive way General Smith-Dorrien had

ridden to within a few yards of a platoon of East Surreys who were performing a leisurely pre-breakfast toilet.

A lance-corporal, face lathered and razor poised for an assault on his face, spotted the General just in time and promptly cut himself. 'Blimey, it's 'Orace!' he exclaimed, blood pouring from his chin; and then, as Smith-Dorrien approached, 'PLATOON! TSHUN!'

Generals, like schoolmasters, tend to have favourites, whatever they may say to the contrary, and the 1st East Surreys were by way of being something of a favourite with Smith-Dorrien.

To the men, in various stages of undress, many of them with heads still dripping soapsuds, Smith-Dorrien said that they had fought magnificently and had acquitted themselves splendidly in the retreat. But this was to be the end of retreating—from now on the B.E.F. would be advancing all the way.

'You mean we're going to turn and knock 'em, sir?' asked an eager young private, ignoring the baleful stare of the lance-corporal, who only spoke to officers when spoken to first and to generals not at all.

Smith-Dorrien smiled, probably for the first time in three weary weeks.

'That,' he said, 'is just what I mean. Good luck to you all.'

News travels fast in the British Army, whether it be good or bad; but this was no latrine rumour—this came straight from the General's mouth. On the morning of September 5 bursts of cheering could be heard from every regiment of cavalry, battalion of infantry, battery of field artillery and squadron of Royal Engineers—all along the line from Villers-sur-Morin to Fontenay: the 'Allemons' would be scuppered and back over the Rhine before September was out, and they'd all be home for Christmas.

In this mood of ebullient confidence the British Expeditionary Force made ready for the Battle of the Marne.

General Joseph Jacques-Césaire Joffre, universally nicknamed 'Papa' in the French Army because of his benign pink countenance and snow-white moustaches, had had enough of retreats and said so vehemently to anyone within earshot: the great and so-far victorious German columns, he declared, were blinding on to destruction if every soldier, French and British alike, did his duty; the time for retreat was over and those who could not advance must die where they stood. It was good fighting talk, and Sir John French soon became a ready convert to Joffre's war aims and promised the unstinted aid of the British Army.

Joffre, however, did little talking on the afternoon of September 5. At French G.H.Q., situated at Bar-sur-Aube, he spent most of the day sitting motionless in the shade of a vine where his staff disturbed him at their peril; much of the time, indeed, he gave the impression that he was asleep.

Something of a gourmet, Joffre had lunched as well as ever —perhaps too well, in the opinion of some of his younger and more flippant staff officers. But the inaccuracy of this diagnosis was very apparent at six o'clock. Joffre rose abruptly from his comfortable anchorage and walked briskly into the Operations Bureau. Ten minutes later he had set in motion plans for the Battle of the Marne—a stupendous struggle which spread from the valley of the Moselle in Lorraine, round Verdun to the Valley of the Ourcq.

History remembers the Battle of the Marne for the rolling back of the German army when it seemed to have Paris at its mercy; for the brilliant generalship of Joffre, Foch, Franchet d'Esperey, Galliéni and Manoury. Perhaps the popular fancy was caught most of all by the rushing up of the 'taxi-cab' army of Paris, when 600 taxis, each carrying five French soldiers, twice made the sixty-kilometre journey to the front line.

The much reduced and battered B.E.F. played its part valiantly enough in the Marne battle, but it was bound to be a small one: the wonder is that they were able to play any part in it at all, because their losses of 589 officers and 18,140 men had not been made good; no substantial reinforcements had yet appeared and there seemed to be no immediate prospect of getting any.

The precious few days' rest at the end of the retreat had worked wonders for the B.E.F., and they were in the same fine fettle they had been in when they had marched to Mons in

August; they were roaring out 'Tipperary' again, although during the misery of the retreat some men had even forgotten the words.

For now there could be no doubt: they were doing the advancing, and the Germans were experiencing the misery and humiliation of headlong retreat. As they marched through Coulommiers, Rebais and La Ferté the B.E.F. already had the appearance of victors.

Let us briefly rejoin the B.E.F. in its static positions on the Aisne and attach ourselves to an august party of senior officers from Corps Headquarters who were about to set off on a tour of inspection.

Peace seemed to have temporarily settled over the tortured landscape which separated the two armies. On this particular day—October 7—there was scarcely a sound of firing to be heard. Cars were stopped at a cross-roads, and thereafter there was no more road—only trenches and subterranean shelters, constructed with loving care and ingenuity by the Corps of Royal Engineers.

Many of these shelters had names: 'The Criterion', 'The Ritz', 'Hotel Billet-doux', 'Wormwood Scrubs', 'Ten Downing Street'. A company officers' mess of the Royal Welch Regiment bore the title 'Tonypandy'. The machine-gun action of the Northamptons was housed in 'Maxim Villa'; a Battalion Headquarters of the Grenadier Guards was labelled 'Potsdam View'.

At the entrance to a sticky path cut in the clay was a neat notice-board announcing that this was the Old Kent Road, heralding the proximity of the Rifle Brigade, and over a stream, which cut a trench at right angles, a rickety bridge of planks was captioned, it seems hardly necessary to say, London Bridge. On through Piccadilly Circus, via the Haymarket to Trafalgar Square. It also goes without saying the 2nd Highland Light Infantry had a communication trench called Sauchiehall Street.

But as the party floundered on through the muddy trenches, there were still grim reminders that unwary soldiers—even red-tabbed ones from Corps Headquarters—could still be killed: as if in protest at this unwarrantable interruption of their siesta, machine guns fired intermittently from both sides and the spiteful whine of snipers' bullets never stopped for long.

And here, as if to emphasise the point that violent death was very near, came a slow-moving procession: a corporal, followed by two men carrying a stretcher; the stretcher bearers were breathing deeply, and on the stretcher lay a soldier, deathly pale, who was breathing very much less deeply and twenty minutes later would not be breathing at all. This mournful procession was followed by yet another stretcher, but the cargo on this one was covered by a ground-sheet. At one end projected a pair of boots, very still and rigid.

The party from Corps Headquarters, with quick murmurs of sympathy for the casualties on the stretchers, disappeared round the curve of 'Shaftesbury Avenue', reached the support line and went along it. Here were soldiers—Buffs, Leicesters, Northamptons and Essex—dozing in the rare and welcome sunshine, and making tea of startling potency brewed over smokeless flames of solid methylated spirit: if the 'base wallas' wanted to get shot at, then let 'em get on with it. . . .

Static trench warfare, it seemed, had come to stay. Some of the senior staff officers, irritated by this inaction, peered anxiously through periscopes, but there was little to be seen between the British and German lines but strips of mud, pocked with shell craters and strands of barbed wire, with tattered corpses hanging upon them like laundry hung out to dry.

At intervals the staff officers paused at a battalion headquarters, usually a dug-out burrowed into the front of a trench —in these dug-outs were telephones which kept the battalion in precarious communication with Brigade, and thence through Division and Corps to Army Headquarters.

From the support line the party struggled along the muddy communication trenches to the front line, but the atmosphere seemed no more warlike: men dozed and smoked on the fire-steps; sentries peered conscientiously through periscopes at nothing at all; the visitors were regaled with whisky and brackish water served in enamel mugs, except in the dug-outs

47

of Guards battalions who boasted chipped glasses and off-white table cloths.

Some of the more offensively-minded staff officers deplored what struck them as being a slovenly, unmilitary and unnatural form of warfare—a war of idleness, immobility, petty ambuscade and sniping. Muttering darkly, they peered through the periscopes and imagined disciplined waves of men swarming across the frail barrier that separated the British and German trenches, although they did not foresee the murderous blood-letting which was to come.

The infantry, on the other hand, took a more phlegmatic view of the stalemate: it was all very well for the gilded staff to bark about taking the offensive, but they would not be doing it. Taking the sensible soldier's view that any fool can be uncomfortable, they lived happily enough in their cave dwellings.

The officers of the 60th Rifles were accustomed to doing themselves well, and in their sector of the line near Troyon they ran true to form. Tucked under the brow of a hill was the officers' mess, but the commanding officer, Lieutenant-Colonel Serocold, was pessimistic when a staff captain called on a routine visit.

'We'll be out of this any day now,' the colonel forecast gloomily.

The staff officer expressed surprise. 'First I've heard of it, sir,' he said. 'What makes you think a move is on the cards?'

'Because,' said the colonel grimly, 'for the first time since this damned war started we've constructed a decent dry shelter. As soon as we make ourselves cosy we move.'

Colonel Serocold was proved an able prophet.

The 2nd H.L.I., unlike the more stoical 60th, did not like this seemingly permanently defensive role which they and everyone else were forced into. It did not suit their temperament, and they said so with truculent insistence.

The fighting record of the Highland Light Infantry has always been a splendid one, although their appearance in a peacetime station has caused garrison commanders to shudder apprehensively, military policemen to patrol in pairs and put

n for transfers, parents to lock up their daughters and publi-
ans to stock up urgently with expendable glassware.

Strictly speaking, the H.L.I. are not Highlanders, for they
ave always been the City of Glasgow's own regiment, re-
ruited largely from the City's less fashionable environs—
Brigton, Bishopstown and the Gorbals. When not fighting
Britain's enemies they have fought other regiments—prefer-
bly Irish ones. In war they fought with rifle and bayonet;
n peace with fists, boots and sometimes razor blades carried in
heir bonnets, with which to wipe the grins off opposing faces
vith a careless backhand swipe.

A private of the H.L.I. has always been famed for doing
nything, including dying, for officers whom he liked and
espected; equally, there is nothing that he *would* do for
officers he disliked—as many a Sassenach officer cross-posted
o the H.L.I. discovered to his chagrin.

'Layabout', 'yobbo', 'tearaway', 'thug'—all these words have
aken their place in the modern English language to describe
young men who regard public houses as legitimate prey for
lestruction. The Glasgow term for such characters is a 'keely',
and from such unpromising military material one of the finest
ighting regiments of the British Army has been recruited.
The H.L.I. have always been known as 'The Glesga Keelies'
—a nickname they cherish with the perverse pride of the dyed-
n-the-wood Glaswegian.

In spite of their sometimes erratic off-duty behaviour—in
letention barracks the H.L.I. have always been well represented, and they were often to be found stationed in Aden,
sometimes called a 'punishment station' because on the barren
ocks opportunities for high-spirited misdemeanour were
severely limited—they have always been found where the fight-
ng was most deadly since their formation in 1777, and many
a hard-pressed commander has been grateful for their presence. Brigadier-General Haking commanding the 5th Brigade
of the 2nd Division certainly was: since the arrival of the
B.E.F. in France the contribution of the 2nd H.L.I. had been
a very considerable one, both in defence and attack. Haking
aad for many nights slept easier in the knowledge that this
battalion was holding a sticky sector of the line.

In the Battle of the Aisne the Battalion was to acquire a Victoria Cross. Private George Wilson, former Edinburgh newspaper seller, won the supreme award for a one-man charge on a German machine-gun section: a marksman of some repute, he shot the officer in command and three of the crew with four slow and deliberate shots from his rifle, and despatched the remaining two with his bayonet.

By the end of September both Allied and enemy troops were living a life closely resembling that of cave-dwellers. The opposing trenches were gradually pushed forward towards one another, but as the distance between the lines lessened the defences increase in strength. An entirely new kind of warfare had taken the place of the old; the infantry sat in their trenches all day, peering almost uninterestedly at the Germans. The Germans, equally unambitious, peered back.

Only a fortnight earlier the 2nd H.L.I. had taken the bayonet to the Germans at Verneuil, and this was the sort of fighting that they understood best. It was unfortunate for these Germans that the Battalion's senior subaltern, Lieutenant Sir Archibald Gibson-Craig, was killed in this attack because Gibson-Craig had been an officer of exceptional popularity with the men: he dished out free cigarettes with gay abandon, rewarded outstanding performers on the rifle range with surreptitious pound notes and had the endearing habit of playing the bagpipes whenever opportunity offered. In this particular attack one hundred Germans were killed by 'D' Company alone, and of these at least fifty were bayoneted whether they put their hands up or not. After the action, one of the bloodiest in the Regiment's very bloody history, the Commanding Officer, Lieutenant-Colonel Arthur Wolfe-Murray, cautiously inquired if any orders had been given regarding the taking of prisoners.

'I didnae hear ony, sirr,' was the usual non-committal reply. The Colonel, who knew his men, did not pursue the matter further.

But now there were no bayonet charges; there were only desultory artillery duels, desultory night raids, desultory patrols. It was no way for a 'Glesga keely' to live.

It was, however, the time of the sniper, and Corporal 'Sixty' Smith was at the top of his specialised world.

He was known as 'Sixty' Smith in the 2nd H.L.I., from the Colonel downwards, because the last two numbers of his regimental number were 60: every regiment of the British Army had its quota of Smiths, and for the purposes of identification they were known as Smith 96, Smith 08 and so on.

On the sleeve of his jacket 'Sixty' wore the coveted crossed rifles of the 'marksman' which carried with it the additional emolument of threepence per day; by 'Sixty's' uncomplicated system of budgeting this represented extra beer (one pint in a pub or two in the wet canteen) or ten cigarettes.

'Sixty' Smith was the undisputed top sniper in the 2nd H.L.I., if not the whole of the 2nd Division, and was guilty of 'wilful damage to War Department property' in advertising the fact with a series of small notches in the barrel of his rifle.

From the cosy vantage point of a sandbagged trench 'Sixty' gazed on the German lines, some 600 yards away, without any great animosity. Sooner or later a German would emerge on man's humblest of all missions, because 'Sixty' had deduced —correctly, as it happened—that a small, crudely erected edifice was a latrine; it went a little against the grain to kill a man in such circumstances—perhaps it might be kinder to shoot him after the mission had been accomplished.

As 'Sixty' watched, his right hand caressed the rifle butt and his left fingered the backsight. It wouldn't be long now. . . .

Then the head and shoulders of a man emerged; he was bent low, but not quite low enough: there was a smashing report from 'Sixty's' rifle and the figure shot straight up like a jumping jack, as men shot in the head usually do, and then fell back out of sight. A second German ran out, intent on the rescue of his comrade, and the rifle slammed again: this man was flung backward and down like a broken doll as the bullet exploded against the angle of his jaw, blowing away half his face and neck.

Half an hour later, 'Sixty' Smith's relief arrived: this was Private McNab (72)—like 'Sixty', he was a marksman, but no stripes had yet come his way because he had a conduct sheet which resembled a full-length novel—and a best-seller at that.

'What's the score, "Sixty"?' McNab enquired.

'Three,' replied 'Sixty' briefly. 'Two bulls and an inner'—the inner was represented by a man he had shot half an hour earlier, and as he had managed to crawl away he could not fairly be claimed as dead.

Then Private McNab assumed the vantage point of killing while Corporal 'Sixty' Smith composed himself for the four hours' sleep to which he was entitled.

This was the overall pattern of life in the trenches on the Aisne: every battalion had its 'Sixty' Smiths, just as the Germans had their 'Sixty Fritzes': these snipers, dedicated killers all, were living proof that to show any part of the anatomy in daylight was swift suicide.

It might be thought that the snipers were the only men to remind both sides that there was still a war on: concealed in their own particular eyries, with their eyes ever laid along their telescopic sights, they kept ceaseless vigil over the ragged outline of the trenches opposite. Wherever a head, or anything resembling a head, showed itself, the sniper fired. Although British casualties were comparatively negligible on the Aisne in the latter days of September, the frequent spectacle of a stretcher, manhandled by two men, and on it a shape covered by a groundsheet terminating in a pair of boots, was a grim reminder that unlucky or unwary men could still die.

During the last week in September rumour stalked the positions on the British lines on the Aisne like a rabid dog; most of the items of gossip were of the type known to the British Army as 'latrine rumours'.

America was in the war; Germany was suing for peace; the Russians were coming to the aid of Belgium; Turkey was coming into the war, but it was not clear on whose side; they would all be home for Christmas; they were going to receive a pay increase; the Kaiser had committed suicide.

For the first time since their arrival in France, the B.E.F. were seeing French soldiers in large numbers, and were not immediately favourably impressed, for they were in the phraseology of the British soldier 'a scruffy looking lot'.

The British soldier of the period always marched strictly in step, whether on a route march, a ceremonial parade or an evening's pub crawl in Aldershot: head up, shoulders back and arms swinging from front to rear—in the words of the song immortalised by Cicely Courtneidge 'There's something about a soldier', their gait was always unmistakable, even in civilian clothes.

They were never less than impeccably shaved, because the British soldier always presented a clean chin to the enemy, providing that soap and water were available and often even when they were not.

Now they saw French *poilus*, shambling all over the road with no thought of marching in fours or keeping in step. Shaving in the French Army, apparently, was optional and whole platoons of men were bearded, looking as if they had stepped from the canvas of some dim cathedral altar-piece of 'The Last Supper'.

There were cavalry in blue and red uniforms with baggy trousers, high jack-boots and long plumes fluttering from their brass helmets, who seemed to have stepped straight out of the first act of *Carmen*. They wore steel breast-plates and back-pieces, just as Meissonier had painted them. Their horses bore no resemblance to the sturdy British cavalry charger; they were small and wiry and of obvious Arab strain.

The British cavalryman always had a tremendous affinity with his horse: he gave it food and drink before he had any himself; he bedded it down with loving care and fed it on carrots spirited away from the cookhouse; using a device known as a 'dock sponge'—for those unfamiliar with equine matters, a horse's fundamental orifice is its dock—they performed the humblest cleansing operation of all.

We, as a nation, are horse lovers, and a frequent bleat from British cavalrymen was that the horses were treated better than they were; not so the French, who regarded them as a conveyance and little more.

'What are all the froggies up to?' was the oft-repeated question asked by the men of the B.E.F. They were soon to know.

Battalions of infantry and cavalry and artillery regiments

were combed for officers whose knowledge of colloquial French extended beyond reading a menu: what started as a latrine rumour was rapidly becoming translated into fact—clearly a French take-over of the British positions on the Aisne was imminent.

Towards the end of September, when it seemed that operations on the Aisne had degenerated into almost total *impasse*, Sir John French approached Marshal Joffre with the proposal that the British Army should move northwards to its former place on the left of the line; more troops were about to be landed in the north of France and French considered it desirable that the British Army should act in one body. French also considered that such excellent fighting material as the B.E.F. should be used in open fighting rather than stagnate in static positions in trenches; it irked French and Haig, cavalrymen both, that crack regiments of lancers, dragoons and hussars should have to moulder in holes in the ground. Most serious of all, from the British viewpoint, was the German menace to the Channel ports: if Boulogne, Calais and Ostend were seized by the Germans they would be able to threaten the transport of troops from England and to block the vital avenues of sea-borne traffic converging on London. They could, in fact, even launch an invasion of England.

Sir John French put it even more strongly. The stakes for which we were playing, he declared, were nothing less than the safety, indeed the very existence, of the British Empire.

The German scheme was to seize the coast and ports of the English Channel; 'to Calais!' was now the cry of every good German, just as he had lately shrieked 'to Paris!' With Calais secured, giant guns could be mounted which could shell Dover at will, thus beginning the total extermination of Great Britain once and for all.

To heap derision and abuse on the gilded staff has always been a favourite pastime of the British soldier. Later in the war red-tabbed officers swilled claret in well-appointed châteaux well out of range of German artillery, but that time was not yet: at Mons, in the retreat, and in the battles of the Marne and the Aisne, brigade and divisional staffs shared many of the dangers of the front line and suffered many casualties.

Even the most rabid critics of the staff could find no fault with the hand-over of the British positions on the Aisne to the French. The organisation was so perfect that when the moment arrived there was scarcely a single hitch: artillery positions were meticulously handed over; communications were rearranged; British battalions moved out and French battalions moved in; and the Germans apparently had no inkling of what was happening, or if they had, they gave no sign of it.

The hand-over was, in truth, a veritable miracle of staff work: the front-line soldiers conceded grudgingly that, for once, the staff wallas had not made a monumental balls of it. British tommy and French *poilu*, each convinced that they were fluent in each other's languages, exchanged traditional greetings which seemed to ensure a lasting *entente cordiale*:

'This place trez bon, eh?'

'*Oui, oui*—Tipperare!'

'Brought any madermerzelles with you?'

Army Headquarters had recently circulated an order instructing men of the B.E.F. to 'lose no opportunity of cultivating the friendliest relations with those of our Allies whom you may chance to encounter'.

'Brought any madermerzelles with you?'

'Never mind about the madermerzelles, Nobby—ask 'im if 'e's got any vin rooge.'

'Aprez la gair fini'—a gesture indicative of drinking, and then of throat cutting—'Allemons soon *kaput*.'

'*Magnifique*—Piccadilly, Leicester Square.'

'Blimey, he savvies a bit of the old parley-voo, don't 'e?'

'We're goin' to alley out of 'ere toot sweet.'

'The tooter the sweeter. . . .'

'*Bravo, mon vieux.* . . .'

'Same to you, mate. . . .'

An anonymous poet summarised the hand-over on the Aisne in these verses:

I met a bloke the other day a-roostin' in a trench,
'e didn't know a word of ours nor me a word of French,

An' ow it was we managed—well I can't understand,
But I never used the phrase book, though I 'ad it in me 'and.

I winked at 'im to start with; 'e grinned from ear to ear;
An 'e sez Tipperary and I sez 'sooveneer';
'e 'ad my only Woodbine, I 'ad 'is thin cigar,
Which set the ball a-rollin', an' so—well there you are!

I showed 'im next me wife an' kids, 'e upped and showed
    me 'is,
Two funny little Froggy kids with 'air all in a frizz;
'Annette', 'e sez, 'Louise', 'e sez, an' 'is tears begins to fall;
We was comrades when we parted, but we'd 'ardly spoke at
all. ...

The hand-over of the British positions on the Aisne to the
French was, in truth, a tremendous undertaking; the British
were holding a winding front of twenty-six miles in length.
Along this front, or in reserve immediately behind, but still
uncomfortably in range of artillery fire, were 70 battalions of
infantry, 15 regiments of cavalry and 84 batteries of artillery,
Horse, Field and Heavy. That was the strength on paper, but
every unit was badly depleted by casualties.

The German lines were, in many parts of the front, a bare
100 or 200 yards distant from the British trenches. In addition, the enemy dominated the situation with their big guns;
but, despite the heaviest attacks, their infantry had nowhere
been able to break through the British lines, and every commanding officer had made it abundantly clear to captive audiences of company commanders that if any battalion lets the
Hun through it will *not* be the Northamptons (or Lincolns,
Bedfords, Leicesters, etc., etc.).

The problem confronting the British and French commanders was to withdraw all the British troops and put French
in their places without letting the enemy know.

On the Aisne, due to the position of the British lines, it was
never an easy task to take a battalion, or even a company, out
of the firing line for a few days' rest and replace it by a new
one. But now the staff were confronted with the problem of
changing whole brigades: the brigade majors, primary archi-

tects of the hand-over, resembled harassed signalmen at a busy railway junction who had to work the points and signals without the help of the interlocking system.

The language difficulty added to the complications: orders had to be so carefully worded that there was no possibility of mistake or misunderstanding when translated—many British officers fervently wished that they had applied themselves more assiduously to their French lessons at school.

Artillery gun positions were handed over, together with the interchange of maps and sketches showing ranges to various targets. Then there were the changes at all the H.Q.s—the rearrangement of communications and telephones, ammunition dumps, routes for ration convoys and all the endless maze of detail which in military parlance at the Staff College is lumped under the heading 'administration'.

The more bile-ridden critics of staff officers contended that the primary function of the staff was to foul up operations, by giving contradictory orders and misreading their maps, in order that wars could be prolonged to a point where every staff officer has become a general.

Undoubtedly several of the staff officers who engineered this move did become generals, and no one could deny their entitlement to high promotion. For when the moment arrived there was scarcely a single hitch: all movement was by night, and during the day the British soldiers stayed out of sight so that they would not be spotted by enemy aircraft. No offensive action was taken by either side, and amazingly the Germans seemed to accept the situation at its face value. The British Army crept away from the positions on the Aisne like a thief in the night.

The soldiers left the Aisne in cheerful mood: any change from the miserable discomfort and tedium of static trench warfare must be for the better. All portents seemed to be good: the capricious French climate underwent a magical change, and days of bright, warm sunshine gave way to nights of radiant moonlight.

Some units went all the way by road, others partly by train and motor-bus. Inevitably, there were long marches but the route lay through beautiful countryside, as yet untouched by war: there were halts in such picturesque places as Mareil-sur-Ourcq, Senlis and Abbeville; there were, almost incredible to relate, baths in which grimy and footsore soldiers could wallow in unlimited hot water. They guarded their meagre pay jealously, but many men counted twenty-five centimes for a small bag of lavender soap-powder as money well spent.

It had been a lovely war in August; a vile one at Mons, in the retreat, and at the Marne and the Aisne. Now it seemed to be lovely once more, and some of the billets on the way were almost luxurious.

There was considerable excitement in the ranks of a company of the 4th Royal Fusiliers when they learned that they were to be billeted in a girls' school; when they gathered that it was a *senior* girls' school for young ladies aged between sixteen and eighteen the excitement became audible, and company sergeant-majors had to remind some of the younger and more concupiscent members of their flock of the message pasted on page one of their paybooks: 'While treating all women with perfect courtesy you should avoid any intimacy.'

'This is a young ladies' school in France, and not Grant Road[1]—got it?' said the sergeant-major.

The columns of cavalry, artillery and infantry trekked ever northwards: left far behind were the level uplands of the Aisne country and the deep forest glades of Compiègne; in their place was a flat manufacturing district reminiscent of the Potteries—the Black Country of France.

The vivid contrast struck everyone forcibly, and was not a little depressing. The weather did not help either, for it grew steadily colder and there were swift, lashing storms—heavy presage of the grim winter months to come.

A new name cropped up in conversation on troop trains or at roadside halts—a curious name, which the soldiers pronounced 'Eeprez' and later inevitably referred to as 'Wipers'. They were headed for the ancient Flemish town of Ypres, and within less than a month those of them still left alive were to wish themselves back in the water-logged slush on the Aisne.

[1] The brothel area in Bombay.

CHAPTER FOUR

The stage is set for tragedy, but the principal actors have not yet appeared on the scene.

Firstly, the town, Ypres; thirty-five miles south of Ostend and twelve miles west of Courtrai on the Yperlé, a small river flowing into the Yser, both of which villages have been canalised.

Ypres was first heard of as a town in AD 960, when it consisted of a cluster of crudely erected wooden huts in a sea of mud. From this frugal beginning it grew to become, during the fourteenth century, the greatest city in Flanders with a population estimated at just under a quarter of a million souls. The prosperity of the city stemmed mainly from the weaving of cloth which was marketed in the famous Cloth Hall.

Ypres, prior to 1914, was no stranger to war and had often suffered siege, bombardment, fire and plunder as the French, the Dutch and the Spanish all took their turn in conquering the town and surrounding countryside. Even the English, under the Bishop of Norwich, besieged Ypres in 1383 until forced to withdraw and admit defeat.

By 1914 Ypres had been reduced in importance to a minor town and the population had shrunk to about 17,500. The celebrated cloth trade had declined, and many of the skilled weavers migrated to Britain where they established their craft, much to Britain's benefit.

Ypres was a quiet, well-ordered and prosperous town, populated mainly by tradesmen and artisans, and some of the older burgher families and property owners. In the surrounding countryside were prosperous farms with a refreshingly constant output, hereditary mansions and magnificent châteaux which housed members of the ancient nobility of Flanders. Ypres in 1914 seemed serene and everlasting.

It has the same benign appearance today: the Grand Place has been changed to cope with the steadily growing volume of traffic. There are well-stocked shops and bright lights, and the highlight of the week is the market on Saturday where almost everything can be purchased from the multitude of stalls. Around the square are numerous bars which enjoy a steady trade from tourists in the summer months.

Ypres has risen from the ashes, and in 1974 is a busy, thriving township of some 18,000 people to whom the future is more important than the past.

But not to one old Englishman sitting at a table outside one of the bars. There is a glass of beer in front of him, which he is sipping without great enthusiasm — thin, wishy-washy, gassy stuff, which compares wholly unfavourably with the nutty and powerful brew which is dispensed at his local at home.

The old gentleman has recently celebrated his eightieth birthday. His hair, what little remains of it, is white, as is his carefully trimmed moustache. He is a little short of sight and hard of hearing; a trifle rheumy; somewhat stiff in the joints. But he can still walk straight-backed, his arms swinging from front to rear.

He is a little bewildered by a world in which income tax at more than 40 pence in the pound, shoulder-length hair in males, women's lib, mini skirts, £25 a week for private soldiers, the Pill, motorways and pornography are separately and collectively supposed to make sense.

His suit of durable blue serge, bought in the years when tailors really knew their job, is well brushed and will, he calculates see him through the evening of his years; his black boots shine as only an old soldier's can. He wears a black tie biased with pale blue and maroon stripes, and in his left buttonhole is a small badge. Pinned to the lapel are four medals: the Military Medal, won as a young corporal on the Somme, the 1914 Star, the General Service Medal and the Victory Medal. The badge and the tie proclaim him to be a member of Great Britain's most exclusive association — The Old Contemptibles, who fought at Mons and Le Cateau; on the Marne and the Aisne; and in the First Battle of Ypres.

He is suddenly conscious of his eighty years; it has been a long and eventful day, and with the passage of time he finds he tires easily. With his eyes half closed, he sees Ypres as he first knew it. . . .   *

He saw the Cloth Hall, but it was robbed of all its dignity: now it was crammed from end to end with wounded British soldiers, and more stretchers were coming in every minute: there were men who were already dead, men who died when the medical orderlies' backs were turned for a second, men who would be dead before the next day dawned, and men who wished they could die now.

He hears the shells which fell in their hundreds on the city. There are huge, gaping holes clawed up in the pavé road and in every corner dead and twisted horses. He sees fragments of what were once men, a motor ambulance standing drunkenly on three wheels, a wagon overturned with four dead horses still fast in the traces. And he smells the sweet, sickly, cloying stench of death which broods like a pall over everything.

Three other 'Chums'—every Old Contemptible, from Field Marshal to Private, uses the appellation 'Chum'—approach the table: they wear the same medals, the same tie, the same little badge in the left buttonhole.

'Time for a pint,' announces one of them.

'If old Bill's left any—had a good kip, Bill?'

Bill opens his eyes, and focuses them on the other three— Sid of the Bedfords, Arthur of the Queen's and Harry of the 9th Lancers.

'Yes,' he says, 'I had quite a nice kip. *Garcong. . . .*'

There is nothing remotely military about the sleepy, New Forest town of Lyndhurst: occasionally a soldier on leave can be seen, but Lyndhurst, unlike Aldershot, Colchester, Catterick or Plymouth, has never been a soldiers' town.

Today Lyndhurst, with its single street, is a bottleneck for traffic heading to and from Bournemouth. Outside the town is a golf course, a playground for casual and not over-dedicated players; New Forest ponies graze and are illicitly fed by hordes of trippers. There are caravans everywhere and, housing the more hardy ones, tents.

In the last weeks of September 1914 the golf course and surrounding country outside Lyndhurst were covered with tents to the exclusion of everything else, and the New Forest ponies had to find new grazing grounds: row upon row of tents, a cornucopia of conical white canvas. In each tent twenty-two soldiers slept, smoked, swore and snored. Each tent smelled robustly of stale cigarette smoke and soldiers' socks.

They were very exceptional soldiers, these occupants of the tents: they were destined to be late on the fighting scene, but when they got there their contribution was a priceless one.

After the departure for France of the 6th Division, there remained in England of regular soldiers only three regiments of Household Cavalry, five battalions of infantry (three of them Guards), seven batteries of Royal Horse Artillery and five brigades of Royal Field Artillery, besides training and draft-finding units.

Britain's Territorial Army—the 'Saturday Night Soldiers' —were bursting with keenness, but were nowhere near to being ready to take the field; Kitchener's 'New Armies'— without uniforms or arms—lived in tents pitched in seas of mud, and were practised in the evolutions of 1870 by sexagenarian non-commissioned officers and commanded by septuagenarian generals.

Stretched to the limit as it was, the British Expeditionary Force in France desperately needed another division, if not an army corps—not in three months' time, not next week, but now. But how was such a division—rather more than 15,000 men—to be found? And from where?

The answer was the garrisons overseas: the 1st Royal Welch Fusiliers, the 2nd Warwicks, the 2nd Yorkshires, the 2nd Royal Scots Fusiliers and the 2nd Wiltshires stood guard over Gibraltar and Malta; the 2nd Queen's, 2nd Bedfords and 1st South Staffords were in South Africa, together with two cavalry regiments—the 1st (Royal) Dragoons and the 10th Hussars; the 3rd Dragoon Guards and the 2nd Gordon Highlanders were sweltering in Cairo.

Soldiering abroad, as any vintage old sweat will tell you nostalgically, was a good life in the pre-1914 era: although a private's pay of one shilling a day seemed to preclude any sort of sybaritic enjoyment, facilities for all forms of sport were excellent and beer and cigarettes were cheap—the soldier of the period asked for little else of life.

In the main, these soldiers were unreflective men, but they

were conscious of a certain feeling of guilt in September 1914. News from France was of the sketchiest—few time-serving soldiers abroad had heard of Mons or Le Cateau—but they knew that for the men of the first six divisions there was no sunshine or beer and very few cigarettes: there was only marching, fighting, mud, meagre rations, mutilating wounds and death. If Great Britain was at war, then the finest regiments of the Regular Army should be in it: bathing in the Mediterranean, route marches on the South African veldt and carousing in Cairo bars were all very well but not for the finest soldiers in the world.

All these regiments—Royals, Queen's, Bedfords, Gordons, Staffords and the rest—felt a little superior to the rest of the British Army and perhaps justifiably so: they had all 'got some service in' and 'got their knees brown', as soldiers in hot weather stations have it: *they* should be fighting this war instead of a mixture of raw rookies and dug-out reservists—a harsh assessment of the first six divisions, but not an entirely inaccurate one.

The troopships were steaming out from Gibraltar, Malta, Port Said and Cape Town: the soldiers, thronging the decks, waved goodbye to the outposts of empire which had been their homes for the past three years; they had had their good times in these places, but it was good to be going home again. . . .

And so these regiments came home and on arrival in England they were shaken up like some military cocktail and became the 7th Division.

But the Division was still far from complete, and during September still more battalions marched into camp at Lyndhurst: the 1st Grenadier Guards and 2nd Scots Guards, who only the week before had been performing ceremonial duties in London, entered the camp with the air of disdain always affected by the Brigade of Guards when they find themselves in contact with the 'Feet'; also from ceremonial duties came the 1st and 2nd Life Guards and the Royal Horse Guards (the Blues)—only the day before they had clattered along the Mall in all their peacetime splendour. Infantry requirements were completed by the 2nd Yorkshire Regiment from Guernsey, full of regret at having to leave that benign Channel island, and the 2nd Border Regiment, who felt no nostalgia for Pembroke Dock whatsoever. Horse gunners from Canterbury and field gunners from Woolwich clattered in, and Royal Engineers from Chatham. The 7th Division was getting into its stride.

The phrase 'Angry Young Man' was not part of the English language in the year 1914, but there were angry young men in plenty of the Yorkshires and Borderers, who laid siege to company sergeant-majors in enraged droves, demanding personal interviews with their company commanders: these were the under-nineteen-year-olds who had not completed their recruits' training, and considered themselves to be victims of a gigantic conspiracy: in wrathful processions they were marched in front of their officers, demanding to see their birth certificates and producing reasons of startling complexity why they should go to war with their battalions. The officers were sympathetic and could only promise them that their chance would come soon enough; possibly sooner than they expected, and they were accurate prophets—many of these young men were to die during the next four years, but King's Regulations decreed that they must stay alive for the rest of 1914.

Resentful company sergeant-majors, who had more important work to do than march saucy young buggers in and out of company offices, marshalled these frustrated young warriors at the rate of one every two minutes. A piece of representative dialogue is produced here:

C.S.M.: Private Smith, 98—request for interview with company commander.

Officer: Well, Smith?

Smith: Permission to go to France with the Battalion, Sir.

Officer: Can't be done, Smith, I'm afraid. Says here that your age is eighteen years and three months.

Smith: That ought to be *nineteen* years and three months, Sir.

Officer: Who says so?

Smith: Me, Sir.

C.S.M.: STOP TALKING!
Officer: Sorry, Smith, but I've got to go by the age shown on your records. March out, sar-major.
Smith: But, Sir....
C.S.M.: STOP TALKING! SALUTE! ABOUT TURN! QUICK MARCH ...

The time at Lyndhurst was spent in hard training: exercises, weapon training and route marches. One rueful and footsore statistician recorded that he had marched three hundred miles about the New Forest.

Sunday, October 4 was like any other Sunday in summer camp: dinner had been eaten and groused at, and in the afternoon the old unwritten law of the British Army 'in bed or out of barracks' was faithfully adhered to.

Lyndhurst's long main street teemed with khaki: although Lyndhurst had never been a soldiers' town, it rose to the occasion manfully. After a lengthy sojourn overseas, most of the men of the 7th Division had, as the British soldier described his rare periods of financial affluence, 'a bit in their credits'. They were predominantly bachelors and were intent on spending their money in the shortest possible time.

They thronged the public houses and threatened to drink them dry; they swarmed into the few cafés and consumed mountains of fish and chips and faggots and peas. They ogled the young women, flattered the middle-aged and called the old ones 'Mum', helping them across the street to the accompaniment of outrageous comment. They spoiled the children atrociously and showered them with sweets; they adopted stray dogs and cats and illicitly fed them on army rations; they wrote their numbers, names and regiments on the wall of the town's only public convenience.

With characteristic perversity the War Office elected to mobilise the 7th Division on a Sunday afternoon — Sunday, the hallowed day of rest for the British soldier, when he slept (about sixty per cent), engaged in marathon sessions of card playing (thirty per cent), or went for a stroll in the town (the remaining ten per cent).

Bored and somnolent orderly officers sat at their posts, waiting for a telephone call which must surely come but not on the afternoon of October 4, 1914: they were looking forward to tea in the mess, a leisurely splash in a canvas bath, gin and angostura and dinner. On Monday the War Office could do its worst, but in the meantime six days they had laboured.

At 3 p.m. that Sunday afternoon the sleepy peace of the camp at Lyndhurst was disturbed by shrilling telephones. Orderly officers reached out for the dreaded instrument, bawled for runners who sped in search of adjutants who, in their turn, sought out commanding officers—most of them were sitting at ease outside their tents on stools, camp, senior officers for the use of, gently savouring the fragrance of the after-luncheon pipe.

The colonels, phlegmatic men who, in the last twenty years, had mobilised for well-nigh forgotten campaigns in Egypt, South Africa and on the North-West Frontier of India, accepted the news without emotion. 'Carry on, and get out the orders,' they told their adjutants; 'there shouldn't be much difficulty—we've practised the thing often enough.'

They had practised it so often that the card players in the tents, after hasty calculations of winnings, were fully accoutred as fighting soldiers in under half an hour. The problem of recalling men in Lyndhurst was solved by sending buglers to high ground near the camp, from which vantage point they blew 'Assembly' at the full pitch of their lungs.

The Seventh Division was ready to march in a miraculously short time: the 2nd Queen's got their orders at 3 p.m. to be ready to move at 3.45, an impossible task in the circumstances. But they were ready at 5 p.m. and other units were no less prompt: the South Staffords, in particular, were warmly congratulated by General Capper on being the first unit which was ready in all respects for war.

Practically the entire population of Lyndhurst turned out to see the 7th off on their nine-mile march to Southampton, and handkerchiefs were unashamedly busy as they swung down the main street: there were young women who had hoped that temporary romantic attachments might achieve some degree of permanency; publicans and café proprietors who looked back on a profit boom such as they had never known before and probably would never know again; the town's police force of three who watched with a mixture of relief and nostalgia—they had only once had to break up a fight, virtually inevitable with Gordon Highlanders and Royal Welch Fusiliers stationed in the same neighbourhood.

So the 7th Division went to war.

In two world wars inter-divisional feuds were inevitable, and usually friendly. But occasionally in rear areas behind the front line, where the off-duty behaviour of soldiers of every nationality frequently fell short of the exemplary, bitterness and rivalry sometimes gained the upper hand: in estaminets and bars, soldiers wearing different divisional signs argued, squabbled and sometimes sanguinarily fought, only to join forces in routing the military police who had been despatched to break up the encounter; in hotels, restaurants and officers' clubs the commissioned ranks sometimes gave rein to their feelings in acrimonious exchanges.

Thus, Division 'A' sun-bathed and caroused in brothels while Division 'B' was being cut to pieces; Division 'C' carried out a brilliant attack, but only with overwhelming artillery and air support—poor old Division 'D' had been decimated, trying to do the same job without either of these ancillary luxuries; Division 'E' had retreated in perfect order, whereas Division 'F' had run like hell in panic-stricken disorder; Division 'G' had held the position to the last man and the last round—that hardy old annual again—while Division 'H' had put up their hands and cravenly surrendered; Division 'I' had carried out an unopposed beach landing whereas Division 'J' had run into scything machine-gun fire, barbed wire and thousands of land mines.

It was mostly good and stimulating talk—esprit de corps, the British Army calls it—but inevitably somebody got touchy and said something out of turn; a fist flashed out and a bottle was broken over a head; accusations of cowardice, casualty figures, statistics of decorations won all added fuel to the disputes.

Some of this, of course, went on in the British Expeditionary Force in the closing days of 1914.

Comparisons are invariably odious, and comparisons between the first seven Divisions is not easy and must inevitably
provoke an outcry from survivors and war historians alike:
the 3rd bore most of the brunt of the Battle of Mons; Le
Cateau was almost entirely a 4th and 5th Divisions affair; in
the Battles of the Marne and at the crossing of the Aisne, the
1st and 2nd possibly showed to the greatest advantage; the
6th, after a slightly shaky start in the Aisne defences, covered
themselves with glory in the later fighting.

It has been said that no single Infantry Division of the
British Army has ever been composed of a more splendid
fighting personnel than was the 7th when it landed in Belgium.

At first sight, indeed, in matters of morale, discipline, keenness and fighting efficiency, the 7th seemed to carry off every
palm. To a soldier this was easily enough understood: like
a top-class rugby football club, the 7th were able to take the
field with all their best players. There were no reservists in
their ranks.

The average regular British battalion had, at its full peace
establishment, no superior in the world as a fighting force.
But when the Reserve is added to bring it to war strength,
something like twenty-five per cent or more is subtracted from
its value. (To stifle any outcry from reservists, three Victoria
Crosses had already been won by men recalled from the
Reserve.[1])

Some explanation of this apparently sweeping statement is
necessary. A reservist, with his colour service and anything up
to five years' civilian life behind him and another thirty or
more stretching invitingly before him, must inevitably be
something of an unwilling warrior; he has, as it were, lost
some of his cutting edge as a fighting soldier (but they soon
acquired it again, as the Germans found to their cost at Mons,
Le Cateau and on the Aisne). The fact remains, however, that
almost every unit of the original B.E.F. had a large proportion of reservists in its ranks, in some as many as sixty per
cent. The infantry battalions of the 7th Division and the

[1] Corporal Holmes — King's Own Yorkshire Light Infantry, Private
Dobson — Coldstream Guards and Private Wilson — Highland Light
Infantry.

cavalry of the 3rd Cavalry Division were peacetime entities—a war was simply incidental; practically every man had at least five years' service, and they were trained to a fine peak of professional efficiency.

They were all crack shots, and their musketry, bayonet fighting, fieldcraft and march discipline were of a higher standard than that of the other six divisions: They were, on the whole, tougher and harder men; predominantly bachelors, there was little bleating from the men of the 7th about the little woman and kids at home and the paucity of separation allowance. If they missed the target on the rifle range, they did not say, 'supposing that had been an enemy?'—they said, fuck it, there goes my proficiency pay'.

So the men of the 7th were, in the main, hard-case professional soldiers whose credo (roughly translated) was fight, fuck and follow the flag, or, as Nietzsche more delicately phrased it, 'war is for man and woman for the returning warrior'.

There were some disgruntled young gentlemen at the Royal Military College at Sandhurst during August 1914; they were worried that the fighting in France might finish before they could reach it.

There were also many apprehensive young gentlemen: these were the cadets who had completed their last term and were anxiously awaiting the results of the passing-out exam. The R.M.C. was then, as now, a forcing house—a place of constant trial and error.

As anxious as any of them was Gentleman Cadet Francis Orme, who had committed more than his fair share of errors. So far, his military career had not been distinguished: he had frequently been called 'an idle gentleman' by the sergeant-instructors, and on one occasion the regimental sergeant-major, an august being of the Grenadier Guards with fiercely waxed moustaches, had uttered the ultimate condemnation, Mr. Horme, sir, you're 'ORRIBLE!'

But Francis Orme need not have worried. His company commander informed him that presumably the examiners had been blind or drunk or both, because by some unexplained miracle he was now Second-Lieutenant Orme of the Royal

Welch Fusiliers. The officer frowned. He hoped—yes, he very much hoped—that Orme would speedily mend his ways and be a credit to his regiment—he had certainly *not* been a conspicuous success at Sandhurst. However, said the company commander with a weighty sigh of resignation, a war must inevitably bring a sharp decline of standards. If it went on long enough, the civilians would start joining up, and if that happened then *anything* could happen. . . . Orme hardly heard him—his commission was safe. Now only one thing worried him: would he get to the war in time?

In the Regimental Depot at Wrexham, Second-Lieutenant Orme fretted and fumed: he went on parade; inspected rifles, counted socks, prepared endless nominal rolls, dined in mess. The war, the Adjutant told him tersely, would last some time yet; in the meantime Orme should not consider that the less glamorous chores of soldiering were beneath him.

News of the conduct of the war in Flanders was scant in the Royal Welch Fusiliers' depot, but casualty lists were all too frequent. It soon became apparent that both the 1st and 2nd Battalions were being systematically knocked to pieces, and it equally soon dawned upon Francis Orme that his days of rifle inspections, nominal rolls and calculations of socks were numbered.

The 2nd Battalion had come through the Battle of Mons and the retreat almost unscathed: such was the fortune of war. True, they had shared in all the hardships of that punishing march rearwards, but the march discipline of the Royal Welch Fusiliers had always been second to none, and few of the men had regarded the retreat as anything worse than a lengthy extension of a peacetime route march.

Indeed, the trials of the 1st Battalion were yet to come, but the 2nd had been blooded in circumstances of murderous ferocity as daily increasing lists of fallen officers sombrely proved: the Commanding Officer, Lieutenant-Colonel Cadogan, had been killed, as were Captains Kingston, Lloyd, Brennan and Lieutenants Chance, Dooner and Egerton; Major Gabbett, Captains St. John and Scaife and Lieutenants Jones and Naylor were wounded; Lieutenants Poole, Wodehouse and Evans were missing—they later turned up in prisoner-of-war camps, as did the Medical Officer, Captain Robertson. In rank and file the 1st Royal Welch Fusiliers mustered barely one hundred.

On a morning in late October, Second-Lieutenant Francis Orme was summoned to the Adjutant's office. Wondering what he had done wrong this time, Orme kept the appointment.

The Adjutant, as frequently was the case with adjutants of British infantry depots, had had a difficult morning: his telephone rang incessantly, and he was bombarded with what the Duke of Wellington accurately called 'a mass of futile correspondence'—most of the documents which the orderly room sergeant relentlessly fed into his 'In' tray had no conceivable connection with war; a few needed to be memorised, but mostly they required his signature. And interspersed between the circulars about treatment of snake-bite in tropical theatres of war, returns of the number of Methodists on the depot strength and homilies on venereal disease, were the inevitable casualty lists—page after page, listed under coldly impersonal headings: killed in action; died of wounds; wounded; missing believed killed; missing believed to be prisoner-of-war.

Colonel Cadogan, then Adjutant himself, had blasted him as a second-lieutenant in 1898; he remembered Major Gabbett as senior subaltern at Shorncliffe; he had been at Sandhurst with Kingston and best man at Brennan's wedding.

Many of the rank and file, too, he knew well, even though they seemed to be predominantly named Jones, Evans, Davies and Williams—he remembered Jones 97 as the scrum half in the Battalion's rugby team and the terror of all referees; Evans 41 who had once been his servant and inevitably wore his shirts off duty; Williams 04 who had urinated on a night watchman's prayer mat in India and all but precipitated a religious riot.

And while all these officers and men were fighting and dying the Adjutant was condemned to a desk at Wrexham. It is scarcely surprising that he favoured Second-Lieutenant Orme with a regulation scowl, when he told him that he would depart for Flanders on the morrow with a draft of 109 N.C.O.s and men.

71

The journey to Flanders took Francis Orme to Le Havre, where he languished in the sea of glutinous mud which went by the misnomer of a rest camp; thousands had sat waiting in this mud before him; hundreds of thousands more were destined to do so later in the war.

On arrival at the front Orme reported himself to Captain Arthur Roberts of the 2nd Queen's Royal Regiment. Roberts, like Orme, had been left behind at Lyndhurst to fret as a reinforcement officer. Now he was in command of the divisional reinforcements—officers and men from every regiment, something like fifteen hundred in all.

Orme gave Roberts a tremendous salute and said: 'I wonder if you could tell me where the 2nd Royal Welch Fusiliers are?'

Roberts jerked his thumb towards a group of sixty or seventy men squatting stoically in a muddy ditch. 'There they are.'

The subaltern stared and gulped: 'And—er—who's in command?'

'I suspect,' said Roberts carefully, 'that you are.'

And so Second-Lieutenant Francis Orme aged eighteen years and nine months found himself elevated to temporary command of the 2nd Royal Welch Fusiliers. It was a tenure of command that he did not hold for long: the remnants of the Fusiliers went back into the line that evening—at this period of the fighting rest periods were rarely of more than six hours' duration—and before another day had dawned the name of yet another officer had been added to the long list of the regiment's fallen officers: Second-Lieutenant Francis Orme.

Captain Roberts in the meantime supervised the distribution of his variegated command—Grenadiers, Gordons, South Staffords, Royal Warwicks, Royal Welch Fusiliers—to their units, and then sought out General Capper at Divisional Headquarters. Capper was holding a handkerchief to a chronically 'weeping eye'; if the truth were known he was very near to weeping in real earnest.

'How many men have you brought with you?' demanded the general.

'Fifteen hundred, sir.'

Capper laughed mirthlessly. 'If it were fifteen thousand,' he said, 'it still wouldn't be enough.'

Although the 2nd Queen's were not in such evil case as the Royal Welch Fusiliers, Roberts found that they could barely muster two weak companies and had been formed into a single battalion with the Fusiliers. Likewise, the 2nd Royal Warwicks were amalgamated with the 1st South Staffords.

Casualty lists of the 2nd Battalion, the Royal Warwickshire Regiment tell of the wounding of Lieutenant Ronald Richardson in December 1914 and of his death while leading his company in the first assault at Loos in September 1915. The topsy-turvy rank structure of the Great War was well illustrated by the fact that in November 1914 *Second-Lieutenant* Richardson, who had recently celebrated his twentieth birthday, was in command of the Battalion which, like nearly every other battalion of the 7th Division, could barely muster one under-strength company.

The 2nd Royal Warwicks were, in fact, a battalion in mourning—in mourning for seven officers killed, six wounded and ten made prisoners-of-war and for over five hundred rank and file. But most of all they mourned the loss of their commanding officer, Lieutenant-Colonel Loring, an officer of almost legendary gallantry.

In the fighting on the Menin Road Colonel Loring, as was his inevitable custom, rode at the head of his regiment. The Second-in-Command, Major Paul Foster, had tactfully mentioned the inadvisability of riding a white horse in such an exposed position, and was consigned to outer hell for his pains. For the Colonel's charger was not a grey, as they say on race-cards, but startlingly and virginally white—a great, prancing seventeen-hand steed which would have befitted Henry V at Agincourt.

In the Second World War many battalion commanders were rapped by their brigadiers for routing about the battle-field like privates in search of glory, armed with such improbable weapons as rifles, tommy-guns and hand grenades, and many of them died; of such men it was often said that they merited a Victoria Cross or a court martial.

Some officers, eye-witnesses of the battle, said that Colonel

Loring's conduct was foolhardy and smacked of bravado, but never in the presence of any officer or man of the 2nd Royal Warwicks. Loring would not have cared what they said, anyway—although two privates of Battalion Headquarters agreed in voices of awed admiration that the old man was barmy: if the 2nd Royal Warwicks were going into action then his proper place was at their head. And if anyone thought that he was going to change his white horse for a flea-bitten bay, then they had another think coming.

Colonel Loring made a splendid target, a fact that was not lost on a German sniper: the Commanding Officer took a bullet neatly through the heel, but beyond uttering an oath of such frightfulness that his soldier servant dropped his rifle, he paid no heed to what he regarded as a trifling mishap.

But later, when the bullets were falling among the Warwicks like hailstones, Major Foster saw his Colonel sway in the saddle and all but fall off. If the white charger took control of the C.O., as seemed ominously likely, it would gallop with him into the middle distance and be lost for ever.

Foster detailed the Colonel's servant and another private to help Loring from his horse and take him to the Regimental Aid Post; a lance-corporal, who would have infinitely preferred to have faced the bullets, was ordered to mount the charger and take it to the rear.

The medical officer examined the Colonel's smashed heel, which not only contained a bullet but pieces of his spur as well: almost certainly, the doctor considered, the wound would turn gangrenous and the best that Loring could hope for would be amputation of the foot.

'You'll have to go back, sir,' said the M.O.

'Go to hell,' said the Colonel succinctly, and bawled to his servant, 'bring me my carpet slippers!'

With his wounded foot encased in a check-patterned carpet slipper, he re-mounted the white horse and once more took his place at the head of his battalion. The white horse was shot from under him, and the flea-bitten bay was brought up at a protesting canter.

The bay, too, went the way of all horseflesh; Colonel Loring was last seen alive, hobbling among his men, encouraging them to greater efforts by the example of his fearless bearing.

Walter Loring was one of three brothers, all killed in the first year of the war. The other two were Major Charles Loring and Captain William Loring, both of the Indian Army.

The 2nd Green Howards, like the Royal Warwicks, were also in mourning for their Commanding Officer: Lieutenant-Colonel Charles King had taken a bullet clean through the forehead while in a forward trench. The Green Howards, however, were comparatively affluent in manpower, for they had Captain Moss-Blundell in command, three subalterns and 300 men out of an original strength of 32 officers and 970 other ranks.

Life was dear to the Regimental Quartermaster-Sergeant of the 2nd Battalion, the Wiltshire Regiment when war broke out in August 1914; not only was life dear, but pension was near —the little cottage near Devizes, which he had set his heart on for his old age was almost a tangible possibility.

The R.Q.M.S., like many another warrant officer holding that august rank, was of comfortable build; the spreading waistlines of 'R.Q.s' was always something of a joke in the old British Army, due, it was constantly theorised, to their inevitable proximity to the ration store.

But on this morning in November the pension seemed twenty years away and the cottage in Devizes a million miles distant. The R.Q.M.S., after twenty-eight years' service, during which time he had never heard a shot fired in anger— he had spent the South African War in the Regimental Depot at Devizes—found himself under incessant shell and rifle fire; he had next found himself in command of a platoon composed of cooks, clerks, transport drivers and officers' mess servants; wrested from his cosy 'bunk' some miles to the rear of main Battalion Headquarters, he had occupied a succession of muddy trenches. It was, thought the R.Q.M.S. resentfully, no way for a senior warrant-officer on the brink of pension, holder of the Long Service and Good Conduct Medals, to live.

But that was not all: beyond a vague hope that he might achieve the rank of Lieutenant and Quartermaster before he retired, the R.Q.M.S. harboured no ambition for further promotion — undoubtedly there was no field marshal's baton in *his* haversack. On the morning of October 25, 1914 he searched for officers of the 2nd Wiltshires and searched in vain: Lieutenant-Colonel Forbes was missing: there were no majors, captains or subalterns. There were just 110 N.C.O.s and privates, and the stark realisation came to the R.Q.M.S. that he was in command of the battalion.

A staff officer of the 7th Division, who was of a literary turn of mind, recorded his impressions of the 2nd Royal Scots Fusiliers in a contribution to *Blackwood's Magazine*: 'We came into a field occupied by the Royal Scots Fusiliers. Here they were drawn up, erect and grim as usual, but what a different regiment from the one which had swung out of Lyndhurst Camp less than five weeks before. That magnificently smart regiment of once a thousand men was now reduced to about seventy, with a junior subaltern in command. The men were mostly without caps, coats or even puttees, war-stained and ragged, but still full of British pluck and pride, with a "never-say-die" look upon their faces, which made the heart swell with pride at being connected with such splendid specimens of manhood.'

An argument was going on at Battalion Headquarters of the 2nd Royal Scots Fusiliers, albeit an entirely friendly one: Second-Lieutenants William Clutterbuck and Alan Thompson were endeavouring to establish which of them was commanding officer of the battalion.

They were both twenty years old, but Thompson was two months older than Clutterbuck, which seemed to establish his seniority; on the other hand, they had passed out of Sandhurst, both of them fairly low down the list, in 1913. Neither of them could remember who had passed out the lowest.

'Only one thing for it,' said Thompson. 'We must get hold of an Army List — one of us must be above the other.'

'Where do we get an Army List from?' asked Clutterbuck.

'You've got me there. Tell you what, though — Sergeant MacWhirter' — he referred to the orderly room sergeant — 'will know; he knows everything.'

'He's dead.'

Clearly, they were getting no further. Eventually they decided on the alphabetical system, and they agreed that Second-Lieutenant Clutterbuck should assume command.

And what of the rank and file of the 2nd Royal Scots Fusiliers? There was no doubt as to who the senior non-commissioned rank was, because Sergeant Forbes was the only sergeant still on his feet. For the rest, the battalion consisted of four corporals, seven lance-corporals and 59 private soldiers.

The casualty list of the Grenadier Guards read like a section of Debrett: Major the Hon. A. Weld-Forester, Captain the Hon. C. M. B. Ponsonby, Captain Lord Richard Wellesley, Lieutenant the Hon. A. G. S. Douglas-Pennant, Major Lord Bernard Gordon-Lennox, Lieutenant Lord Congleton.

The Commanding Officer, Lieutenant-Colonel Earle, was seriously wounded and taken prisoner and the Medical Officer, while dressing his Colonel's wound, had been killed. The Second-in-Command, Major Hugh Stucley, was killed half an hour after assuming command from Colonel Earle; fourteen other officers were dead, wounded or missing.

The losses of the officers of the 2nd Scots Guards were also representatively patrician: Captain Lord Esme Gordon-Lennox, Captain the Master of Kinnaird, Second-Lieutenant Lord Garlies, Major Viscount Dalrymple, Captain the Hon. J. S. Coke, Lieutenant Lord Gerald Grosvenor, Captain Sir Victor MacKenzie, Bart., Lieutenant Sir George Ogilvy, Bart., Lieutenant Sir John Dyer, Lieutenant the Earl of Dalhousie.

In the Great War—and, indeed, in every other war—the Brigade of Guards suffered astronomical casualties: proportionately, regiment by regiment, probably the highest of the entire British Army. The reason is not hard to find: their attacking line was always that little bit straighter and more determined—'by the right', as the Brigade's drill book has it; in desperate last-ditch stands the position was always held that little bit longer; the order 'to hold to the last man and the last round' was always interpreted in its most literal sense.

The Brigade of Guards are, and always have been, a law unto themselves: the Household Brigade has changed but little in the past century because, as is fiercely argued by guardsmen, there is nothing about it that needs to be changed.

In peace or war the Household Brigade subjected its would-be officers to searching inquiries about their social and financial status: failure to satisfy these exacting requirements frequently resulted in social extinction in the despised infantry. A Guards officer was never allowed to travel on public transport, carry cigarettes in a packet or refer to London as 'Town'.

Guards officers have always behaved in a manner which, to the outsider, seems strange. It is not done to express enthusiasm about military matters at any time; they give the impression that they are slightly sorry for anyone who is *not* an officer of the Brigade of Guards; they are parochial to a degree which may seem insufferable to the casual observer or lesser beings in less fashionable regiments. More specifically, they heap derision on the other regiments of the Brigade of Guards. Thus, to a Grenadier the Coldstream are the last word; the Scots are the end; the Irish are beyond the pale; the Welsh are the Foreign Legion and only good at singing; and the Household Cavalry merely laughable. It goes without saying the other Guards regiments dispose of the Grenadiers with the same degree of cordial malice.

Unaccountably, officers of the Foot Guards wear their forbiddingly-peaked caps in the mess, whether drinking sherry before lunch or eating breakfast. Ask them why this is so, and they will produce the unanswerable rejoinder: 'But, my dear fellow, why not?'

It is no good trying to understand them. One can call them 'debs' delights', 'chinless wonders', 'scarlet-tunicked popinjays' and all the other things that spring easily to the minds of their most rabid critics; all these appellations are a matter of supreme indifference to the officers of the Household Brigade.

They have always given, and will continue to give, the impression that they know little and care less for the job that they have at heart. Nevertheless, beneath this dégagé façade is the simple desire to prosper in their chosen profession and a cold professional efficiency. It was precisely this same rather rarefied attitude which led the commanding officer of a Guards battalion who had been ordered to surrender, to reply that the regiment had not practised such a manœuvre in peace and was therefore unable to carry it out in war.

In peacetime London, in the splendour of bearskins and scarlet tunics, it was sometimes difficult to imagine them at war. But students of military history and others with long memories recall that where the fighting was most deadly in any of Great Britain's wars, there would always be found a company of Guards and many a hard-pressed commander in the field was grateful for their presence. And their smartness, even in the vilest conditions, always excited the admiration — tinged, perhaps, with envy — of other regiments.

The uniforms and kit of a Guards battalion were always that little bit neater than those of their neighbours; their bivouacs or camp lines were that much straighter and better ordered; their movements on parade were that much more impeccable. And as it was on ceremonial parade, so was it in battle.

The scene on a morning in late November 1914 might have been Chelsea or Wellington Barracks before the war.

Before the war Guardsmen spent most of their waking hours cleaning and polishing: they expended gallons of spittle and mounds of blacking on their boots; rivers of metal polish on buttons, cap badges and brasswork on web equipment — it was sometimes said that, freely translated, the motto of the Brigade *'honi soit qui mal y pense'* meant 'after you with the Bluebell'.

The men of the 1st Grenadier Guards and 2nd Scots Guards were doing all these things on that November morning: boots were in a deplorable state and there was an acute shortage of polish, but soon every Guardsman's toe-caps shone like glass; carefully hoarded tins of 'Bluebell' were passed from hand to hand, and in a miraculously short space of time buttons, cap badges and brasses glittered like burnished gold. Other units might be lying in supine exhaustion in their billets, but one thing was certain—the Guards were going on a drill parade.

Such a state of affairs today might bring some twenty-five pounds-a-week private soldiers to the brink of insubordination: the 'bull after battle' routine could hardly be expected to stimulate recruiting. But the Guardsman of the period saw nothing incongruous about it, and if he did he was wise enough not to say so.

The 1st Grenadiers fell in in two ranks, to the accompaniment of the usual Grenadier endearments from Drill-Sergeant Capper who informed them that they looked like the wrecks of the Hesperus and a lot of old whores at a virgins' meeting.

The two ranks of Guardsmen stood as if they had grown straight out of the ground, their heels exactly twelve inches apart and the butts of their rifles mathematically in line with their highly polished right toe-caps in the position known as 'properly at ease'. Sergeant Capper then dressed the front and rear ranks in such a way that each man could just see the chin of his neighbour but no further. He then bawled 'Front rank, STEADY!' and 'Rear rank, STEADY!', followed by 'EYES FRONT!' with 'As you WEAH!' shouted three times for good measure. Eventually, satisfied with the symmetry of the battalion, he marched one hundred paces, for all the world as if he were taking part in the Trooping the Colour ceremony on Horse Guards, and reported to Captain Rasch, who was commanding officer, second-in-command and adjutant. With him were four other officers: Lieutenant Lord Claud Hamilton, Lieutenant Teece, 2nd Lieutenant Darby and Lieutenant Mitchell.

At a range of approximately three feet Sergeant Capper bawled in Captain Rasch's face: 'Battalion ready for your inspection, SIR!'

Rasch returned Capper's salute, but when he tried to say 'Thank you, Sarn't Capper' the words would not come. It was then that Sergeant Capper saw that his commanding officer was crying.

Sergeant Capper brought his hand to his rifle in a butt salute which sounded like a pistol shot, about-turned with a crash of heels and marched back to the battalion.

The orders that morning had said an hour's steady drill;

that order had not been countermanded—therefore one hour's steady drill there would be. 'FORM FOURS! SLOPE HIPE! FORM FOURS! MOVE TO THE RIGHT IN FOURS! RIGHT TURN! BY THE RIGHT, QUICK MARCH! SWING THOSE ARMS! LOOK UP! LEFT-RIGHT, LEFT-RIGHT, LEFT . . . !'

The strength of the 1st Battalion The Grenadier Guards was five officers and 125 rank and file.

An almost exactly similar scene was enacted in the 2nd Scots Guards. But when Company Sergeant-Major MacBride reported the Battalion ready for inspection, there was only one officer on parade. The 2nd Scots Guards consisted of Captain Strachey and 69 men.

Billeting officers of the B.E.F. in the early days of the Great War were harassed individuals, whose job normally approximated to the vexed question of introducing a quart into a pint pot: in the early days there had been too many soldiers and too few buildings in which to house them: they crowded into farms, barns, schools, convents, churches and estaminets. The quality of the billet depended on the unit billeting officer, and ranged from the almost luxurious to the downright squalid. These billets were for men about to go into battle—400 officers and 12,000 men.

In this manner did the 7th Division, a crack formation, one of the finest that Great Britain had ever put into the field, prepare for battle: they were trained to a hair; they were a superbly disciplined force with the highest possible morale; whatever the first six divisions had achieved, they would do better.

But what was this? A column of men were coming back from the salient about Kraseik: they were indescribably filthy, and their mud-clotted clothes were in rags. They trudged along like sleep-walkers, in a sort of cosmic slow motion; their eyes wandered and their mouths hung open. They looked like old, old men, for their faces were stubbled with beards, and the colour of them was a queer pallor, pitted with mauve powder marks as are the faces of miners who have spent a lifetime in the pit.

It seemed that their legs were not strong enough to hold them; many were wounded, with rough head bandages and arms in slings; others carried wounded men on stretchers or hobbled along, using their rifles as a crutch.

Two staff officers, enjoying a brief respite from the feverish activity of Corps Headquarters and feeling in need of exercise, rode towards them. Their horses were also in need of exercise; over-indulgent grooms had fed them too many oats and they had to be ridden on a harsh curb.

The staff officers were immaculate, with gleaming Sam Browne belts and field boots that shone like chestnuts. Their red tabs seemed almost indecent when set against the grimy shuffling throng who struggled along the road.

'In God's name,' said one of the staff officers, 'who are they?'—his province was 'Q' Branch, which dealt with ammunition and rations rather than human bodies.

'The 7th Division,' said the other, who was of 'G' Branch which dealt with battles and fighting soldiers, 'or what's left of it.'

The weary column came closer, and the staff officer of 'G' Branch experienced a sudden cold feeling in the pit of his stomach. For he had noticed the distinctive black silk flash on the back of the tunic collars of the men who staggered past him: they were of his own regiment, the Royal Welch Fusiliers.

He raised his hand to halt them, and beckoned to the sergeant at their head. The sergeant came to attention in front of the staff officer, swaying like a drunken man, and somehow contrived a salute.

'What's happened?' asked the staff officer.

'We're all that's left of the battalion, sir,' said the sergeant, and in spite of his crippling fatigue there was a note of pride in his voice.

'Who is in command?'

'I am, sir,' said the sergeant, and his voice seemed to grow stronger. 'Mr. Orme joined from the depot yesterday morning. He was killed.'

The staff officer nodded, for he was beyond speech. Momentarily he cursed the military permutations which had permitted him an extended period of military education at the Staff College, Camberley, which had placed him in a position of comparative comfort and safety. Then, with a cold feeling returning to his stomach muscles, he realised that he could, at worst, be dead; at best wounded or a prisoner-of-war. He said curtly: 'Carry on, sergeant.'

The sergeant favoured him with another tremendous salute, and barked at the semi-conscious men, 'Right, get moving.'

The Royal Welch Fusiliers—just seventy strong—shuffled on, and the two staff officers sat erect in their saddles, their hands at the peaks of their caps. Both wanted to cry, but dared not; they could not mutter 'Well done, well done', as the Royal Welch Fusiliers passed by.

More remnants of battalions struggled past these two staff officers, who suddenly felt puny and impotent and ashamed of their glossy horses, red tabs and glittering field boots: Grenadier and Scots Guards came past—they marched at the slope, they were impeccably in step, but even the Brigade of Guards could give the appearance of having been shattered, and the 1st Grenadiers and 2nd Scots Guards were shattered almost beyond recall; came Gordon Highlanders, with two pipers at their head defiantly playing 'Cock o' the North', a bare company strong and only kept conscious by the music of the pipes; Borders, Bedfords, Royal Scots Fusiliers, Yorkshires, Wiltshires, Queens, Royal Warwicks, and South Staffords completed the melancholy procession—the whole of the 7th Division could barely muster two complete brigades of infantry; no one brigade could show a complete battalion on its strength.

They were a mere wreck of the fine force which had landed at Zeebrugge just a month before. Their fighting power was all but exhausted, but their fame was secure for all time.

The two staff officers, as they hacked their horses back to Corps Headquarters, asked one another over and over again, 'How did it happen?' At G.H.Q., Sir John French asked himself the same question, as did other staff officers as the casualty lists poured in. How had it happened? What had gone wrong?

In every unit of the 7th Division, the melancholy story was the same: on November 7, of 400 officers and 12,000 men who sailed from Southampton, only 44 officers and 2,336 other ranks remained.

How had the 7th Division, the veritable cream of Britain's regular army, arrived at this sorry state? What had gone wrong?

The war had not started auspiciously for the newly arrived 7th Division. Like the men of the original B.E.F. they had crossed the Channel in a mood of high-spirited exuberance, which boded ill for the Germans: they would get this war finished with, go home for Christmas and two weeks' home leave and then back to the sunshine again.

On disembarkation at Zeebrugge the men of the 7th and the 3rd Cavalry Divisions were accorded the same rapturous reception as their predecessors at Le Havre and Boulogne, but unlike the 1st and 2nd Corps they did not go straight into a battle like Mons, Le Cateau, the Marne or the Aisne; nor did they find themselves forced into precipitate retreat. They did not, in fact, go into battle at all on arrival, but within a week they were almost as exhausted and footsore as the men who had taken part in the Great Retreat from Mons.

They did not advance, neither did they retreat—they just marched; marched hither and thither, reasoning not why. Long marches, of course, were nothing new to them—the 2nd Queen's, 1st South Staffords and 2nd Bedfords thought nothing of fifty-mile route marches across the South African veldt— but as they plodded backwards and forwards across Belgium they swore roundly; if all they were going to do was more route-marching they might just as well have stayed in Lynd-hurst, for there, at least, the population did not clutter up all the roads.

As they marched and counter-marched from Zeebrugge to Bruges; thence to Ghent; and from Ghent to Pitthem, via Roulers, they were caught up in the flight of the refugees pouring out of Antwerp and the remnants of the shattered Belgian Army.

The 7th Infantry Division and the 3rd Cavalry Division had been despatched to save Antwerp, but there was no help devised by man for a city so sorely stricken, for Antwerp, that once proud bastion of Belgium, was doomed.

Imagine, if you can, Liverpool suddenly abandoned by its entire population, the people crowding on to the shipping in the harbour or streaming out across the countryside with such few possessions as they can carry.

Every road was thickly clogged with the long and hopeless columns, a shuffling, wailing throng; the most tragic jetsam of war—the civilian refugees.

There were enormous horse-drawn wagons with anything up to thirty persons huddled in the backs like the wares of a rag and bone man: girls clinging listlessly together on heaps of bedding; aged women like shrunken walnuts lying haphazardly, buried in shawls; children sleeping fitfully, waking suddenly, wailing for food; and babies howling interminably. There was a broken-down two-wheel cart with a horse dead between its shafts; the owner, an old man nearing seventy, had gone out of his mind: he stood by the roadside, swearing and shaking his clenched fists in the air, pausing every so often to tear at his hair and beard. Here and there were lone horsemen, riding bareback or on rough farm saddles.

There were bicycles with shapeless bundles fixed to them, protruding on either side of the wheels; and some of them had a child tied to the handlebars and another seated on the rear mudguard, clinging precariously to its rider's waist. There were perambulators, loaded with children and the few pathetic household belongings that had been salvaged; young men pushed wheelbarrows containing their aged parents and other men carried their children in chairs slung from their shoulders. Herds of animals added to the overall confusion: bevies of baa-ing sheep, goats, bellowing cattle, dogs barking distractedly, cats miaowing despairingly.

Here came a man with an old woman, his mother, in a wheelbarrow; also balanced on the barrow was a clock—a real, antique grandfather clock which periodically let out a macabre chime.

Some of them, in a state of utter exhaustion, could go no farther and dropped out on the side of the road: a woman stood weeping hysterically by the roadside with the one possession she had managed to salvage—a huge harp with a gold frame; another sat dully alone, gazing blankly at a hen-coop laden with crockery; there was a woman suckling her baby in a ditch, while in this same ditch another felt the first labour pains; standing nearby a small boy, aged four or five, stood sucking his thumb, wide-eyed with fright, hunger and bewilderment.

These people were the population of Antwerp, by this time a dying city.

Before the war Antwerp had been considered to be impregnable; it was admirably adapted by nature for a prolonged siege, having access to the sea on one side while to landwards the city was practically encircled at an advantageous distance of about 3,500 yards by the rivers Scheldt, Rupel and Nethe.

'Antwerp', wrote Winston Churchill in *The World Crisis*, 'is not only the sole stronghold of the Belgian nation; it is also the true left flank of the Allied front in the West. It guards the whole line of the Channel Ports (Dunkirk, Calais and Boulogne); it threatens the flanks and rear of the German armies in France; it is the gateway from which the British Army might emerge at any moment upon their sensitive and vital communications.'

Nor was the German High Command slow to appreciate the importance of Antwerp. As early as September 9, before the Allied crossing of the Aisne, orders had been issued by the Kaiser that 'immediate steps should be initiated for the reduction of the fortress'.

Belgium's soldiers had fought the Germans with all the strength and courage that God had given them: man for man, they considered themselves superior to the enemy in fighting qualities and had already proved this in many bloody encounters. But they were exhausted after two months of continuous fighting; they were woefully ill-equipped and hopelessly outnumbered. Although he managed to blind himself to the fact, General de Guise, Commander-in-Chief of the Belgian Army, realised that the surrender of the city was inevitable.

But it seemed that the salvation of Antwerp was at hand. The first detachment of the Naval Division arrived in the city in the late evening of October 3, and the effect on the people of the city and the bone-weary and dispirited Belgian soldiers was electrifying: comely Belgian girls pinned miniature flags made of silk on to tunics; jugs of beer appeared as if by magic; kisses were bestowed on officers and men alike with a fine lack of discrimination. But all the time the distant boom of guns told that the Germans were getting nearer to Antwerp every minute: they had established themselves on ground from which they were able to bombard the city with their powerful howitzers with insulting ease.

The men of the Naval Division, their spirits in no way deflated by the shells which were falling on the city, marched, still singing lustily, to their trenches. The effect was astonishing: the Belgian soldiers were half-way to being convinced that Antwerp would be held; the civilians went about their occupations with lighter hearts.

The melancholy fact remained, however, that there was no hope for Antwerp—there never had been—although the Belgian High Command were optimistic to the last: they believed, even as late as October 6, that some 35,000 crack regular British troops were on their way to Antwerp; with a force of this size, the city could be held indefinitely.

The city's newspapers, like the Belgian High Command, was unquenchably optimistic: the evening editions of October 6 declared merrily in large type 'La Situation est bonne', and went on to say that the invaders would be hurled back beyond the river Nethe. On the morning of the 7th it was no longer possible to ignore the gravity of the crisis, but Le Matin was determined to allay the fears of the population: 'Whatever the future may have in store,' declared a brave editorial, 'all our people have behaved worthily and like heroes. We must now prepare to face the time of trial which we have to go through. Whatever bitterness it may contain, Belgium will emerge from the ordeal greater than ever.'

La Métropole, too, was buttressing the fortress with defiant print: 'Although there is evident recognition of the gravity of the hour, nowhere does one see any sign of depression. . . . Antwerp awaits events with serenity and confidence.'

These were the last newspapers to be published in Antwerp.

*

In spite of the brave utterances of the press, melancholy fact had to be faced that British help had been too little and too late. It was argued that if five times the number of men and ten times the number of guns had been sent a fortnight earlier the city could have been held. This was probably true, but instead of 35,000 British soldiers all that was available to defend Antwerp was the shattered remnants of the Belgian Army and about 8,000 belligerent but bewildered and at best half-trained sailors and marines.

On the evening of October 9 the Burgomaster made formal surrender of the city to the Germans and Antwerp's agony was at an end: it was now no longer a city, but only the husk of one; the streets, usually a hive of activity and gaiety, were shuttered, silent and deserted; the population was now reduced to nurses and their wounded, a few city officials, half a dozen newspapermen (including one from *The Times*) and a sprinkling of dubious citizens who had good reason to know that they had nothing to fear from the Germans.

A gazetteer will tell you that Menin is a town in Belgium; that its principal industries are flax, tobacco, textiles, rubber goods and soap. Its population numbers approximately 20,000 souls, and its best-known landmark is the British Memorial at the Menin Gate.

Few people in Britain, other than battleground tour enthusiasts, have heard of Menin. But to survivors of the 7th Division and 3rd Cavalry Division—today probably less than two hundred in number—the name has in its very sound the tone of a deep bell pealing a fateful note.

The 7th Division were fed up to a man on October 12: expecting to go into action almost at once, they merely marched and cursed an enemy that they could not see; spoiling for a fight, they heard rumours of the presence of concentrations of Germans, only to find still more miles of foot-bruising pavé to be covered. In the first week in Belgium the 7th saw nothing of the war, although the sound of the guns was coming ever nearer. But they saw a great deal of war's beastly aftermath: the wailing, shuffling throngs of refugees, the sight of which might have depressed and come near to demoralising a less well disciplined formation.

Paradoxically, the 7th Division, which was destined to fight one of the greatest defensive battles in the history of warfare, was initially used in an attacking role. The news was well received in the ranks; anything would be better than this endless marching.

'Marching, marching, marching!' they sang to the tune of 'Holy, Holy, Holy, Lord God Almighty'; 'always bloody well marching! Christ send the day when we'll bloody well march no more!'

It was good to be advancing against an enemy at last, with a full magazine in the rifle and one up the spout. There was, of course, still more marching but at least they knew where they were going.

The objective was Menin.

The job was entrusted to Brigadier-General Sydney Lawford's 22nd Brigade, which consisted of the 2nd Queen's, 1st Royal Welch Fusiliers, 2nd Warwicks and 1st South Staffords.

At first the attack on Menin seemed assured of success, but very early in the advance things started to go wrong.

Sir John French, when he ordered the attack on Menin, had been under the misapprehension that the town and its environs were weakly held by the Germans; he considered that an assault by four determined battalions could effectively brush aside all opposition: Menin cut through the German line of communications, and French wanted to throw all the enemy operations into disorder by the sudden occupation of the town.

Here was faulty British intelligence with a vengeance. Far from being weakly held, a large force of German cavalry held the Flemish town of Roulers, just north of Menin. The 22nd Brigade were advancing against an enemy force which outnumbered them by six to one.

The advance continued, so far against no opposition whatsoever: the Royal Welch Fusiliers on the left, the Royal Warwicks on the right, with the South Staffords and Queen's in support.

In total ignorance of the vast German forces in front of

them, Lawford's brigade continued to advance. Indeed, on th
morning of October 10 the brigade advanced 4,000 yard
against what appeared to be negligible opposition: there ap
peared to be few Germans in their path except for a fe
standing patrols which beat hasty and undignified retrea
after firing a few rounds. Those that stood and fought wer
contemptuously swept aside; to the men of the 7th it seeme
that these Germans were scarcely worthy of their steel.

At his Headquarters General Capper was jubilant as report
of still more successes poured in: all four battalions of Law
ford's brigade were making steady progress and killing a
encouraging number of the enemy. It seemed that the firs
independent operation of the 7th Division was to be crowne
with victory, and a resounding victory was badly needed b
the British Expeditionary Force.

It was an officer of the Royal Flying Corps who finally pu
the damper on victorious advance and sounded the knell fo
British victory at a single stroke.

October 10 had been a tough day for Captain Lawrenc
Strange of the Royal Flying Corps. He had spent all th
morning and most of the afternoon on aerial reconnaissance :
he had been shot at by Germans; naturally enough, Strang
did not complain about this because they were the enemy, an
it was their bounden duty to shoot him out of the sky; he wa
not altogether surprised when the French shot at him as we
—admirable soldier that he was, the French *poilu* was notori
ously trigger-happy and tended to fire indiscriminately at any
thing that moved, whether on the ground or in the sky. Bu
the ultimate insult was to be shot at by British soldiers, especi
ally as he had spent many painstaking hours painting the red
white and blue of the Union Jack prominently on the wing
of his machine.

Consequently, Captain Strange was not in the best of tem
pers when he landed his Blériot at 7th Division Headquarters :
to the junior staff officer who greeted him he gave a slangy and
racy account of what he had seen: 'Columns of Huns comin
along the road from Courtrai—country black with the sods
Pretty foul job altogether—don't mind the Jerries potting a
me, that's what they're there for. Good job the Froggies ar

such rotten shots. But I reckon our own chaps shooting at us was a bit over the odds.'

But Strange gave a more sober assessment of the situation to General Capper: the 7th, he told the General uncompromisingly, were advancing against a German force which outnumbered them by at least six to one. Clearly, one division could not take the offensive against four; Capper, therefore, had no choice but to call off the assault on Menin.

After the abandonment of the attack, the 7th Division went back to Ypres: to the weary men who entered the town on October 14, it seemed as peaceful and welcoming as Lyndhurst after a long route march through the New Forest. At first sight, the quaint, old-fashioned Flemish town, lying sleepily by the side of a tree-shaded canal, seemed very remote from war.

At every cottage door there were rosy-cheeked women with tempting jugs of wine—there were few teetotallers in the 7th —and the usual wide-eyed children, demanding souvenirs. In spite of the proximity of the Germans, life continued normally: the Mayor and Corporation were functioning, and seemed to be filled with more than ordinary importance; everywhere was to be seen the bewildering bustle of military movement—British, French and Belgian troops passing through the streets, billeted in the houses and public buildings.

The men of the 7th were paid for the first time since their arrival in Flanders, and speedily set about spending it in the open-air cafés, which dispensed the gaseous beer which incurs the displeasure of present-day Old Contemptibles, 'vin blank' and 'vin rooge'. 'Wipers', decided the men of the 7th and 3rd Cavalry Divisions, was quite a place.

But this sybaritic period was to be of short duration. More reports from Royal Flying Corps pilots told of a force of Germans, estimated at a quarter of a million men, advancing on Ypres. The 7th and 3rd Cavalry Divisions took up their positions five or six miles east of Ypres, on the line Houthem-Gheluvelt-St. Julien and they got there in the nick of time. They were the only British soldiers between the Germans and the Channel Ports. This point was forcibly made to brigade commanders by General Capper of the 7th and General Byng of the 3rd Cavalry: 'You're all there is between the Germans and Le Havre. There's nothing behind us. If we give way the war's lost. Positions will be held to the last man and the last round.'

For three weeks from October 16 there was not an officer or man of the 7th Division and 3rd Cavalry Division, save the dead and desperately wounded, who was not fighting continuously by day and by night. For the first few days they fought the Battle of Ypres alone and unsupported.

Between infantry and cavalry there was no difference in role. The cavalry were superbly mounted and had arrived on Belgian soil bristling with confidence, but by the evening of the 16th there was no sign of peacetime glitter or even of horses. The shine on leather and brass had been replaced by stinking mud, and the horses were in charge of the very minimum of horse-holders.

Captain John Dorrington of the 1st Dragoons (the Royals) described his transition from dashing horse soldier to the mole-like existence of a front line infantryman thus: 'I have half my troop, twelve men in all, with me in a shallow trench . . . the rest of the squadron is spread out a hundred yards on each side of us . . . in ten days I have washed twice and had my boots off once. Horses? I've almost forgotten what a horse looks like. . . .'

There were other officers and men of the 3rd Cavalry Division whose presence seemed to bring to the Battle of Ypres a new extreme of incongruity.

To the regiments of His Majesty's Foot Guards—Grenadiers, Coldstream, Scots and Irish (the Welsh were not born until 1915)—the Household Cavalry had always been something of a joke: clad in polished helmets and cuirasses, scarlet (Life Guards) and blue (Royal Horse Guards) tunics and gleaming, long black jack-boots they stood guard outside Whitehall, a perpetual target for tourists; when Royalty and foreign dignitaries ventured forth, the Household Cavalry, superbly mounted on prancing black steeds and with sabres drawn, were in attendance. To the regiments of foot guards, who occasionally forsook London and Windsor for service in Egypt and Palestine, the Household Cavalry were known as

'The Donkey Wallopers', and it was said that their foreign station was Pirbright, that bleak hutted and tented camp in Surrey, where they went for one month of musketry training every year.

In spite of their ceremonial appearance, which made Life Guards and Royal Horse Guards, apart from the different colour of their tunics, as indistinguishable as rows of hard-boiled eggs, a Life Guard and a Blue resembled one another as a Scot resembles a Senussi. Between the two regiments has always existed a traditional and cordial dislike: to a Life Guard a Blue was a 'tasty blue'; to a Blue a Life Guard was a 'ticky tin'.

On a morning in late October 1914 a woman walked along Whitehall with determined steps and positioned herself three feet away from the mounted Household Cavalry sentry at the entrance to Horse Guards Parade. The sentry eyed her out of the corner of his eye without any particular interest: in his five years' service he had grown used to admirers; it was all part of the day's work.

But this particular lady was no admirer of the Household Cavalry. She was a female of waspish tongue and nature; a fervid patriot, who distributed white feathers to men of military age wearing civilian clothes. The fact that once, later in the war, she presented one to a recipient of the Victoria Cross deterred her not at all—the country's young men had to be made aware of their responsibility to King and Country. To add emphasis to this admirable theory, she demanded in ringing tones of the sentry why he was not with a fighting regiment.

The sentry stared straight in front of him, but his lips under his moustache just perceptibly moved. He was, in fact, prophesying such a fearful fate for the militant lady that had she heard him she would have swooned there and then. As it was, she brandished her umbrella at the sentry and strode off to sow the seeds of patriotism elsewhere.

Now, to those who still tend to regard the Household Cavalry as mere symbols of military pageant, certain facts about them be made known.

The King's Life Guard was founded by a very small body

of officers, N.C.O.s and men who were, for some reason, unfit for overseas service: they had all, practically without exception, done their best to convince medical officers that such was not the case, but in the meantime they formed the Reserve Regiment.

The truth of the matter was that there was not an officer, N.C.O., or man of the 1st and 2nd Life Guards and the Royal Horse Guards who was not fighting continuously by day and by night.

Consider the appearance of the British cavalry soldier, ready for mounted action, in 1914.

In marching order each man's horse was equipped with a saddle with two blankets under it—one for the horse, the other for the man. But the saddle, daily saddle-soaped and polished to a dazzling hue, was not just something on which the mounted soldier sat: on the off-side was a leather rifle bucket with a flat, round metal mess-tin strapped to it, and a feed-bag containing seven pounds of oats; on the near-side, a leather sword-frog and pouch—the pouch contained spare horseshoes, a feed-bag, a folding canvas bucket from which the horse drank and an emergency ration of more oats.

In the peacetime riding school the recruit prayerfully clung to the front arch of the saddle as a fractious young remount pranced, kicked, bucked and farted its way round the arena: if he was unseated, as he frequently was, a liverish rough-riding corporal inquired acidly and without a great deal of humour, 'Who gave you the order to dismount?'

In marching order the front arch of the saddle supported a bewildering panoply of gear difficult to take in at a single glance: a pair of leather wallets containing grooming kit—dandy brush, curry comb, dock sponge and a lethal-looking device known as a hoof-pick; over the wallets was a rolled mackintosh cape.

On the rear arch of the saddle, which saved insecure cavalry recruits from sliding over the horse's tail if it suddenly decided to rear up on its hind legs, was a rolled great-coat. In addition, each horse carried round its neck a leather bandolier containing sixty rounds of ammunition.

The individual soldier was equally heavily-laden: over his right shoulder was a haversack, bulging with authorised and unauthorised items; the authorised items included a knife, fork and spoon, but to make room for extra supplies of cigarettes cutlery was often tucked into the top fold of the puttee. Over his left shoulder was a leather bandolier containing thirty rounds of rifle ammunition and a felt-covered water bottle; in the early days in France, hardly a day passed without a man of the Cavalry Division being put on a charge for substituting wine, 'blank' or 'rooge', for water.

The cavalry regiment was ill-adapted for use as infantry because no one had ever foreseen such an eventuality. By the time one man for every four horses, farriers and the necessary N.C.O.s had been subtracted, no regiment could produce many more than 200 men for dismounted action—about the strength of two infantry companies. Yet the 600 men of a cavalry brigade were expected to hold the same length of line as an infantry battalion.

Machine guns – each cavalry regiment had two – had assumed a new importance. Before the war no one had wanted to be machine-gun officer, and in some regiments the job was given to the subaltern with the most slovenly seat on a horse. Suddenly the machine-gun officer had become one of the most important people in the regiment, and a regiment's reputation had come to depend to a remarkable extent on how much experience he had acquired at his job.

Horse-holders, riding one and leading two, were peremptorily hustled away to the rear; machine guns were sited; bayonets took the place of lances and sabres; foraging parties went in search of barbed wire; commanding officers thanked God for the appearance of a consignment of spades.

If anyone had told a cavalry officer before the war that the time was not far off when he would be clamouring for reel after reel of barbed wire and spades with which to dig trenches, he would have put it down to some strange neurosis: barbed wire was merely a tiresome obstacle occasionally encountered in the hunting field; digging was for the Royal Engineers and the Infantry, but not for the cavalry—indeed, some regiments evaded throughout their corporate existence the annual two hours' instruction in field fortification which War Office Regulations prescribed for cavalry.

As each regiment of cavalry came into the line the orders were the same: 'Get the men dismounted and horse-holders told off.'

It was an order that commanding officers of cavalry regiments sternly resented: it was only natural that cavalry regiments should remain mounted and ready for mounted action in the absence of express orders to the contrary; consequently, regiments of lancers—the 5th, 9th, 12th and 16th—arrived in the environs of Ypres in long columns of flashing lance-points. Household Cavalry, dragoons and hussars, hands itching to draw their sabres, rode towards the sound of the guns. They were all determined, in the cavalryman's axiom, to add tone to what would otherwise become an unseemly brawl.

In the British cavalry the 'sabre versus lance' argument had been going on for centuries: it was argued that the lance as a killing weapon was lethal and conclusive—a man run through by a lancer at stretch gallop represented a well-nigh certain kill. But hussar and dragoon regiments were quickly ready with a counter-argument. How could a lancer be sure of getting his weapon back? For once a lance was plunged through the body of an enemy, the lance—an expensive item —was lost. True, admitted the lancers, but they had sabres as well, sabres with which to thrust and slash without encumbrance.

It was all good and stimulating discussion in the Cavalry Club and the wet canteen (but not in the officers' mess, because such a conversation would have been interpreted as 'shop'). At Ypres it had no significance whatsoever, because in this battle sabres and lances were as out of date as bows and arrows and powder-horns; machine guns and rifles, spades, barbed wire and small arms ammunition represented top-priority requirements. And a cavalry officer was well advised to cast away any image of Balaklava if he wanted to remain alive.

Probably no other regiment of Allenby's Cavalry Division felt this transition into an infantry role more acutely than the

12th Royal Lancers: in common with other more fortunate cavalry regiments, the 9th and 16th Lancers and the 4th Dragoon Guards, the 12th had been privileged to take part in real cavalry actions—at Moy, in August, they had charged with lance-points and fluttering pennons and had speared no fewer than seventy Germans: loud and envious had been the cheers from the rest of the Cavalry Division as the 12th ro͏e͏ back to their billets.

But the heavy cavalry panache of the *arme blanche* w͏ speedily deflated when the cavalry were rushed into the lir before Ypres in that last week of October 1914. The experi ence of the 12th Lancers was typical of many another cavalr regiment.

Lieutenant-Colonel Francis Wormald was the conventiona cavalry commanding officer of the period: brave, bigoted͏ hide-bound; he had seen much active service in the South African War, and in peacetime had performed prodigies of valour on the polo field and in steeplechases. After the Boer War he set his lips firmly as he impressed upon the subalterns of his squadron the necessity of teaching the men to be soldiers again. Lancer regiments, he was convinced, should never be clad in anything but blue and gold, schapskas and plumes, or accoutred with anything else than lance pennons and em-broidered saddle-cloths. As he gazed upon the magnificent and glittering ranks of the 12th in peacetime his men feared him exceedingly, and would cheerfully have died for him—as many of them did in war.

Wormald had led the 12th in the charge at Moy, and his sword had gone in and out of four Germans like a knife going into butter. But after Moy it seemed that an era had come to an end: throughout September and early October the 12th marched endlessly; they were moved hither and thither, not knowing where they were going or why; they endured the misery of the retreat from Mons; horses fell away in condition —they went ungroomed for days on end; far from galloping, it was often as much as their riders could do to urge them into a spiritless trot.

For the cavalry regiments the war was beginning to assume a nightmare unreality and, as successive regiments arrived to strengthen the sagging line, sulphurous scenes sometimes developed.

Colonel Wormald found himself involved in one of these. Arriving at the head of his regiment, he was greeted in a somewhat less than cordial manner by Brigadier-General Sir Philip Chetwode, who gave him peremptory orders to get his men dismounted and horse-holders told off because they were going straight into the line.

It was unthinkable, but it was true: horses and lances, the very sinews of the regiment, were wantonly cast aside or 'returned to store', as the British Army has it. All that was wanted now were men armed with rifles who could fire at least fifteen rounds to the minute and trenches from which to fire them. Household Cavalry, lancers, dragoons and hussars were all told this in uncompromising terms by brigadiers and senior staff officers, who only a short six months earlier had been arguing vehemently about the respective merits of sabre and lance.

Digging trenches and lying down to fire—both these things came naturally to infantry. Every cavalryman was an expert rifleman—indeed, the cavalry frequently boasted that they could outshoot the infantry on any range—but *digging trenches*? This was near madness.

A number of cavalry subalterns, when ordered to get their men digging, said reasonably enough: 'Yes, sir. But what are they going to dig with?', only to be blasted by majors and colonels who told them not to ask damn fool questions. If a man wanted to stay alive at Ypres, he dug, if necessary with his bare hands—and many men did just that, for they found themselves in muddy fields the soil of which yielded to hands and bayonets alike; the shallowest hole in the ground quadrupled a man's chances of staying alive.

CHAPTER FIVE

The time has come to introduce on to the scene a very exceptional soldier, Major-General Edmund Allenby. If some space is devoted to Allenby, it is because he was a subject worthy of it.

He was a big man in every way—physically, mentally and morally. He was universally nicknamed 'the Bull', and had many of that animal's external characteristics. There is a certain irony in the qualities of this gallant but low-brow animal being attached in the military mind to one who was, in fact, of very high intelligence, if not actually scholarly.

In speech he resembled the bull most of all, and he was given to violent outbursts of temper; his explosive utterances and crushing rudeness to senior officers delighted all those who were fortunate enough to be listening. He rarely lowered his voice at any time, and certainly not when administering rebukes. To one brigadier-general who had incurred his displeasure, he said: 'There are fools, damned fools—and you sir.'

Yet at bottom he was kindly and tolerant, and he had a sympathetic understanding of soldiers' problems. Although a strict disciplinarian, if not a martinet, he hated to punish a man; indeed, some officers thought him too easy by the standard of those days. When he was in command of the 5th Lancers, a trooper stood in front of him in the orderly room, quivering with nervous anticipation. The erring trooper fully expected at least fourteen days' field punishment, which he probably richly deserved. Colonel Allenby's face, as was habitual with him when he was about to deliver a blistering rebuke, was the colour of a ripe damson plum; his veins stood out on his forehead and he gripped his desk as if it might run away from him.

The Colonel seemed to be fighting for breath; the Adjutant and the Regimental Sergeant-Major gazed at the ceiling, while the prisoner and his escorts stared fixedly at a portrait of the King behind the Colonel's chair.

Then the blast came: 'Go away!' roared the Bull in a voice clearly audible at two hundred paces; 'I am far too angry with you to trust myself to punish you.' So yet another malefactor of the 5th Lancers stamped from the orderly room, dismissed with no punishment save a painful tongue-lashing. This was typical of the man; the fear of Allenby's wrath was a greater deterrent to many soldiers than a sojourn in the cells; a dressing-down from him was not an experience that the hardiest cared to repeat.

Nor did he spare his officers the rough side of his tongue. The story is told of a senior captain—a squadron commander of lengthy service—who collapsed altogether while being re-proved by Allenby. 'The Bull' was genuinely surprised. 'What affected him like that?' he asked. 'I wasn't even really angry with him.'

All generals had, and still have, their individual phobias: with one it was bootlaces, and he was fond of saying that a broken bootlace could stop a whole division on the march; another swooped on cookhouses, demanding to sample the men's dinner for that day; an illustrious cavalryman even went so far as to chew horses' fodder, until brought up sharp by the observation of a roughriding sergeant 'them little black bits is rat shit'.

Allenby's phobias centred round chinstraps and socks. The pre-1914 British soldier was considerably less fastidious on the subject of foot hygiene than he is today: soldiers' socks *en masse* have an indescribable smell, not unlike the cloying, sickly stench of death, and some soldiers disdained to wear them at all, but not during Allenby's tenure of office as Inspector-General of Cavalry from 1910 until 1914.

On one memorable day he pounced on the 5th Lancers—his own regiment—and told a squadron commander to order a certain trooper to dismount from his horse and remove his boots. The man was barefooted.

The squadron commander wore an expression of comical dismay; he well knew that the Inspector-General had an eye like a hawk, but it could hardly penetrate an army boot.

'That man was my servant in the regiment,' said Allenby with grim enjoyment. 'I could never persuade him to wear socks, and it seems that you have been no more successful.'

The chinstrap was neither comfortable nor popular. But woe betide the soldier or officer who was seen by Allenby on his horse without his chinstrap down.

Although Allenby puts in a late appearance in this story, he had, of course, been there all the time. But so far his Cavalry Division had been given little opportunity to shine. The Battle of Mons had been an entirely infantry affair, and the cavalry had no chance to add tone to this particular un-seemly brawl; in the retreat from Mons they had plodded wearily ever rearwards, covering Smith-Dorrien's 2nd Corps; the battle of the Marne had been fought largely without cavalry assistance, and on the Aisne they had floundered about in trenches knee-deep in mud, which was a perfectly suitable role for infantry but definitely *not* for cavalry.

Cavalry were essentially mobile troops, whose essence was speed of movement. Their primary functions were scouting and reconnaissance—they were the ears and eyes of the army—but at the back of every cavalryman's mind was the prospect of charging, squadrons in line, with sabre or lance.

In both world wars there were a number of senior officers who have been accused of having a 'Balaklava mentality', thus implying crass stupidity, stubborn rigidity of purpose, reaction-ary idiocy and a host of other defects.

Rightly or wrongly, this attitude of mind was to be found in generous measure in Allenby's Cavalry Division and, let it be whispered, in Allenby himself—he had charged Zulus and Boers in South Africa.

It irked Allenby inexpressibly that there had been so few real cavalry actions in the war so far, although he crashed down on any officers who complained about this state of affairs with his habitual crushing rudeness; when confronted with Allenby on the warpath, the old adage 'never complain, never explain' stood the objection in good stead.

The regular cavalry officer of the period, before the out-break of the war in 1914, sometimes escaped being a figure of fun by mere inches. The story is often told of an officer of a

British cavalry regiment who was so stupid that even his brother officers started to notice it; another anecdote, unkind but not without a grain of truth, concerned a retired officer who attended a guest dinner night of his old regiment.

The officer in question was regaled with cocktails on his arrival in the ante-room; the regimental band discreetly played selections from Gilbert and Sullivan until, to the muted strains of 'The Roast Beef of Old England', the officers of the Regiment filed into the dining-room. They settled themselves up and down the long table, banked with flowers and candles. The mess silver, easily worth five years of a field-marshal's pay, stood bravely on the table.

The port circulated and the King had his due. As he lit a cigar, the retired officer—he had only recently left the Regiment, but was to reappear from the reserve and be killed on the Somme—looked up and down the long table and said under his breath: 'Same dear old faces, not a gleam of intelligence on one of them.'

This was, of course, a cynical and unfair assessment of the cavalryman of the period, but in the years between the end of the South African War and 1914 cavalry officers were seldom called upon to do anything which called for sustained mental effort, and absolutely nothing happened to disturb the even tenor of life in Dragoon, Hussar and Lancer regiments. Regiments, in rotation, went to India where the officers shot tiger, snipe, gaur, ibex, snow leopard and giel; they charged, four squadrons in line, on manœuvres; they stuck pigs, played polo and rode in steeplechases.

Cavalry officers led a spacious and unreflective life on infinitesimal pay. And the subject of the paucity of that pay— a subaltern received five shillings and threepence per day— earned many a young officer a crushing rebuke from grizzled colonels and majors who had charged at Omdurman. 'You can't have it both ways, young man,' the colonels grated at the complainants. 'Either we're privileged people and have to pay for our privileges, or we're ordinary public servants. And if we're public servants, then the tax-payer is entitled to wonder why we don't do a damn' sight more work—and that goes for *you* too.'

*

Now, much of this had been changed by the reality of war; the pre-1914 inertia, however, seemed to linger on. Some cavalry regiments, through no fault of their own, had been in the ignoble position of heading the column during the retreat from Mons; others had been twenty miles away from any action when the Battle of the Marne was being fought and, in the view of fermenting colonels, might just as well have stayed in Aldershot for all the good they were doing in France; others again, thirsting for action, arrived on the Aisne just as the battle petered out into mud-bound stalemate. There were colonels of cavalry regiments who took it as a personal grudge that their regiments should have had no casualties save stragglers during a month's active service.

But on the Messines-Wytschaete Ridge, between Rawlinson's 3rd Corps and Haig's 1st, every cavalry regiment of Allenby's Cavalry Corps was at least occupied, though in an unorthodox form: they had all been transformed into identical attenuated lines of riflemen, whose function was not to charge with lance or sabre but to fire a rifle as fast as they could work the bolt, until it was too hot to hold; they were digging feverishly in a frantic effort to improve the line; there were no horses to be seen, and many a cavalry officer observed during that grim period, 'I've almost forgotten what a horse looks like.'

Lieutenant Kenneth North of the 4th (Queen's Own) Hussars was at the top of his specialised world. More, he was probably the only officer in the Regiment who was really happy in his work; the others were putting a brave face on their transition from cavalry to infantry, but they were without their horses, and in the early days of the Great War there was something strangely pathetic and helpless about a dehorsed cavalryman—although this state of affairs did not last for long.

North was happy because he was the machine-gun officer, and did not miss his horse at all; indeed, he had not been sorry when a horse-holder had led it away. A wall-eyed brute of a remount, it had a disconcerting habit of kicking out backwards and shying at imaginary ghosts encountered on the march.

The post of machine-gun officer was not eagerly sought

after by the 4th Hussars, or in any other cavalry regiment: machine-guns had no conceivable connection with mounted action and there was certainly no place for them in a hell-for-leather charge across open country. North had been given the machine-guns, not as the most promising machine-gun officer in the Regiment (a distinction the whole mess scorned), but because he had the most slovenly seat on a horse that had ever disgraced the ranks of the 4th Hussars.

The 4th Hussars were busily making the village of Hoolebeke impregnable. The more fortunate established themselves in a drainage ditch which ran in the right direction and afforded natural cover, but the remainder were digging trenches with any tools that came to hand—and spades were in short supply. Men dug with bayonets and even their bare hands; the executive order from the officers was 'Dig if you want to stay alive' and it had a very real meaning. The troopers swore horribly, and the sergeants answered them in the same language, promising death to those who did not dig as an alternative to a liberal dose of detention if they were lucky enough to be alive after the German attack which they all knew was inevitable. Infantrymen were trained to dig and did so uncomplainingly, but the fear of death or dishonour made even cavalry dig and the 4th Hussars sank into the ground like moles.

Aloof from all this sordid spade work, Lieutenant North was engaged in siting his beloved machine-guns in a position from which they could do the maximum execution. He had found an angle of a tributary ditch. Lieutenant-Colonel Howell came to inspect North's efforts. Howell, something of a fanatic on the subject of mounted perfection, had given the machine-guns to North when the Regiment had been stationed in Aldershot; he now realised with a twinge of anxiety that the reputation of the Regiment depended to a great extent on how much efficiency North had acquired at his job.

Impressed by the obvious competence and keenness of North and his section, Howell left him to his own devices; however little North knew about machine-guns it was more than the Colonel did.

*

Before sailing for France, the officers of the Cavalry Division had viewed the outbreak of a major European war with a mixture of excitement, boredom, irritation, disdain and downright peevishness: the hunting season was about to start and polo was just getting into its stride again. At the Headquarters of the 2nd Cavalry Brigade at Tidworth, whither the officers of the 9th Lancers, 4th Dragoon Guards and 18th Hussars were summoned on the morning of August 5, 1914, the atmosphere was scarcely warlike: standing about in chattering groups, waiting for the arrival of their brigade commander, Brigadier-General Henry de Beauvoir de Lisle, C.B., D.S.O., they might easily have been discussing a 'needle' polo match: the war would undoubtedly be over by Christmas, even if it lasted that long; it seemed unlikely that it would interfere with the Grand Military meeting at Sandown Park in 1915. Their tunics were rather long in the skirt; their breeches miracles of Savile Row tailoring; their field boots shone like chestnuts. They all spoke with slight drawls and sprinkled the floor of Brigade Headquarters with dropped g's. The whole business was, by and large, a bit of a bore.

General de Lisle brought them down to earth in very short order, as did Brigadier-General C. J. Briggs, C.B., commanding the 1st Brigade, Brigadier-General H. de la P. Gough, C.B., of the 2nd, Brigadier-General the Hon. C. Bingham, C.V.O., C.B., of the 4th and Brigadier-General Sir Philip Chetwode, D.S.O., of the 5th: these were all officers who knew what war was about, from hard experience in the Sudan, South Africa and the Tirah. They all quelled undue optimism with similar words: 'Make no mistake, gentlemen. We are in for a long and bitter war.' Their warning came as a cold douche to the younger and more insouciant officers; suddenly the polo field and Sandown Park seemed very far away.

Now every British cavalry regiment, without benefit of horses, was in the front line of Ypres: they were all exclusive regiments, and therefore expensive—the officers all had private means, ranging from a comparatively humble £750 per year (about the minimum on which a cavalry officer could maintain a standard of gracious living) to five or six times that amount. Their outlook on life was severely equine, and they were expected as a matter of course to play polo and ride in steeplechases; any other forms of off-duty endeavour, other than hunting, shooting and fishing, were classified as 'poodle faking' and therefore suspect.

There were Dragoons, usually classified as 'heavy cavalry': the 1st (Royal Dragoons), the 2nd Dragoons (Royal Scots Greys), the 3rd Dragoon Guards, the 4th (Royal Irish) Dragoon Guards, the 5th Inniskilling Dragoon Guards, the 6th Dragoon Guards (Carabiniers).

There were Hussars in plenty: the 3rd, 4th, 10th, 11th, 15th, 18th and 20th. Lancers were represented by the 5th, 9th, 12th and 16th. There was a Composite Household Cavalry Regiment, an uneasy mixture of Life Guards and 'Blues', the 1st and 2nd Life Guards and the Blues.

And while the battles of Mons, Le Cateau, the Marne, the Aisne and Ypres were being fought, the 7th Dragoon Guards, the 7th Hussars, the 8th Hussars, the 13th Hussars, the 14th Hussars, the 17th Lancers and the 21st Lancers, all stationed in India, fretted in sweltering frustration. It looked as though they might miss 'the Great Adventure', for the war would surely be over by Christmas.

For the infantry the name of Menin had in its very sound the tone of a deep bell pealing a fateful note. For the cavalry, the town of Messines gave out the same ominous ring.

Messines had had its share of wars in bygone days, and been razed to the ground in the eleventh century and again in the seventeenth. Its demolition in the twentieth eclipsed its former woes.

The 9th Lancers, of course, were in the forefront of the battle from the start; indeed, they would have taken it as a deadly insult if they had not been.

Of the 9th Lancers, Field-Marshal Lord Methuen, when Commander-in-Chief in South Africa, said: 'I cannot speak too highly of this regiment and do not suppose there is a finer regiment in the service.' It was an assessment with which few soldiers would quarrel, and one with which the officers and men of the 9th agreed wholeheartedly: their bearing on ceremonial parades had invariably been superb; their conduct in South Africa may have been equalled by other cavalry regiments, but can hardly have been surpassed; they had been magnificent at Balaklava, invincible in Afghanistan. In the Indian Mutiny their prowess with the lance had earned them the proud nickname 'The Delhi Spearmen'.

Lancer regiments regarded Hussars as bounders and theatrical popinjays; Dragoons were overweight louts; the Household Cavalry were merely laughable. Other Lancers were classified with varying degrees of amiable condescension. The 5th were Irish, and therefore suspect; they had been disbanded in 1799, and a damn' good job too—God only knew how or why they had been revived (steady, 9th, the 5th were Allenby's old regiment). The 12th rode like ploughboys. The 16th couldn't carry their liquor like gentlemen. The 17th couldn't play polo properly and invariably fell off in steeplechases. The 21st, who had charged at Omdurman in 1898 with the not inconsiderable addition of Second-Lieutenant Winston Churchill, carried only one Battle Honour—'Khartoum'—and therefore merited no classification whatsoever.

But the 9th were stiff with Battle Honours; they acknowledged no peers on the polo field; on ceremonial parades their glittering ranks were inevitably faultless; their Commanding Officer, Lieutenant-Colonel David Campbell, had ridden his own horse, The Soarer, to victory in the Grand National; the 9th . . . and so it could go on.

It was no bad state of mind for a regiment to be in, and not inaccurate. The 9th Lancers would not have been one half as good unless every officer, N.C.O. and trooper had believed it to be the best regiment of all.

Unlike many other cavalry regiments, the 9th had got away to a flying start, for they had taken part in proper cavalry actions: with the 4th Dragoon Guards they had charged suicidally and in true Balaklava style at Audregnies in August; at Moncel in September they had routed a squadron of German dragoons in one of those hell-for-leather gallops so beloved of 9th Lancers.

But at Messines on October 31, there was nothing to distinguish the 9th Lancers from any other regiment of the Cavalry Corps, or any infantry regiment either: they were just part of a ragged line of khaki, hastily entrenched in muddy ditches.

On that day Messines stuck out like a bastion in front of the Cavalry Corps line. The village was a small one—1,400 inhabitants, a church, a lime-house and the mill. The 9th Lancers held the jut-out east of the village, and on their left were the Queen's Bays. The second line of defence ran straight through the village, and was held by the 11th Hussars. Squadrons of the 5th Dragoon Guards filled gaps in the sagging line, and they were many—in places there were a full hundred yards bare of defenders.

The 9th Lancers were comparatively affluent in manpower on October 31, and their strength was twenty-seven officers and 416 non-commissioned officers and troopers, not unduly below the full war establishment of 531 all ranks. It was unfortunate that, at a time when every rifle was needed in the line, a large party had been detached from the Regiment to bring up remounts: the 'Balaklava mentality' had not been entirely eradicated, and cavalry regiments must still be ready for mounted action. Consequently, only 150 men were available for trench duty.

Lieutenant-Colonel David Campbell, himself a fanatical disciple of mounted action—he had charged at the head of his regiment in the two most spectacular cavalry actions of the war so far, with a panache that Lord Cardigan himself would have envied—deplored the lack of horses, but the lack of 250 riflemen even more; his line was woefully thin—a line of small and hastily dug pits some fifteen yards apart with at most two, and frequently only one man in each; there was only a pretence of touch with the Bays on the left.

'Handsome is as handsome does'—the old tag had never applied so forcibly as it did to the 9th Lancers at Messines. They were subjected to a hail of shells. As a bombardment it was a puny affair, not to be compared with the later bombardments of the war when mathematical calculations showed that every patch of ground was hit by three separate shells— but by the standards of 1914 it was shattering: it seemed to reduce men to the significance of ants, but, like ants, they found shelter in cracks in the ground and the pits dug by the shells gave them some form of protection.

The pattern of German assault seldom varied. Towards dusk the bombardment was lifted and, supported by machine-guns, infantrymen advanced in suicidal waves, climbing over their heaped dead, to leave fresh swathes of corpses a few yards further on. Every man of the 9th – cool as a cucumber and full of that glorious pride of regiment that makes the super-soldier—fired steadily into the oncoming mass. But the 9th Lancers could not kill them fast enough. To the music of bugles and loud singing, which sounded like some sort of insane chorus, they still came on . . . from the immediate front and from the right and left flanks.

No man went back unless he was wounded, as were four officers and thirty men, to be tended by the Medical Officer, Captain Middleton, who performed near-miracles of life-saving by the last glimmerings of a fast-dying electric torch.

There was no sleep for the 9th Lancers on the night of October 30, and as dawn broke on the 31st a solid mass of grey infantry, marching as steadily as if on a ceremonial parade and supported, at each end of the line, by a Maxim which belched forth a stream of fire every few yards. Every man of the 9th who could hold a rifle poured shot after shot into the oncoming mass and it was scarcely possible to miss: every bullet found a billet, and some even two.

The first attack was beaten off, but only with fearful effort. There were encouraging heaps of German dead in front of the 9th's trenches, but the shelling was hotting up again and the Maxims firing from the flank tore great gaps in the Lancers' line; in places there were gaps of ten yards between riflemen. Artillery support was limited to about four rounds per day, and Colonel Campbell knew with awful clarity that one more full-scale attack would swamp them and the 9th Queen's Royal Lancers would cease to exist.

Then, later in the morning, still more shells came and the air was one mass of rending flashes. Shock succeeded shock and deadly missiles fell like hail—so fast and thick that no living thing could long remain untouched beneath the torrent of metal that sprayed over the trenches.

Retreat was abhorrent to Colonel Campbell—it was a word that never figured in his vocabulary—but it was clearly time to go.

There was one 9th Lancer who did not receive the order to withdraw, and would probably have disobeyed it even if he had. Corporal Tom Seaton was manning a machine-gun in a forward trench and was doing deadly execution; Seaton, in fact, was at the top of his specialised world.

A lantern-jawed and normally somewhat taciturn man, Seaton, with his thumbs on the firing lever of a machine-gun, became a veritable artist of destruction. He had poured something like a thousand rounds into the advancing German infantry, and they would be coming back for more. This suited Seaton admirably.

It did not suit his Number Two, whose job it was to feed the belts of ammunition into the gun, quite so well; true, the gun had accounted for astronomical quantities of Germans, but it was showing ominous signs of boiling over. Clearly, Corporal Seaton wanted to be a hero; Trooper Saunders was harbouring some doubts about this.

During a brief lull in the slaughter, Seaton produced a packet of Woodbines and considered its contents with morose fatalism; there were only two of the precious weeds left, and after mature consideration he gave the other one to Trooper Saunders.

To Saunders it seemed that the roar of musketry from the 9th's trenches was receding rearwards, and he diffidently suggested to Seaton that it seemed possible that the Regiment was retiring. The answer was all that he had expected: 'Maybe they are, and maybe they ain't,' said Seaton briefly, 'but you and me ain't going anywhere. Now, hand over that belt of ammo and look sharp about it.' Trooper Saunders sighed, a faintly mutinous sigh; but if he was going to die, as seemed very probable, then Corporal Seaton was undoubtedly a good man to die with.

No 9th Lancer liked the idea of retreating, but Captain Francis Grenfell disliked it most of all; Grenfell had already won the Victoria Cross in the very early days of the Battle of Mons, and there were many Lancers who swore that he earned a bar to it at Messines.

The order to withdraw did not reach Grenfell; like Seaton, he would probably have ignored it. He was holding a house with two weak troops—about twenty men, all that remained of 'A' Squadron—when he noticed that the advance of the German infantry had ceased. Then he heard another sound, which told him conclusively that for him retirement was out of the question.

Grenfell was cut off from Regimental Headquarters, and no orders could have reached him in any event: the sound that he heard was unmistakably the 9th Lancers' only remaining machine-gun—the other one, together with its crew, had been blown into small pieces just an hour earlier. The noise of firing told Grenfell that there were still 9th Lancers in action against Germans, and if the 9th were still in the fight then Francis Grenfell was going to be in it as well. To the remnants of 'A' Squadron, he said 'come on', and they went forward.

Grenfell found that the 9th Lancers represented by Corporal Seaton and Trooper Saunders, fired or perhaps frightened by Seaton's example, were very much in control of the situation. When the German infantry drew off just long enough for Seaton and Saunders to inhale the last two Woodbines, Seaton had re-sited the machine-gun under a low bush. To the by now resigned Saunders Seaton said grimly: 'Let 'em come again, son, and we've got 'em cold.'

He had. As Grenfell and his men ran up to the position the Germans attacked again. Waiting until the Germans were almost upon him—until some, indeed, were actually climbing the parapet to his left and piling into the trench—Seaton loosed off his deadly quick-firer. He poured a thousand rounds into the enemy at such close range that the execution was almost beyond realisation and they were mown down like grass in the path of a motor-scythe. The surprise of the manœuvre added to its effectiveness. Leaping out of the death trap the Germans, by now panic-stricken and demoralised, rushed rearward in a close crowd for cover, the machine-gun in Corporal Seaton's deft and exultant hands playing on them as they ran. Grenfell's men, not to be outdone, emptied the magazines of their rifles into the fleeing enemy.

It was absolute victory for the 9th Lancers and total rout for the attacking Germans. But it was the end of Corporal Seaton's machine-gun, for this lethal piece of ordnance had been pierced by bullets which had punctured its water jacket and finally rendered it useless. To Seaton and Saunders, Grenfell said: 'Damned well done, you two. Now get out of it.' Seaton retired reluctantly, Saunders with considerably more alacrity—there seemed to be too many bloody heroes about that day, and he'd had just about enough. He and Corporal Seaton were both subsequently awarded the Distinguished Conduct Medal, and as Saunders freely admitted afterwards he owed his award entirely to his corporal, 'for if it hadn't been for that bloody Seaton I'd have buggered off out of it a long time before'.

Grenfell and the remnants continued to fight until the Germans were twenty yards away and closing in for the final kill; Grenfell himself was the last to leave, but not before he had collected a bullet in the thigh and emptied his revolver ammunition into the advancing enemy.[1]

By November 1, there was scarcely a regiment of Allenby's Cavalry Corps which could muster the equivalent of a full-strength squadron. But their contribution had been a priceless one: in the trenches around Messines Dragoons, Lancers and Hussars had proved themselves equal to any infantry; deprived of the chance of charging in open country with sabre and lance, they had taken the bayonet to the Germans with devastating effect. Their musketry was of such a high order that a captured German officer said that he could not believe that Messines had been held for so long by cavalry—he was certain that it had been defended by a picked corps of machine-gunners. As no cavalry regiment had more than two machine-guns, the rifle shooting of the cavalry was only excelled by the manipulation of their bolts.

[1] Francis Grenfell's wound did not detain him in England for long. He was back in action with the 9th Lancers in early 1915 and was killed in the Second Battle of Ypres.

'J' Battery, R.H.A. (5th Cavalry Brigade) in open positions

French and British troops digging trenches

Battle of Messines 1914. 129th Baluchis in a front line
trench on the outskirts of Wytschaete, October 1914.
There were 345 casualties in one day's fighting

Remnants of the London Scottish after Battle of Messines,
31 October 1914

Scots Guards arriving at billets in Zillebeke after being
relieved by French troops in the Salient, 15 October 1914

Men of the 7th Division discussing the news during a halt
by the roadside, near Ypres

'J' Battery, R.H.A., passing through a village near Amiens

British soldiers advance in single file

The Scots Guards snatch a hasty meal before going into the line

A London furniture van, pressed into military service, stands outside the Cloth Hall in Ypres

First line transport, 2nd Cavalry Division, in reserve
behind Hollebeke Château

A Highland Regiment passes through the peaceful
Flanders countryside

Men of the 2nd Scots Guards in a hastily dug trench
near Zandvoorde

French Cavalry on the march passing the 1st Cameronians
in bivouacs where, with the rest of the 19th Brigade,
they lay hidden all day marching by night

The Cavalry Corps held the line because it had Allenby in command and he, in himself, was a positive denial of defeat; it was held because there were generals in command who, far from sitting in spacious headquarters miles to the rear and running the battle on the telephone, set an example of courage and leadership which cannot have been equalled in any war — Briggs, de Lisle, Gough, Bingham, Chetwode, Makins and Kavanagh.

It was held because the regiments of the Cavalry Corps had commanding officers like Colonels Campbell, 9th Lancers, Wormald, 12th Lancers, Mullen, 4th Dragoon Guards, and Gore-Langton, 18th Hussars. It was this kind of leadership for which all their native talents were best suited; with commanders like this at hand, not the most fleeting thought of retreat crossed any man's mind. When defeat and annihilation seemed certain, they put new heart into their men with their total disregard for danger. It seemed as unlikely that they should survive as that a spun coin would come down heads ten times running, and yet they did.

It was held because there were majors like Combe of the 3rd Hussars, Ing of the 10th Hussars and Beale-Brown of the 9th Lancers who, although wounded, continued to command their squadrons after the most cursory medical treatment; captains like Grenfell, 9th Lancers, and Dorrington, Royals.

Subalterns like Lieutenant Roger Chance, 4th Dragoon Guards, who was elevated to the command of a squadron at the age of twenty-one and continued in command with a hand smashed by shrapnel; Lieutenant North, machine-gun officer of the 4th Hussars, who fired all his ammunition and brought his two guns out of action on a wheel-barrow.

Sergeants like Wright of the 3rd Dragoons who, while carrying a vital message to regimental headquarters, found his way blocked by twenty Germans — he drew his sabre, put spurs to his horse and carried out a one-man cavalry charge, literally cutting his way through, and killing five of them; like McLellan of the Royals and Seddons of the 4th Hussars, who, after their troop officers had been killed, led a succession of bayonet charges.

There were corporals like the gallant Seaton, machine-gunner of the 9th Lancers, and Colegrave, the oriental linguist, who infused new fighting spirit into the temporarily leaderless and demoralised Baluchis; privates like Saunders, Seaton's 'Number Two', and Smart, 5th Lancers, who continued to fire a machine-gun after being shot in the mouth.

It is small wonder that Allenby, in one of his less explosive utterances, rhetorically demanded of one of his staff: 'Where do we get such men?'

To these regiments and names must be added the London Scottish.

On the Messines front the 6th Dragoon Guards (Carabiniers) were in a singularly unenviable position: they were in hastily dug trenches full of thick, black mud; they were almost without cover of any sort; there were a full hundred yards bare of defenders between the 6th Dragoons' right and the beginning of a drainage ditch wherein was established the left of the 3rd Hussars.

Two Carabiniers crouched in one of these stinking, mud-filled holes, trying to keep their rifles out of the mud. They had killed upwards of twenty Germans each and their rifles were almost red-hot to the touch.

'How long we been here, George?' said one Carabinier.

'Gawd knows,' said the other. 'I reckon I was born in this bleedin' trench.'

It seemed, however, that help was at hand; a battalion was on its way to plug the cavalry line.

'Who are they?' asked the first Carabinier.

'Some Scotch mob — the London Scottish.'

'Never 'eard of 'em.'

'Territorials, they are. 'Spect they'll run like 'ell.'

No such disparaging remark was made about Territorials after that.

The London Scottish had come to France with an *esprit de corps* which was at least as strong as in any regular unit. Locally a London organisation, the London Scottish had from the very beginning a strictly Scottish character. It was, as it still is, a Scottish regiment which happens to be in London — the guardians of the Stone of Scone, on which the Scottish kings were crowned. The feeling in the Battalion was always that it represented before London, in visible form, the Scottish people.

For the London Scottish there was no preliminary training on arrival in France, and no 'shake-down' period in a quiet sector of the line (in the First Battle of Ypres there was no such thing as a 'quiet sector' anywhere). They were desperately needed on the Wytschaete-Messines ridge, which was under ceaseless attacks from two and a half German Army Corps; here was the centre of the line of battle and, had it given way, disaster would have resulted for the entire left flank of the Allied line.

The London Scottish, first Territorial Battalion to go into action in the Great War, were in sharp contrast to 'hard case' regulars of the original British Expeditionary Force. They were inspired with at least as much, and frequently more, patriotism as the regulars.

Indeed, the pre-1914 regular usually enlisted for economic, alcoholic or amatory reasons, but rarely from motives of patriotism. It is sometimes said that soldiers are born and not made, but this was not strictly true of the regular of the period; for every man who joined because he wanted to, there were ten recruits who could find nothing better to do. They were sometimes referred to as 'work-shy riff-raff'—'it's Tommy this, and Tommy that, and chuck 'im out the brute'—but although there was an element of truth in this, it was hardly fair: work was scarce in the early twentieth century, and the treatment meted out to the 'lower classes' was scarcely calculated to turn a young man into a blazing patriot. The young soldier of *circa* 1910, when asked if he had enlisted to fight for King and Country, replied truthfully enough and from the heart, 'Not bloody likely. I joined to get three square meals a day and a pair of trousers with an arse to them.' Others freely admitted that the Army got them before the police did.

There were no soldiers like this in the London Scottish when they mobilised in August 1914. The ranks were largely filled by public school and university men and were of what was known as 'officer material': indeed, the officers of the London Scottish were nearly always commissioned from the ranks, although many served throughout the Great War without aspiring to commissioned rank.

Prior to 1914 the British regular was not encouraged to think—'the officers do the thinking for you,' their N.C.O.s told them uncompromisingly. In those days, as now, a private soldier's excuse for some dereliction of duty invariably began: 'I thought . . .' and was followed by the inevitable interruption from an unsympathetic N.C.O.: 'DON'T THINK! Know what thought did? Thought shit its breeches.' And to this improbable theory the private himself gave no answer.

The situation at Messines was rapidly becoming desperate. General Allenby had told Sir John French that his numbers were too weak to hold the position for much longer unless reinforcements were quickly forthcoming. Pending their arrival, the cavalry had a truly colossal task before them: they were absurdly outnumbered, and had opposed to them the 14th and 2nd Bavarian Corps, some of the best fighting men of the German Army. The Bavarians had the Kaiser himself breathing down their necks, and the Kaiser was in no mood to listen to excuses for failure.

Infantry battalions from the battered 2nd Corps were hurriedly scraped together and rushed up to plug the gaps—Lincolns, King's Own Yorkshire Light Infantry, Royal Northumberland Fusiliers and King's Own Scottish Borderers. But none of these battalions was more than one full company strong and each successive parcel of British troops, as it arrived, barely sufficed to patch or extend the wavering front in the face of the masses of Germans hurrying to the same point.

Major-General de Lisle, commanding the 1st Cavalry Division, hardly had time to notice that the last batch of reinforcements to arrive looked rather fitter and fresher than the 2nd Corps battalions, or that they wore dark blue glengarries and kilts of an unfamiliar shade of brown, known as 'Hodden Grey'. He only knew that there were 800 more rifles to stem the tide.

Nor did he waste much time or many words in giving his orders to Lieutenant-Colonel Malcolm: 'You're going into the line at once, and if you go back the war's lost. You have no other orders and no discretion—except to hold on to the last man.' He had hardly finished speaking when the First Battle of Ypres engulfed the London Scottish.

The battle inoculation of the London Scottish started with a furious bombardment; as they extended into line a hail of bullets and shells fell all about the Regiment. It would have been a shattering experience, even for battle-hardened troops, and Colonel Malcolm, mindful of the gloomy prophecies of some regulars on the fighting potential of Territorials, made frequent forays up and down the line to see how his men were taking it. He exposed himself fearlessly to shot and shell on these journeys, many of which turned out to be unnecessary: the London Scottish took their initiation in shellfire like veterans.

Nor were they found wanting when the massed German infantry attacks came in. They rolled on in dense masses, to the accompaniment of brass bands blaring out *'Deutschland, Deutschland, über Alles'*; if the rifle fire of the London Scottish did not quite match the murderous 'mad minute' fusillades of the regulars—no man had fired a shot from his rifle since arrival in France—there were encouraging heaps of German dead in front of the London Scottish. At no point was their line pierced.

In peacetime the soldiering of the London Scottish consisted of one or two 'drill nights' a week at the Headquarters in Buckingham Gate and the annual two weeks' summer camp on Salisbury Plain. At Hogmanay and Hallowe'en there were celebrations of a homeric nature at Buckingham Gate, but on Hallowe'en, 1914—October 31—the London Scottish were called upon to prove that bayonet fighting had not been neglected in their military education. Their bayonet charge excited the admiration of the whole British Army at Ypres; no one called them 'Saturday Night Soldiers' after that.

They certainly excited the admiration of General Allenby, and in a memorandum to French he wrote:

'The London Scottish came under my orders on the evening of October 30, 1914, and were detailed to the support of the 2nd Cavalry Division on the following morning. They were into action at 10 a.m., October 31, with a strength of 26 officers and 786 men, and occupied trenches throughout the day, being subjected to heavy artillery and machine-gun fire. From 9 p.m. onwards, during the night October 31–November 1, the Germans attacked the trenches of the London Scottish continuously, and at 2 a.m. they succeeded in turning the left in large numbers. The situation was restored at the point of the bayonet, and in this charge the London Scottish inflicted heavy casualties on the enemy. Throughout these operations, which lasted for two days, viz. October 31 and November 1, the losses of the London Scottish amounted to 278, or about 34 per cent of their strength. Rarely, if ever, have second line troops sustained unshaken so high a percentage of casualties.'

It was only after the battle that the London Scottish (and all the other territorial regiments) differed sharply from their regular comrades. It was their attitude to the death in action of their comrades.

The regular had a casual, cynical, almost callous view of death, as witness this conversation of a burial detail engaged in interring their comrades in a mass grave:

'Anyone know this bloke?'

'Yes, it's Brown 98—"C" Company.'

'Owed me a couple of bob when we left Aldershot.'

'You won't get it now.'

'Room for one more in there. . . .'

'Right—tip 'im in, then.'[1]

The men of the London Scottish, while there was work to be done and an enemy to be held at bay, thought of nothing more than to die fighting, if necessary, to the last man: those had been the Colonel's orders, and they were prepared to carry them out to the letter. But the heavy losses among their friends bowed them down with grief; for they necessarily lacked as yet the professional training and stoicism of men whose real business is war.

[1] I have some personal experience of this attitude. On the Imphal Plain in 1944 my battalion relieved the 2nd Border Regiment on a hill position. Prior to moving out, the Borders were carrying out a casualty check. A private seized a corpse by the hair, lifted it into a sitting position and shouted in ringing tones, 'Anybody know this fucker?'

Sir John French visited the London Scottish after the battle of Messines, and described it as a profoundly moving experience: 'the exhibition of natural feeling only excited in me a deeper admiration for the splendid courage and endurance they had displayed when unsustained and unassisted by the influence of that iron discipline which only a long course of military training can inculcate. They were urged only by the spirit of *noblesse oblige* and the higher ideals which inspire all who have taken up arms against the Germans in this war.'

CHAPTER SIX

Massive help was on the way from India—it had to be from India, because the regular British Army in Great Britain was a mere skeleton: a quartermaster, a mess orderly, a sanitary orderly, a veterinary officer and a thousand red-tabbed staff officers, as one cheerful cynic assessed our island's military might in October 1914.

The Territorials, of course, were bursting with keenness and raring to go—they could not get out to France fast enough—but only a chosen few were so far considered eligible for that most exclusive club, the B.E.F.: the London Scottish, the Oxford and Northumberland Hussars were in France already, and fiercely determined to prove that anything that the Regular Army could do, they could do better. Their opportunity, as has already been seen, was not slow in coming.

There were many other Territorial regiments who were not quite ready, although their commanding officers made any available general's life a constant misery by repeatedly reiterating that they were; Artist's Rifles, Queen's Westminsters, North and South Irish Horse (these two formations were particularly truculent in their insistence that total defeat faced Great Britain if they did not get to the fighting soon), the Honourable Artillery Company (older in years than any regular regiment of the British Army, including the Life Guards), Hertfords, Monmouths, Liverpool Scottish and regiments of Yeomanry from every county of the British Isles. The regular cavalry sometimes referred to the Yeomanry as yokels on plough-horses, who might conceivably be ready for a form of limited warfare in ten years. They, too, were to get their chance to disprove this theory very soon.

In England recruiting offices were thronged from morning to night by under-age boys, still in the virgin state and yet to experience their first shave; over-age men with dyed hair, strenuously insisting that they were only thirty-five; unfit men with hammer toes, bronchial disorders and suffering from malnutrition. But they could not possibly be ready for another six months at the earliest: Kitchener's New Armies, many of them still without uniform or arms, were practising the evolutions of 1880 which very few of them would live to carry out.

So the 'massive help' had to come from India: it was massive on paper only, for even with the arrival of the Indian Corps under General Sir James Willcocks, the Germans still had a numerical preponderance of something like six to one.

The decision to send Indian troops to France was only arrived at after considerable mental wrestling in high places. The Army of India was little understood in Great Britain. Occasionally deeply tanned and hawk-eyed men appeared in England and were immediately identifiable as British officers of the Indian Army on long home leave. They shivered in the unaccustomed cold and blinked about them in a bewildered fashion—it was often their first sight of the Mother Country for seven years or more—and, like schoolboys long deprived of tuck, laid violent siege to Ascot, Henley, Goodwood, Lords, Wimbledon and as many restaurants and night clubs as they could afford. To these men England resembled a gigantic *hors d'oeuvre*, difficult to take in all at once. So they grabbed haphazardly and found it good, for soon another seven years of blistering exile awaited them.

Within the 'snob fabric' of the pre-war regular army, British officers of the Indian Army had no social status whatsoever. The Indian cavalry were tolerable—one had, of course, heard of the Bengal Lancers and the Guides, who were invested with a certain glamour in their magnificent ceremonial uniforms, and when it came to polo some of them could even teach the 9th Lancers a thing or two. The Gurkhas, too, sounded exciting: they were small, grinning, murderous Mongolians who slew their enemies with vicious-looking curved knives called *kukris*. The Sikhs sounded mildly interesting, because apparently they had some strange religion which forbade them to cut their hair or shave their faces. But the rest—Baluchis, Punjabis, Pathans, Rajputs, Dogras, Mahrattas, Garhwalis, were lumped together under the contemptuous heading 'black infantry'.

Equally abysmal, if not more so, was the ignorance of the

British press on the subject of the Indian Army. They, too, had just heard of the Bengal Lancers (not for nothing did Hollywood later latch on to them for one of the greatest ever motion pictures, starring Gary Cooper as a somewhat improbable Scottish-Canadian called MacGregor); but one eager scribe referred to a Sikh squadron of cavalry as 'fierce turbaned Moslems on fiery Arab steeds', and another got Gurkhas and Sikhs mixed up—'Gurkhas,' he wrote, 'are those tall, bearded warriors, who storm into action armed with their razor-edged *chalumchis*' (*chalumchi* is the Hindustani word for a wash basin).

The Army of India in 1914 was trained for a frontier war, practically a permanent state of affairs, or for a minor overseas expedition, but nothing else. This was due to the parsimony of a Government which spent money lavishly on everything except the Army; money could be had for anything except preparation for war. Consequently, the Army was short of almost everything—machine-guns, artillery, mechanical transport, medical and signalling equipment. But there was never a shortage of soldiers.

At the outbreak of war in 1914 the response of the Overseas Dominions was uniformly magnificent. As the B.E.F. retreated from Mons, advanced on the Marne, slogged it out on the Aisne and formed up for the First Battle of Ypres, the troop transports were on the tide from Canada, Australia, South Africa, New Zealand and Newfoundland. But no Dominion gave its sons more unstintingly than India, 'the fairest jewel in the Crown'.

Germany had made deep-laid plans for a reckoning with Great Britain as soon as France and Russia had been disposed of, and counted on an insurrection of native India. This was one of many striking instances of Germany's ridiculous belief that other people must think and act as Germany would; and of her complete failure to appreciate the real meaning and purpose of Empire as viewed by Great Britain. It is the fashion today to belittle and even to condemn the acquisition of an empire, but the British Empire was based upon not materialism but imagination.

When the call came, India rose as one man to stand by the

side of the British Raj. The Princes of the peoples did not wait to call for evidence nor to argue about the rightness of the cause; it was enough for them to know that the British Empire was at war with Germany, and any enemy of Britain was India's also. They knew the cause must be a righteous one, and they offered themselves, their men and their treasure to further it.

But there was no compulsory service, no 'Derby Scheme', no call-up; the Indian Army was the largest volunteer army the world has ever known.

There were men from every caste and race in the sub-continent: Sikhs, Dogras, Pathans, Madrassis, Mahrattas, Kumaonis, Garhwalis, Jats, Baluchis, Punjabi Mussulmans, Rajputs; there were men who had sniped at British Army columns on the North-West Frontier, and the Gurkhas, in all their tribes and sub-tribes, from Nepal; there were men who had barely heard of Great Britain or Germany.

They worshipped God according to the rites of a hundred different religions and spoke in as many different languages. There were men who had four wives, men who shared one wife with four brothers and men who openly practised sodomy. There were Hindus and Muslims, who had rioted bloodily against one another and been dispersed by stoical British soldiers. But they all had one thing in common—they wanted to fight in the 'Sahibs' War.' John Buchan never uttered a greater truth than when he wrote: 'The British soldiers and civilians who had found lonely graves between the Himalayas and Cape Comorin had not lived and died in vain when the result of their toil was this splendid and unfailing loyalty.'

The Indian Corps comprised two divisions, the Lahore Division (Major-General H. B. Watkins, C.B.) and the Meerut Division (Lieutenant-General C. A. Anderson, C.B.). It was a magnificent formation, containing some of the most illustrious regiments of the Indian Army—the 15th and 47th Sikhs; 57th, 58th and 59th Rifles (Frontier Force); 129th Baluchis; 6th Jat Light Infantry; 9th Bhopal Infantry; 125th Rifles; 39th Garhwal Rifles; 41st Dogras. There were also the 1/1st Gurkha Rifles, 2/3rd Gurkha Rifles, 1/4th Gurkha Rifles, 2/8th Gurkha Rifles and 1/9th Gurkha Rifles.

On the outbreak of war there was audible gloom in British battalions in India and, in the 1st Connaught Rangers, 1st Highland Light Infantry and 2nd Black Watch, a state bordering on near mutiny. For it seemed that they were to miss the Great Adventure and would be condemned to more sweltering years of cantonments, riot-duty, gut-rotting native spirits, cholera epidemics and perilous liaisons with diseased women—the life of the British soldier in India was not the riot of fun as portrayed in Kipling's *Soldiers Three*.

But there were wildly celebratory scenes in wet canteens when it was learned that each Indian brigade would be leavened with a British battalion (the other three were the 1st Manchesters, 2nd Leicesters and 1st Seaforth Highlanders). The Adjutant of the 1st Highland Light Infantry breathed a sigh of relief when he heard the news—there were twenty-three men in detention, seven court-martial cases pending and two more bars had been wrecked, which made three in a week. . . .

Between British and Indian soldier—particularly the Gurkhas—there was a wonderful *camaraderie*, based on mutual respect and liking. This had nothing to do with language; hardly any Indian or Gurkha soldiers, even the most senior, spoke English, and the British soldiers, although firmly convinced that they were accomplished Oriental linguists, usually murdered Hindustani with all-embracing thoroughness, as they did French and Arabic.

In India, they inevitably pronounced everything wrong; the Punjab was the Pun-jab, to rhyme with Hun and nab; a Pathan (correctly pronounced P'than) was a Paythan; Razmak, the North-West Frontier outpost, was Razz-mack.

Tea, as every old soldier and nearly every civilian knows, was 'char'; jam was 'pozzy'; food (*khana*) was konner; any vehicle, horse-drawn or mechanically propelled, was a 'garry'; women were 'bibis', and so on and so forth, up and down the Hindi tongue.

They called the Baluchis the 'Bollockys', their pronunciation of Jats, some of India's finest warriors, rhymed with cats, Sikhs were hairy-arsed bastards (a term of endearment) and the Gurkha was inevitably Johnny—to the British soldier he is, and always will be, 'Johnny Gurkha'.

In spite of their lowly station in British military society in England, the British officers of the Indian Army were very exceptional men—'the salt of the earth,' said General Willcocks, and he did not use the phrase lightly. Admittedly, some of the more glamorous cavalry regiments were referred to derisively by British service officers as 'government subsidised polo clubs', but basically they were all born leaders of men, comrades and friends of their men, and inspired in their soldiers a devotion and loyalty unsurpassed in any other army of the world. But they were, alas, far too small in numbers and in two World Wars they suffered astronomical casualties; this was particularly true of Gurkha regiments, because in size the British officers, conspicuous always, were rendered still more so because they topped their men by anything from six inches to a foot.

The embarkation of the Indian Corps did not go as smoothly as General Willcocks would have wished.

The British battalions, mostly long-service men, festooned with webbing equipment like Christmas trees, humped their rifles and kitbags up the gangways with their habitual stoicism: apart from the fact that they were headed for a major European war, this looked like being just another voyage in a trooper, and like all the others probably would not be worth the trip. There would be the usual vile food, the usual smell of sweat and vomit on the troop-decks; they would be packed like sardines in conditions which would drive any present-day soldiers to the edge of mutiny. On the credit side, it was rumoured that there might be a beer issue on these transports, and there was always the chance of picking up a month's pay in one of the endless games of housey-housey.

The Gurkhas, none of whom had ever seen the sea before, eyed the Indian Ocean dubiously. 'Where does it all come from?' they asked their officers. 'And where does it all go to?' Reassured on this point, they stumped cheerfully up the gangways, wearing the broadest of grins.

But to many of the Indians, who had never seen the sea— some of them, indeed, had hardly seen a river—it represented a hazard of the most daunting and terrifying description. Eastern races are not troubled over-much with nerves, and normally they take things as they come with philosophical resignation. But this vast and menacing expanse of water, on which great castles rocked up and down, was something far beyond their ken. This was the *kali-pani*—the black water—the sea, and they feared it exceedingly.

Like parents taking tearful offspring to the dentist, the British officers shepherded their men on board. The oration of a giant Pathan of Wylde's Rifles, a man who feared nothing on two legs or four, has been preserved: on the subject of sea travel, he had this to say (freely translated from *pushtu*): 'our hearts and entrails became as water and heaved within us', which is probably as accurate a description of seasickness as has ever been uttered in any language.

Throughout the voyage, the convoy was stalked by rumour. It seemed that France was not the destination at all, but Egypt, where they would relieve British troops; and no one was surprised when on arrival at Suez orders were issued to disembark and proceed to Cairo.

Cairo has always been popular with British officers of the Indian Army—many a promising military career has suffered a set-back within its hospitable confines—and in September 1914 the city ran true to form. The Heliopolis Hotel became an officers' club and there was every opportunity for a modicum of immoderate behaviour: champagne was consumed by the magnum; the band played 'Rule Britannia' to the accompaniment of tumultuous cheering; a stout German was debagged by a party of Connaught Ranger subalterns and threatened with immersion in a water trough.

But amidst all the gaiety in the Heliopolis there was grave concern: news of the German defeat on the Marne had filtered into Egypt and it seemed that the war might be over by the time they got to France, if indeed they ever did. As the convoy neared Malta, yet another rumour started to go the rounds: the Indian troops were to garrison the island, thus releasing British battalions for more serious work in France. This irked everyone except the old hands in the British battalions who had served there before.

Having left Malta behind, however, there was no further doubt and here, on Saturday, September 26, 1914, was the port of Marseilles to prove it.

For many of the soldiers the voyage had been a continuous nightmare. In any war, the fortitude of wounded Gurkha and Indian soldiers has been a constant source of admiring amazement to the medical officers who tended them. Bullet, bayonet and knife wounds were the normal occupational hazards of a soldier's trade; seasickness was something abnormal.

The more grievously afflicted lay in rows on the decks, tightly clasping their bodies lest their stomachs should melt away altogether, and in a dozen dialects called upon as many Gods to witness their piteous plight.

But as the transports drew alongside, all traces of *mal de mer* vanished. The sight of the quayside and the teeming masses of cheering people settled the stomach and magically cleared the brow; the rails of every ship were lined with a sea of turbans, brown faces and flashing white teeth.

A young lieutenant of the 129th Baluchis leaned over a bulwark and hailed an officer of the embarkation staff: 'Is it over yet?'

The embarkation staff officer had had a difficult morning, and the afternoon promised to be worse. 'Is what over?'

'The war.'

'Over? It's hardly started. . . .'

The welcome accorded to the Indian Corps was at least as vociferous as that given to the original B.E.F. in August, and within an hour of the last soldier filing down the gangway, East had met West in the most cordial manner.

The people of Marseilles took the Indians to their hearts: in 1974 the spectacle of Indians in Britain is commonplace, but in 1914 it needed a world war to bring Asia to Europe.

Picture, if you can, the mediaeval church and a homely market square which are as French as Joan of Arc, where voluble French housewives haggle over the price of carrots and potatoes; turn a corner and, apart from the houses, you could be in a corner of an Indian bazaar.

There is even the smell of India—the curious parchment odour of the East mingled with the smoke of wood-fires, the faintly acrid smell of ghee (Indian cooking fat) bubbling in a pot; the cooking scents of strange spice-laden concoctions, the staple bill of fare of the Indian soldier: mountains of boiled rice; chapattis (discs of unleavened bread made from whole wheat flour in the shape of a pancake) and dhal, a kind of lentil stew. The main course of the evening meal was probably still alive, but presently there was heard a terrified bleating from a goat, its moment of execution at hand.

A large contingent of the Indian Corps was encamped on Marseilles race-course, for all the world as if Sandown or Kempton Park had been transformed into a giant tented camp. Here, too, the East had taken over from the West and over the whole concourse was the smoke from hundreds of fires and a babel of sound in all the languages of India.

A large part of the Indian Corps was fortunate enough to have a reasonable period of acclimatisation: they had come straight from brilliant sunshine to the cold, biting sleet, icy slush and rain-soaked fogs of Flanders. But two Indian battalions, the 57th Rifles and the 129th Baluchis, were rushed forward almost immediately to plug the sagging line of the Cavalry Corps.

It would have been a shattering experience for battle-hardened troops, which the Baluchis and 57th certainly were not—not in this form of modern warfare, at any rate. Most of the officers and men of both battalions had certainly experienced a form of limited war on India's North-West Frontier, a war which never ceased for long, a seemingly never-ending conflict against the wily Pathan, who considered it his sacred duty to kill British soldiers and any Indians foolish or misguided enough to wear the uniform of the British Raj. The Pathan was as brave as any man alive and, in his own place and manner, as good a fighting man as any in the world: there were many Pathans in the ranks of the 129th Baluchis and 57th Rifles who endorsed this with feeling; many of them, indeed, had cousins, brothers-in-law and even blood brothers on the other side.

However, everyone has his little fancies and dislikes, and the Pathans, who were the sworn enemies of the King Emperor and not his servants, disliked the bayonet. It was not that they had a distaste for cold steel: on the contrary, the Khyber knife was his favourite weapon and he would as soon face it as use it. But determined, deadly and murderous as he was at hand-to-hand fighting, he knew nothing of parrying a shrewdly delivered thrust with the bayonet. With his sword-like knife he cut and slashed, decapitated and disembowelled, but never thrust; consequently, being accustomed to the receipt of thrusts, he had never learned how to parry one. So against the 'in, out, on guard' of the British and Indian soldier, trained in the use of the bayonet, he had no chance. He did not understand it, and he did not like it; wisely enough, against an opponent who used such outlandish weapons, he got out of the way. Consequently, using the disciplined bayonet charge, the men of the 129th Baluchis and 57th Rifles had come out on top in nearly all their encounters on the North-West Frontier.

The men of both battalions were confident of achieving the same superiority over the Germans; almost certainly their musketry was of a higher standard, and when it came to bloody and close quarter work with the bayonet—then God help any of the *dushman* (enemy) foolish enough to stand up to them.

As it transpired, the 129th Baluchis and 57th Rifles were plummeted into a war about which they knew nothing and had never believed possible; they had never even encountered machine-gun fire before, let alone the murderous hell of suffocating high explosive and quick fire. Bemused and bewildered, but always brave, they were dumped into a maelstrom where death was showered upon them from guns five miles away. Many of the older soldiers had seen men die in battle before from Pathan bullet and sword, but in this new terrible war men were blown into small pieces and buried alive.

The problem besetting the British officers of the Baluchis and 57th Rifles was to get their men to stay under cover, for the sepoys seemed to find it degrading to crouch in a trench. The lesson, taught though it finally was by bitter experience, took a long time to be assimilated: the battle-ardour of those men, soldiers from their childhood (many of them had had fathers, grandfathers and even great-grandfathers in the regiment) was unquenchable—they could see the serried ranks of blue-grey uniforms which represented the *dushman*, but they could not get to grips with them because of the incessant shelling and machine-gun fire.

There was a world of pathos in the remark, uttered over and over again, by sepoys to their British officers: '*Sahib*, why did you not tell us that it would be like this? Why did you not teach us this warfare?' Like mothers with fretful children, the officers could only tell them that they knew nothing of such warfare themselves, adding the promise that they would soon be given the chance to show their mettle with rifle and bayonet.

Typical of these belligerent complainants was a huge Pathan of the 129th Baluchis: a magnificent specimen of his race, great and hard of sinew and, like so many of his compatriots, loyal to the core and faithful unto death from the moment when loyalty and fidelity had been won and given.

The distance from the top of his high-piled puggri to the soles of his size-eleven ammunition boots must have been close to seven feet; for, bare-headed and bare-footed, Sepoy Shere Khan was six feet and four inches in height, a man of tremendous shoulder-breadth, barrel-like chest, mighty girth of arm and thigh. Shere Khan did not like being forced into a defensive position; it did not suit his character. When he approached his British officer, during a lull in the shelling, he spoke for every man in the Indian Corps: '*Huzoor*,' he said, 'we are not children and cowards to sulk behind earthworks.'

His officer, Lieutenant Lewis, who himself desired nothing more than to get to close grips with the Germans, was sympathetic. 'Just keep that big head of yours down, Shere Khan,' he counselled, 'and you'll get your chance—probably sooner than you think.'

The village of Chakwal may or may not still exist: possibly it has been swept away by flood; laid waste by famine, pestilence or fire, or a combination of all four; destroyed by war.

Half a century ago, however, Chakwal was as much a living part of India as Clovelly is North Devon. The river lapped listlessly by, and on the north bank were the mud-walled houses which were Chakwal; over the whole village hung the smell which is the smell of all India—a combination of wood-smoke and excrement.

The old men and women, their faces seamed and withered like old apples, squatted on their haunches and watched the sluggish course of the river. The middle-aged and young women staggered back and forth, carrying what seemed to be impossibly heavy loads of wood and water; naked children frolicked, fought and shrieked in the dust and darted in and out of the river like impatient otters; the men of the village were straggling back from the fields. Within the mud walls of the houses babies were being conceived, born and suckled.

Outside one of the houses sat a man aged about thirty: he sat in a manner traditional to the Pathan, squatting on his heels with his arms hanging loosely over his knees. At first sight he seemed indistinguishable from any other youngish man of Chakwal, but a longer and closer look revealed that he sat very straight, almost in a position of attention, and his moustache was not straggling and unkempt but fiercely up-swept.

It had been a long and a hard day in the fields, because in a village like Chakwal long and hard hours of back-breaking work were the only passport for survival. He noted with appreciation that a fire was burning outside his house, and an encouraging odour testified to the imminence of the evening meal.

Everyone who passed this man of an evening gave him a courteous *salaam*; the young men, several of them ex-soldiers and future soldiers, knelt and touched his knee. This ritual was insisted upon by the headman of the village, himself a former *Dafadar* of the Guides Cavalry; if the headman had had his way he would have had a flagpole in the village with the Union Jack fluttering at its mast, and a trumpeter to play the Last Post every evening.

Who was this man, and what had he done to inspire such homage in the people of Chakwal? His name was Khudadad Khan, formerly sepoy of the 129th Baluchis, and somewhere within the mud-walls of his house was the dark red ribbon

131

and bronze cross, inscribed with the words 'For Valour'—the Victoria Cross.

Sepoy Khudadad Khan, the first Indian soldier ever to be awarded the Victoria Cross, won the supreme award for valour in the furious fighting in the environs of the village of Hollebeke.

The 129th Baluchis had been rushed up in support of the 2nd Cavalry Division, which was holding a stretch of line measuring three and a half miles between the canal bridge east of Hollebeke and Messines. The Baluchis were desperately needed because the cavalrymen were under persistent and heavy attack by day and night; so far all these attacks had been repulsed, but the continuing strain on the defending troops was never relaxed and casualties were mounting at an alarming rate.

The Baluchis went straight into trenches, which were under murderous artillery fire; none of them had experienced artillery or machine-gun fire before, but their commanding officer, Lieutenant-Colonel Southey, reported that they 'stuck it splendidly'. Then waves of Germans attacked, and the machine-gunners had a chance to show their mettle.

There were two Maxim machine-guns in the battalion, and the machine-gun section was under the command of Captain Dill, an officer of exceptional gallantry. One gun was blown to pieces by a shell, as were two of its crew; the remaining three —Naik (Corporal) Sar Mir, Lance-Naik Hobab Gul and Sepoy Redi Gul—joined Captain Dill who was doing deadly execution on the Germans with the other gun.

The bronze emblem of the Victoria Cross was manufactured from the metal of guns captured at the Alma. The second machine-gun of the 129th Baluchis might well have been used in the making of future Victoria Crosses for the Indian Army, for this gun has a famous story attached to it, resulting in the award of the Victoria Cross to Sepoy Khudadad Khan.

Captain Dill had lost one gun, but he remained with the other. He was severely wounded, but refused to be evacuated; only when he became unconscious from exhaustion and loss of blood was he taken to the rear. His gallant team continued to serve the gun and there were piles of German dead in front of their position; as each man fell, another took his place. When the final German assault swept over them, only Khudadad Khan was still alive—all the rest were shot or bayoneted at their posts. Khudadad, although badly wounded himself by three separate bayonet thrusts, feigned death and crawled back to the battalion. Captain Dill recovered from his wounds and was awarded the D.S.O.

There was an air of suppressed excitement in an Indian field hospital on a freezing morning in mid-December, 1914. Outside the hutments there was frenzied sweeping of snow; a Guard of Honour of the Grenadier Guards had been hustled out of their billets with instructions to scour and polish themselves as for a 'Jimmy' or a 'Buck', as guards on St. James's Palace and Buckingham Palace were called in the Brigade of Guards; medical orderlies scurried to and fro and corridors were swept with demoniac energy; anxious-faced medical officers darted in and out of wards, finding fault with everything; a retinue of red-tabbed staff officers stamped into the hospital, leaving incipient panic in their wake.

Sepoy Khudadad Khan lay in bed in a ward full to bursting point of wounded from the 129th Baluchis and the 57th Rifles: his right leg was immobilised and practically the whole of his body was swathed in bandages, for he had been peppered by shrapnel in addition to his bayonet wounds. But in spite of this and the fact that two of his comrades, who had occupied beds on either side of him, died during the night, Khudadad Khan was not unhappy: he had, he considered, fought a good fight, even though he had lost his machine-gun; apparently the Colonel *Sahib* thought so too—a man of few words and ever-sparing with his praise, Colonel Southey had visited him in hospital and told him that he had done well. Many good comrades had been killed on that day, and Khudadad Khan wondered why he had been allowed to live.

He also wondered what all the excitement in the hospital was about. He wondered still more when three medical orderlies bore down upon his bed. One helped him into a clean suit of pyjamas, which was several sizes too small; another shaved him so conscientiously that he drew blood; a third manipulated his flowing black mane of hair into an immaculate 'Pathan bob', as the Pathan soldiers' hair style was sometimes called, and with loving care restored his luxuriant moustache to Baluchi trimness.

Khudadad Khan asked one of the orderlies: 'What is this *tamasha*?'[1]

The orderly grinned broadly. 'You will find out,' he said.

Suddenly the ward seemed to be full of red tabs; among the staff officers Khudadad Khan recognised his own Colonel. There was another face he recognised instantly—a grave, kindly, bearded face: the face of His Majesty King George the Fifth, who pinned the Victoria Cross to Khudadad's pyjama jacket.

That is why Khudadad Khan was a deeply honoured and respected man in the village of Chakwal. For how many men in Indian villages could say that they had been decorated with the greatest *bahaduri*[2] of them all by the King Emperor himself?

Any Indian soldier of the Indian Corps, if asked by his British officer what his function in war was, would have answered something like this: '*Sahib*, with you, I will hold the position alive, and if I cannot hold it alive I will hold it dead; I will follow you in the attack, if need be to hell and back again; I will happily die for you.'

He would face bullets, shells and cold steel; hunger, thirst, dirt and discomfort without complaint; he would dig trenches at the *Sahib*'s order until he broke the shovel, his back or something else; he would march with the *Sahib* until he fell dead from exhaustion.

He would shirk nothing except one thing, and here was uttered the *crie de cœur* of the Indian: 'Spare me nothing, *Sahib*, save one thing—*jimmiwari*—responsibility.'

This preamble leads up to one story of what happened during the fighting round Messines.

A certain sector of the line became untenable, and the order came from the 3rd Cavalry Brigade for a general retirement. The orders did not reach Captain Forbes, commanding the

[1] Party.
[2] Gallantry award.

134

Punjabi Mussulman Company of the 57th Rifles, and they were attacked frontally, from both flanks and surrounded. They fought back valiantly with bayonets, rifle butts, boots and fists, but Captain Forbes received severe wounds from which he subsequently died and Lieuteant Clark was killed. A bare half company—some forty men in all—managed to escape.

All the Indian officers had become casualties, and there was no one above the rank of *naik* left alive in the company: the bugbear of *jimmiwari* was ruthlessly exposed.

Obeying some herd instinct the survivors sought the temporary shelter of a shell-torn barn, where they huddled together in miserable groups, awaiting what fate had in store for them.

It may seem that the conduct of these men was not entirely creditable. They had no British officers and no orders; they did not know where they were. But one and all had fought with the greatest gallantry against an enemy who had outnumbered them by something like ten to one; they were not afraid, they simply did not know what to do. They needed a leader, and they needed him quickly.

They were soon to get one, in the improbable shape of Corporal Colgrave of the 5th Lancers.

Colgrave was a Kiplingesque character. Once, a long time ago, he had been a Squadron Quartermaster-Sergeant. But a fondness for liquor, first in a trickle, and then in a rush, had brought him down. He claimed intimate acquaintance with General Allenby, which was true in a way because Allenby, then Commanding Officer of the 5th Lancers, had 'busted' Colgrave to the ranks.

Now Corporal Colgrave was climbing the weary promotion ladder once more. His officers had looked for qualities of leadership in him and looked in vain; it seemed almost certain that the two stripes he wore, precarious at that, represented the peak of his promotion prospects.

Colgrave and a squad of a dozen men had been looking after horses about a mile in rear of Messines, when an urgent order summoned them forward to a point in the line where the addition of thirteen more rifles would be of incalculable value. The barn on which they happened looked tempting and Corporal Colgrave ordered five minutes' halt for a smoke.

'Got a fag, Corp?' asked a trooper hopefully outside the barn.

'Only got one,' said Colgrave.

'I only want one.'

'Less of your lip. Get inside.'

Corporal Colgrave had done many years' service in India and regaled newly joined young soldiers with largely untrue stories of gory encounters on the North-West Frontier against the wily 'Paythan', massive commercial deals in bazaars and gargantuan copulation in native brothels. Like many another vintage British soldier, he was firmly convinced that he was a fluent speaker of Hindustani.

The Lancers entered the barn and gazed upon forty miserable Indian faces; when he is really downcast, no race of man can wear a darker mask of woe than an Indian.

'Blimey, what a bunch,' said the corporal; then loudly *Sab thik hai idher?*'

Clearly, everything was very far from being '*thik*'. The Indians eyed him warily and without enthusiasm. On the other hand, although he was not a *Sahib* he had a white face and wore the two stripes of a *naik* and might take on the *jimmiwari*.

'*Kis waste*[1] this 'ere?' asked Colgrave. '*Sahib kidher hai?*'

'*Sahib margya,*' said a dozen sad voices.

'Well, blimey,' said Colgrave, in trouble with the language already, 'you want to *marrow* the fuckin' Germans, don't you *malum*?'

[1] Some sort of glossary of this strange conversation is required. *Sab thik hai idher* is 'everything all right here?' (clearly it was not) *margya* is dead; *malum*, literally translated, means 'know'; *jee-ha* is 'yes'; *idher ao* is 'come here'; *abhi wapas* roughly means 'we are going back now'; *achi bat*, in the language of a British N.C.O., can be construed as 'right, then'; *chalo*, literally translated means 'drive' but in this context can be taken as meaning 'let's go'; *kis waste thi 'ere* almost explains itself — it is 'what's going on here, then?', the rhetorical question asked by English policemen in almost any circumstance.

136

The idea was beginning to catch on. 'Jee-*han*!' said a dozen voices.

Corporal Colgrave winked at the other Lancers, one of whom was heard to say 'old Charlie fancies 'isself as a fuckin' general'.

Smiles were beginning to appear on downcast brown faces; there was something about the gamey, ribald approach of Corporal Colgrave which seemed to be a positive denial of defeat. Murderous shelling, which had blown men to pieces and buried men alive, had taken some of the heart out of the Punjabi Mussulmans, but Colgrave was putting it back.

'Right, then, you miserable-looking lot of buggers,' said Corporal Colgrave with affection, '*idher ao*[1]: *Abhi wapas*, got it? *Marrow* all the German *soors. Abhi thik hai?*'

'Thik *hai*!' said forty voices in unison.

'*Achi bat*. Now, then, who's going to win the bleedin' V.C.? *Chalo*!'

And so thirteen Lancers went into the line, with the priceless addition of forty by now one-hundred-per-cent belligerent Indians, and that particular sector of line was held for the next twenty-four hours.

In one of the 'little wars' on India's North-West Frontier—a war about which the British public read little or nothing in its newspapers—a young British officer found himself in command of a half company of young soldiers, unfortunately men of one of India's less martial races. They were pinned down by a murderous and accurate fire from Pathans concealed behind rocks. Ammunition and water were dwindling to a decimal point and the relieving force were five miles away. The men were tired, hungry, thirsty and frightened; the Pathans were none of these things. The young officer, thinking aloud, said, 'Oh, for a hundred Sikhs with fixed bayonets', and he spoke from the heart.

The Sikhs have ranked high among India's great fighting men, ever since the Sikh war of 1845 when they gave the British Army more than enough to worry about: the Sikhs, those fierce and proud bearded warriors with their strange and rigid religious customs—the hair on the head and face must never be cut; they must not smoke; every man wears a steel bracelet on his wrist; they must invariably wear white underpants (other soldiers of the Indian Army, particularly Gurkhas, went in for gaily-coloured checks and stripes).

The British soldier rises an hour before first parade (and later if he can get away with it). The Sikh sepoy must be astir at least an hour earlier if his shoulder-length hair is to be neatly coiled under his *puggri* and his beard arranged in a state of military perfection—the more dandified Sikhs place their beards in a hair-net.

A company of Sikhs on parade is a splendid sight: they are mostly six-footers, and the rows of grave faces from which flash fierce and unfathomable brown eyes create an impression of disciplined arrogance calculated to warm the heart of any commander.

In battle they charge with an *élan* which has struck terror into Germans, Turks, Pathans and Japanese; also, let it be said, into British soldiers in the Sikh wars. Men think twice before standing up to rifles and bayonets wielded by these men who are transformed by the heat of battle into hairy nightmares. Their battle cry '*Sat sri kal!*' is as frightening a sound as any man can dread to hear. To command Sikhs, however, has never been the easiest of tasks—ask any veteran Colonel of a Sikh battalion, including one of the greatest Sikh commanders of all: Brigadier Jackie Smyth, V.C., M.C., who has probably seen more active service than any living soldier of any nationality. 'Finest soldiers in the world,' they will tell you, 'as long as you watch 'em like a hawk round the clock and work 'em into the ground.'

They tend to be moody; they are prone to intrigue; they are not averse to homosexuality; like good soldiers the world over, they have a pronounced fondness for alcohol. But a British officer who had won their respect would count on extraordinary devotion and loyalty and would not exchange them for Guardsmen, Highlanders, Gurkhas, or any other breed of soldier who has brought glory to British arms.

Of all castes of Indian who made up the Indian Corps, the Sikhs—sepoys of the 15th, 34th and 47th Sikhs—probably resented static, trench-bound warfare, when they were a sitting target for a rain of shells, most of all. The Gurkhas, more stoical mortals, stood the shelling better—the trenches were deep; too deep, indeed, for men whose average height was five feet three inches, and they often had to stand on tip-toe to fire over the parapet at advancing Germans. The Gurkhas hated shellfire as much as soldiers of any other nationality, and they could not understand why they had to sit still under it without retaliation of a personal and murderous sort. But their British officers, who also disliked shellfire, strode unconcernedly among them and assured them that there would be plenty of opportunities for close and gory work with the *kukri* before long—and so it turned out to be.

The Sikhs, more volatile and less phlegmatic than the Gurkhas, found this static warfare intolerable, and said so loudly and forcibly: to be forced on the permanent defensive did not suit their temperament: they wanted to get to grips with their enemy with cold steel—the Sikh is probably unsurpassed by any soldier of any nationality with the bayonet—and the sooner the better. On October 28 they got their chance, and took full and sanguinary advantage of it.

In the desperate fighting around Neuve Chapelle the 47th Sikhs took the bayonet to the Germans, with devastating effect: in this desperate struggle they fought an action which was seldom equalled in the annals of the Indian Army.

This was the moment that the 47th had been waiting for: with bayonets fixed they surged over the parapet. There was not a stick of cover and German machine-guns tore great gaps in their ranks, taking particularly heavy toll of British officers —the inevitable melancholy pattern in the Indian Corps.

The 47th Sikhs got into the town with perhaps half their number still on their feet, then as soon as they arrived in a village on the outskirts of Neuve Chapelle they came into their own with a vengeance. Now it was the time for cold steel; many Germans, in no mood to stand up to these huge bearded men, their *puggris* crimson above their swarthy faces and the blood-lust in their eyes.

When the term 'seeing red' is applied to Sikhs or Gurkhas, it is used quite literally, for their eyes become clouded over with a reddish film; the sight of the Sikhs seemed to fascinate and paralyse the Germans, striking them helpless. Many of them fled in terror, only to be overtaken—for the Sikh can cover the ground like an antelope—and bayoneted; some raised their hands in craven surrender, but the 47th had recently taken part in a small war against the Pathans on the North-West Frontier, where no prisoners were taken—the Sikhs saw no reason why the 'Sahibs' war' should be any different. A few—but only a very few—Germans were taken rearwards as prisoners, and counted themselves the luckiest men in the German Army.

No soldier of the 47th Sikhs was more intent on slaughter than Naik Rangal Singh, a veritable giant who topped the tallest man in his company by a clear two inches. The 47th, more fortunate than many other battalions, were going into action with full bellies: Rangal Singh had partaken generously of good, fat-tailed sheep and there had been an issue of rum (Rangal Singh, taking heed of the adage that 'rank hath its privilege', had been round twice).

Rangal Singh, temporarily cut off from the rest of his section, who were hunting Germans in another part of the village, was at the summit of his particular world; he had already skewered one German by the simple expedient of thrusting into the stomach and ripping upwards; he had skilfully parried a bayonet thrust by another and brained his assailant with the butt of his rifle. Now, in search of further targets, he found himself outside a derelict farm building. From inside he could hear muted voices, and Rangal Singh listened warily—he knew no English, although he recognised it when he heard it; they were certainly not speaking Hindi, Punjabi or Pushtu. Therefore they must be the *dushman*, and must be most thoroughly slain.

Inside were indeed eight German soldiers; they had had enough of fighting for the time being, and this building seemed to offer a haven of sanctuary.

It is possible that they thought Naik Rangal Singh was the devil, and he was no bad substitute: roaring out the choicer Punjabi imprecations and whirling his rifle round his head like a cane, he became a one-man wave of destruction, dedicated to the most elementary butchery.

With five Germans dead, Rangal Singh surveyed the remaining three, who were cowering and whimpering in a corner. Rangal Singh had received no orders regarding the taking of prisoners, and would in all probability have ignored them even if he had, but it occurred to him that if he took back three live *dushman* the Captain *sahib* might feel more kindly disposed towards him—only two days earlier he had threatened Rangal Singh with demotion to the rank of sepoy for some minor misdemeanour.

When Rangal Singh reported to his officer, the Captain asked him: 'Why did you not kill them all?' To which Rangal Singh replied with a disarming smile: 'My right arm got tired.'

The introduction of Indian troops at such a time has been severely criticised, mostly by armchair pundits with scant (if any) knowledge of the Indian soldier and by many others who should have known better. These experts contended that it was near madness to send Indian soldiers, children of the sun which shone all the year round, to a land which would play havoc with their health and morale. This may well have been true, but the sick parades of Indian soldiers were seldom larger than those of British battalions—and frequently much smaller. In every British unit there has always been a small hard core of professional malingerers, who rehearse an assortment of groans on sick parade, and whose all-consuming desire is an appointment with a specialist—the average medical officer of any British unit could detect men like this at fifty paces.

But there was no such thing in the Indian Army as a malingerer; the dreaded words 'Medicine and Duty', written in red ink, never defaced an Indian Army battalion sick report. An Indian soldier only reported sick if he was really ill, and not always even then.

The main troubles of the Indian Corps were lack of British officers, who in the early days in Flanders were killed and wounded at a terrifying rate—as indeed they were in the later years of the Great War and in the Second World War.[1]

[1] In the Imphal fighting in 1944 my own battalion, 3/3 (Queen Alexandra's Own) Gurkha Rifles, were reckoned to have got off com-

On occasions the men of the 129th Baluchis and 57th Rifles seemed to be in a state of disintegration (the saga of Corporal Colgrave of the 5th Lancers was not an isolated incident); they were many times driven out of their trenches, although blasted out would be a fairer description; they sometimes seemed to resemble a leaderless and purposeless rabble.

Of course, they were too dependent on their British officers; certainly it was in their nature to be, but their training had encouraged them in this. It added enormously to their fighting power, providing their officers were not shot; and the Indian Army, organised from frontier fighting in India, presumed that all the British officers would not be shot in one day or, say, a week. But having lost his British officer the Indian soldier lost fighting efficiency. Sometimes he failed to go on with his natural determination and *élan*, not because he was afraid but because he simply did not know what to do.

Another grave disadvantage, which was overlooked by the critics of the Indian Corps, lay in the lack of reinforcements. It was bad for the survivors of an Indian battalion—and this situation arose in almost every unit of the Indian Corps in the early days in Flanders—which had lost heavily in battle to be left a mere skeleton, to contemplate annihilation. The ranks should have been filled with new men as quickly as possible so that fresh spirit could be immediately infused.

Yet in spite of the vile weather conditions, which none of them had ever experienced before, the conduct of the Indian soldiers was, in the main, superb. If they did not come up to standard on all occasions it was because too much was asked of them by those who were ignorant of their psychology and needs.

Psychologically the Indian soldier had much greater demands made upon him than had the British and still more the French.

The French soldier was motivated by hate for a country which was ravaging his homeland; he therefore fought with hate in his heart as well as the fear of total destruction. The

---

paratively lightly: we had four British officers killed and four wounded out of a total of sixteen—exactly fifty per cent casualties.

British soldier was short on hate—Thomas Atkins has never been a good hater—but he was learning fast, and he knew that he must win this war or be destroyed.

The British and French were fighting for national survival. The Indian soldiers fought for their officers, their honour and fifteen rupees a month.[1]

[1] Reckoning the rupee of the period at one shilling and fourpence in old currency, the pay of the 1914 Indian sepoy can be assessed at just £1 sterling per month.

CHAPTER SEVEN

Of the entire British Expeditionary Force, only Lieutenant-General Sir Douglas Haig's 1st Corps bore any resemblance to a cohesive fighting force in that last week in October, 1914. Smith-Dorrien's 2nd Corps had, since its arrival in France, suffered 26,505 casualties, which had not been made good; the 7th Division had practically ceased to exist; the Cavalry Corps was still hanging on grimly, but hardly a regiment had half its original strength.

In the course of the next three weeks the 1st Corps was to find itself in little better case than the shattered 2nd and the skeleton 7th Division.

Haig's 1st Corps, hastily entrained northwards from the bogged-down trenches on the Aisne, came into the line to the left of Ypres on October 19 — the 1st Division around Poperinghe, with the 2nd Division beyond it, covering Cassel.

The men of 1st Corps left the Aisne positions in almost holiday mood: any change from the miserable discomfort and tedium of static trench warfare must be for the better. All portents seemed to be good, and the fickle French climate took a significant hand; days of bright, warm sunshine gave way to nights of radiant moonlight.

The conditions of the train journey — hard wooden seats and men crammed like sardines — would have reduced present-day British soldiers to a state of near mutiny, but the men of Haig's Corps put a brave face on it. Halts were frequent, occurring in such picturesque small towns as Mareil-sur-Ourcq, Senlis and Abbeville, and all these places represented to the grimy and battle-weary men from the Aisne front a brief glimpse of Paradise. There were comfortable billets and baths, and for the first time since their arrival in France men could wallow in unlimited hot water. Perhaps it was going to be a lovely war after all.

No one knew their exact destination except that it was 'somewhere in Belgium'. The country was becoming flatter, and cavalrymen, always incurable optimists, noted this with satisfaction—flat ground with good galloping surface pointed to mounted action. (It is no coincidence that a number of former cavalry officers have become racehorse trainers in their retirement, for a cavalryman always had an eye for the 'going', be it hard, soft, good or yielding.)

Not all the scenic changes, however, were for the better: the vineyards and beautiful uplands of the Aisne country and the peaceful forest glades of Compiègne had been left far behind and in their place was a flat manufacturing district; only men of the South Staffordshire Regiment viewed this with pleasure, for it closely resembled their own inhospitable-looking 'Black Country' of England.

Nor was the new climate encouraging. Like an unpredictable English summer, the fine weather went as quickly as it had come; it grew steadily colder; the azure-blue sky became grey and frequently almost black; there were swift, lashing storms, with the promise of snow to come.

A new name cropped up in conversations on troop trains —a curious name, which the British soldiers pronounced 'Eeprez' and later referred to as 'Wipers'. From all accounts, it seemed that Ypres was quite a place and the men of the 1st Corps looked forward to a sojourn in a town where they might re-live the brief golden age that they had enjoyed only a short two months before in Boulogne, Le Havre and Rouen. They remembered the gargantuan steaks, the wine and the women, who, in spite of Lord Kitchener's austere directive, were frequently hospitable and accommodating.

Within less than a month those men of the 1st Corps who were still alive were to wish themselves back in the chalky and waterlogged trenches on the Aisne.

At first sight, Ypres seemed to fulfil all expectations: officers, who had previously existed on an exclusive diet of bully beef and issue rum and whisky and water in enamel mugs, set off on gastronomic forays and consumed food of exquisite tenderness and wine to set the palate reeling, served on snowy white tablecloths by comely young women who seemed intent on making the *entente cordiale*, in its most intimate sense, come true there and then.

Word soon got round that British soldiers had an insatiable hunger for a delicacy known as fish and chips. Fish and chips were not on the menu in French cafés in October 1914, but the local populace did their best: villainous-looking fragments of fried fish changed hands for a consideration and hot potatoes in various guises appeared as if by magic; some of the more enterprising British soldiers gained admission to kitchens, commandeered frying pans and actually manufactured their own chips.

Such beer as there was was amber-coloured, thin, flat and gaseous, but there was red and white wine of remarkable strength and delicious coffee, which bore no resemblance to the pale grey outrage doled out in British army canteens at home.

The 1st Battalion the Irish Guards were an instant hit in Ypres. To the music of melodeons, they danced Irish jigs on the pavements. They also sang seditious songs—songs of the wilds of Ireland and the old Fenian days—from a very seditious repertoire. In the midst of all this gaiety a squadron of French cavalry, resplendent in plumes and cuirasses, clattered through the town at the trot, to add a colourful touch to a scene that was soon to become a sad and nostalgic memory for those few who were ever to see 'Wipers' again. The news that the large majority of the Irish Guards were Roman Catholics soon circulated, and as they made ready to march out of Ypres nuns distributed rosaries.

The consensus of opinion among the soldiers was that 'this 'ere Wipers is a bit of all right. Old 'Aig can leave me here as long as he likes'.

But there was a grim reminder that the war was near, and very far from being lovely: in the distance, from the east and north-east, the sounds of the booming of guns and the crowds of Belgian refugees streaming along the roads, were dreadful harbingers of the calamity that was to overcome the ancient city of Ypres.

Suddenly playtime was over for the 1st Corps and it was time to go to war again.   *

At 5 a.m. on October 29 the battalions stood to arms: with no reserves and no supports they waited for the final annihilating attacks which they knew must come—the assault by an enemy at least twice their strength and with an overwhelming preponderance of heavy artillery. The orders issued to every brigade and battalion commander were the same, and owed nothing to Staff College training: 'The position will be held to the last man and the last round.' The more pessimistic commanding officers averred that it would not be long before the last man was dead and the last round shot.

They were all in the front line at Zaandvoorde, Kruiseik, Polygon Wood, Zonnebeke and Gheluvelt: grooms, signallers, cooks, orderlies, trumpeters and drummers—particularly drummers. Charles Downham was a drummer in the King's Company, 1st Battalion Grenadier Guards; his lack of inches (he stood only five feet three inches tall) made him a somewhat incongruous figure in the King's Company, for the minimum height requirement for this exclusive body of giants was six feet three inches.

The job of a drummer in action was a hazardous one: the carrying of messages from company headquarters to battalion headquarters or to one of the other companies. Many were the messages that Charles Downham carried, although he seldom knew what they were all about: folded scraps of paper, torn from field message pads, the writing blurred and shaky, the signatures barely decipherable, but the meaning always clear. These scraps of paper contained news of a new enemy breakthrough, trenches lost, trenches regained, platoons wiped out, companies reduced to half a platoon.

Every journey undertaken by Downham was perilous in the extreme; there were no communication trenches and he had to travel across expanses of broken ground, swept by artillery, machine-gun and rifle fire. But the messages to and from the King's Company always got through.

There was another drummer who was performing prodigies of valour, Drummer William Kenny of the 2nd Battalion the Gordon Highlanders. He was to gain the first Victoria Cross won by the Gordons in the First World War.

There is something irresistibly funny about a very small

man beating the big drum in a military band. The big drummer, one would have thought, should be a big man with mighty arms and a chest like a barrel, for the big drum was no light weight. Drummer Kenny had a chest like a barrel, but like Charles Downham, stood five feet three inches in his ammunition boots. In ten years before the war the pipes and drums of the 2nd Gordons had delighted audiences from Edinburgh to Delhi and from Aldershot to Cairo. During these ten years William Kenny had lent his very considerable presence to the proceedings, making up for his lack of inches by the fervent vigour with which he belaboured the big drum.

In addition, he played back in the band's football team, if not with great skill then with immense keenness. He had exactly the figure for a zealous full back, and was of the type who kicked with such vim that when he missed the ball—which he usually did—he invariably fell heavily to the ground.

During the desperate action which was fought by the 2nd Gordons at Zonnebeke, Kenny seemed to bear a charmed life; he carried messages of vital importance under the heaviest fire, enabling small and often isolated groups to co-operate in resisting every tactical device of the enemy.

To every Gordon Highlander, from the Commanding Officer downwards, the sudden and unexpected appearance of 'wee Wullie' in a score of desperately hard-pressed sectors of the line acted as an immediate tonic.

Drummer Kenny did not only carry messages. A sergeant, a corporal and three privates, all of them wounded, owed their lives to him; showing incredible strength, he carried them to safety under heavy fire.

The ferocity of the German attacks on the 7th Infantry and 3rd Cavalry Divisions multiplied every hour, and the plight of one unit differed little from that of another. It is doubtful, however, if any two battalions found themselves in more dire straits than the 1st Grenadier Guards and the 2nd Gordon Highlanders at Gheluvelt, astride the notorious Menin Road.

The 1st Grenadiers, the left-hand battalion of the 20th Brigade, had suffered the most severely: they were attacked frontally, from both flanks and from the rear. Before the German infantry swarmed into their position, they had been subjected to the most intense artillery fire. In spite of the overwhelming numbers of the enemy, the Grenadiers held on grimly and lost scarcely a hundred yards of ground.

They did, however, lose all their officers except four: the commanding officer, Lieutenant-Colonel Maxwell Earle, was wounded and taken prisoner; the second-in-command, Major Hugh Stucley, was killed within five minutes of assuming command. Altogether the 1st Grenadiers lost nineteen officers killed, wounded and missing, and 470 men.

A party of about one hundred Grenadiers and Gordons were lying in a ditch: they had no officers and few sergeants —possibly three in all. They had been literally *blasted* from their positions, for the so-called trenches which they had been occupying afforded no cover whatsoever, and they might as well have been lying out in the open.

They were unhappy and a little shamefaced, for there was no gainsaying the fact that ground had been lost, and the loss of ground was abhorrent to Grenadier and Gordon alike. They wished nothing more than to re-take the position from which they had been so murderously ousted, because its loss meant that the Germans were one hundred yards nearer to the Channel Ports.

Most of the Grenadiers and Gordons were in favour of counter-attacking immediately; there were a few, but only a very few, who wanted to go back even farther, but they were speedily silenced by dreadful oaths and dire threats from the few remaining N.C.O.s.

The artillery barrage had, for the time being, slackened— something for which the men were profoundly thankful. But the irritating and shameful fact remained that the Germans were still in *their* trenches—the trenches *they* rightfully owned.

To the leaderless but still belligerent force came Lieutenant Otho Brooke of the 2nd Gordon Highlanders, who had been sent up the line with an urgent message for the officer in command. Undoubtedly the message was urgent, but there was no officer to take delivery of it; far more urgent, Otho Brooke .decided, was the restoration of morale and fighting spirit in the motley collection of Gordons and Grenadiers lying in a muddy ditch.

Otho Brooke, at first sight, was the epitome of a true 'Gay Gordon'; his uniform, although liberally bespattered with Flanders mud, was impeccably cut; his cap was worn at a rakish angle; his left hand rested lightly on his sword hilt, as if he were about to fight a duel.

At the sight of these men the 'Gay Gordon' was quickly transformed into the hundred-per-cent functional soldier. The senior sergeant present, a giant Grenadier, jumped to his feet at the appearance of an officer and favoured Brooke with a slashing salute, as if he were on the parade ground at the Guards Depot at Caterham. Bullets zipped around them, but they paid no heed: to the sergeant it seemed that this debonair young officer of the Gordon Highlanders had appeared at exactly the opportune moment, and he was right.

'Things not too good here, sergeant?' said Brooke casually.

'They are not, sir,' said the sergeant—he jerked his thumb in the direction of the Germans—'them Jerries are in our trenches.'

'They won't be in them for long,' Brooke assured him. With the bullets still zipping round him—one, indeed, ploughed a neat furrow across his cheek—he strolled nonchalantly up and down the line of recumbent men; here and there he cracked a joke with his Highlanders—they were not particularly funny jokes, but Brooke knew that they were the sort of jokes the men must have. To a group of Grenadiers Brooke asked: 'Are you gentlemen of the 1st Guards averse to going into action with humble Highlanders?'

'Not bloody likely, sir,' said a guardsman, forgetting his language in the heat of the moment.

'Good man,' said Otho Brooke. Then, all the soldier again, he went on: 'Now, then—who's going to win the Victoria Cross? Fix bayonets and give 'em hell.'

The roar from a hundred desperate throats struck terror into the hearts of the Germans as the Grenadiers and Gordons charged across a hundred yards of open and bullet-swept ground, where there was no stick of cover of any description. Otho Brooke carried them all: waving his sword and shouting encouragement in a tongue which several Gordons swore was Gaelic, he was shot through the heart just twenty yards from he Germans. The Grenadiers and Gordons still on their feet —a bare forty N.C.O.s and men—surged over his body into he trenches and beyond, for many of the Germans had fled panic-stricken before this murderous onslaught; Grenadiers nd Gordons swore horrible oaths and stabbed and hacked with their bayonets; triggers were pulled at a range of a few nches; rifle butts cracked down on heads, driving spiked helmets into brains.

The senior Grenadier sergeant rammed his bayonet into a field grey tunic and pulled the trigger of his rifle before he kicked the man in the testicles; a brave and foolhardy German called upon a corporal of the Gordons to surrender: 'Hands up, Englishman!' he ordered, as he pointed his rifle at his attackers.

'Englishman be fucked!' howled the Gordon, as he shot the man dead.

A private of the Gordons, who had seen Otho Brooke fall, went berserk: as a German lunged at him with rifle and bayonet, he pulled his legs from under him, thrust his bayonet into his stomach and ran on. He drove his bayonet into the throat of another who tried to kick him in the groin; he freed the bayonet just in time to blow the jaw from the face of a man who had his rifle raised to club him. Firing from the hip, he shot the teeth out of a man behind him and rushed on, bellowing with glee.

In this annihilating attack no prisoners were taken: Germans were shot down or run through with bayonets whether they put their hands up or not. Just ten minutes after Otho Brooke had given his last order, the Grenadiers and Gordons were back in their original positions.

'And this time,' said the grim-faced Grenadier sergeant, his bayonet dripping with blood, 'we stay here.'

And they did.

The popular misconception of World War One generals is of stout, choleric, port-wine-complexioned incompetents who swilled quantities of claret in well-appointed châteaux miles behind the front line. Undoubtedly, alas, there were such generals in the later stages of the Great War, but not in the closing months of the year 1914.

The generals of the period were front-line soldiers; they did not wish to command their brigades or division by telephone — indeed, most of them had a great loathing of the instrument and left the answering of it to more willing hands.

Typical of these generals was Major-General Sir Hubert Hamilton, whose leadership of the 3rd Division at Mons, Le Cateau and on the Aisne had been of the very finest order. Hamilton was essentially a 'soldier's general': office work irked him ('What the hell have I got a staff for?' was one of his frequent complaints when confronted with a mountain of paperwork demanding his attention).

Hubert Hamilton gave the lie to the theory that in the First World War generals sent their troops into hopeless battle, while they themselves stayed in the rear and eventually toddled home to die in bed with twenty thousand good dinners behind them. Hubert Hamilton was, in fact, the prototype of many Second World War generals — men like Pete Rees, Bill Slim, Frank Messervy, Frankie Festing, Jim Cassells and Joe Kendrew — who were usually to be found a good deal farther forward than was strictly necessary. But what generals like this lost in control they gained in the morale and confidence of their troops. A dead general was always a great morale builder; all these men did their best.

General Hamilton was universally admired by his staff, but he sometimes moved them to near despair when he disappeared from his headquarters for anything up to three days at a stretch. One of his A.D.C.s, who thought he was on to a 'cushy' job, found that life was every bit as hard and dangerous as in a front line battalion and bewailed his lot to unsympathetic audiences. It was on a visit to the 2nd Royal Scots — a once-a-day visit to a front line trench was a 'must' in Hamilton's programme — he was killed by a stray shell.

The Gilded Staff, as they were known, have always been a target for the regimental soldier — the man in the front line — to snipe at: 'The Staff,' declare their more bigoted critics, 'is a bloody nuisance, inefficient when it isn't actually crooked'; 'the Staff,' say their still more extremist opponents, 'has only one function: to foul up operations by giving contradictory orders and misreading its maps, in order that wars will be prolonged to a point where every staff officer has become a general'.

In 1916 and 1917, when men were dying on the Somme at a rate comparable to the Great Plague, bitterness against the staff increased: while fighting men floundered and drowned in liquid mud and were crucified on barbed wire, red-tabbed staff officers shot partridges and complained about the temperature of the champagne and quality of the cognac far from the front line. Of course, it happened in the Second World War as well. Not for nothing were the exquisite beings at G.H.Q. in Cairo known as 'The Gaberdine Swine' — the most daunting military crisis that came their way was a mild sandstorm or a defective refrigerator.

In the Great War, it was darkly rumoured, a senior officer of the Quartermaster-General's department was admitted to the Companionship of the Distinguished Service Order for devoted service in issuing plum and apple jam; another supposedly received the D.S.O. for counting intimate undergarments for the women's services.

But in the opening months of the First World War relations between the fighting soldiers and the staff were cordial enough because no divisional or brigade headquarters was ever far out of range of shellfire. During the battle of Le Cateau General Sir Horace Smith-Dorrien was frequently in the forefront of battle, and often far farther forward than a corps commander should have been — but Smith-Dorrien was a fighting infantryman, a soldier's soldier, who knew from hard experience what mud, death, mutilation and short rations were all about.

For all that, it seemed at first sight that the headquarters of Major-General Lomax's 2nd Division was taking a luxurious view of the war: Divisional H.Q. was housed in the Hooge château, an imposing edifice standing in the midst of a beautiful park in strong contrast to the ugly industrial land surrounding it.

For a visitor, it was like emerging from a recurrent nightmare to enter the gates of the château, to have a guard turn out to him, and to give his horse to a groom who, in spite of his uniform, looked like an old family retainer in an English country house: almost, one could think of a house party in aristocratic and rural England with the prospect of a day's hunting, a pheasant shoot, tennis, a leisurely game of croquet and perhaps a hunt ball on the morrow.

The visiting senior officer would be given a good stiff whisky and soda, served by a white-coated mess waiter, which made a nice change from his last drink which had probably been tea or issue rum from an enamel mug. He would dine well, and the cuisine and service would be impeccable, because the officers of a Divisional or Corps Headquarters saw no point in discomfort for discomfort's sake—any fool, they were wont to say, could be uncomfortable. Later in the war the air of sybaritic luxury in Headquarters officers' messes became still more pronounced, and units were combed for ex-waiters, ex-cooks and ex-maîtres d'hôtel.

Yet although Headquarters of the 2nd Division was well in range of enemy guns—at night red gun-flashes and the yellow flashes of bursting shells could be seen and the crackle of rifle and machine-gun fire plainly heard at any hour of the day or night—the scene in the Headquarters offices (the nerve centre of the Division) was not appreciably more warlike than in the officers' mess.

There were long, green baize tables where red-tabbed staff officers with incessantly shrilling telephones in front of them worked amidst a very pleasant aroma of cigars; officers of 'G' Branch pored over huge maps covered with tiny flags; despatch riders, during brief respites from hurtling along muddy and shell-pocked roads, cleaned their motor-cycles outside the windows; typists clicked away at their machines; 'Q' Branch officers wrestled with ammunition and ration returns, while 'A' Branch dealt with casualties, recommendations for honours and awards and pending courts-martial; red-capped military policemen strode from the building marked 'Provost-Marshal', intent on keeping traffic moving, herding together stragglers and apprehending wrong-doers.

There never seemed to be a hint of hurry or worry; Divisional Headquarters resembled a well-oiled machine. Indeed, you could see more hustle and bustle in a busy office in London or any other big city in Britain.

But all this changed on the morning of October 31 — the day that Sir John French described as the worst of his life.

Major-Generals Lomax and Monro, commanding the 1st and 2nd Divisions respectively, were in conference in an annexe organised as a studio. With them were a proletariat of staff officers: General Staff Officers, First and Second Grade; Deputy Assistant Quartermaster-General; staff captains and aides-de-camp.

Four shells straddled Hooge château; a fifth scored a direct hit and the nerve and brain centre of the 1st and 2nd Divisions became a charnel house. Colonel Kerr, G.S.O.2 of the 1st Division, Colonel Percival, G.S.O. of 1st Division, and Lieutenant-Colonel Paley, G.S.O.2 of 1st Division, were all killed instantly; General Lomax received wounds from which he died shortly afterwards and General Monro was stunned. Two junior staff officers were killed; one was totally obliterated by the shell, but there was no discernible mark upon the other — he had been shocked out of life by blast.

In the pantry of the Headquarters staff officers' mess the mess sergeant, Sergeant Wilkins, looked at the clock and heard the crash of the shell simultaneously: too bloody close for comfort that one, he thought, but shells or no shells the officers were having a break for sherry at 12.45 pip emma. He snapped his fingers at two of his minions, and bearing trays laden with decanters and glasses, the two waiters headed for the annexe.

They found only dead officers, wounded officers and red-ribbed fragments of what had been officers.

It was a crippling blow: the directing brains of the 1st and 2nd Divisions were shattered and the two divisions themselves were perilously close to being shattered as well.

Sir John French accurately enough described October 31, 1914 as the worst day of his life, for the 31st was a day of practically unrelieved disaster.

October 28 had been a comparatively quiet day: there was merciful respite from shelling and only a few half-hearted infantry attacks which were beaten off without difficulty or heavy casualties.

'Not so many of them now,' remarked the second-in-command of the 1st Queen's, Major Watson, to his commanding officer, Lieutenant-Colonel Pell.

'Nor of us,' replied the C.O. grimly.

On this day, all along the line, the German guns were almost silent, but it was like the silence that broods over an eastern sea before a typhoon. The British infantry could only work feverishly to improve their shallow trenches and wait for the attack which they knew must come.

If few Germans shells came over on the 28th, the British artillery could reply with still fewer, for there was a desperate shortage of artillery ammunition; there were no more shells for howitzers and eighteen-pounders and most of their crews were fighting as infantry. Every field-gun was placed on a daily allowance of ten shells when ten times that amount was barely sufficient.

At daybreak on October 29 the storm burst. Heralded by a whirlwind of shells of every size, massed infantry attacks were hurled at the British line: in ferocity and weight of numbers they surpassed anything that had gone before. There was about these attacks a new mood of reckless desperation and disregard for casualties. Clearly, the German generals had paid careful heed to the Kaiser's order that Ypres must be captured by November 1.

The 1st Corps did not abandon their trenches, they were literally blasted out of them: it was more than human flesh and blood could stand, and they could no longer stand against artillery fire which was killing, blinding and maiming men at the rate of something like thirty every five minutes.

On that day it seemed that Haig's 1st Corps were totally defeated and routed; that, for the Germans, the way to the Channel Ports lay wide open; that Great Britain and, indeed, the British Empire, were doomed to total destruction.

There seemed to be every ground for such gloomy prognostications when Sir John French set off in his staff car on a visit to Haig's Headquarters. What he saw on the journey was not encouraging.

In Ypres there were manifest signs of unusual excitement and some shells were already falling in the streets. Clearly, the contagion of panic was spreading through the civilian population and a mass evacuation of the town seemed to be at hand.

On the road to Haig's Headquarters the situation seemed even worse: the road was crowded with evidence of a crushing defeat, if not a rout, and it looked as if the whole of the 1st Corps was about to fall back in confusion on Ypres: heavy howitzers—their ammunition was exhausted—were moving west at a trot, always a significant feature of a retreat; ammunition and other wagons blocked the road almost as far as the eye could see; ambulances, overflowing with wounded, were pouring down the road. In the midst of this press of traffic, and along both sides of the road, crowds of walking wounded came limping along, all headed for Ypres. Shells were screaming overhead and bursting in adjacent fields.

To French it seemed that this must be the end, and his first feeling was one of crippling despair: it seemed that the British line was irreparably broken, and the immense numerical superiority of the enemy would render retreat well-nigh impossible, particularly in view of the fact that Ypres and the River Yser lay to the immediate rear. The only hope seemed to be to make a new stand on the line Ypres–Messines, but in the face of such a close and determined pursuit this seemed barely feasible.

But if Franch felt near to despair, it was tempered with admiration for the men of his command. 'What grieved me more than anything else,' he wrote in his book *1914*, 'was that the 1st Corps should at last be forced back after the glorious stand they had made. I felt that they had done far more than could be expected of any men, and that even if they were driven into the sea they had earned their country's lasting gratitude for the determined fight they had made. No shadow of blame could be laid upon them or their commander.'

The B.E.F. needed a miracle, and in the First Battle of Ypres miracles were at a cripplingly high premium. But it seemed that a miracle was at hand, in the not wholly likely form of His Majesty's 36th Regiment of Foot—the 2nd Battalion the Worcestershire Regiment.

*

A number of military historians, none of them fools or melodramatic romantics, have attributed the salvation of the British Army in France to a single battalion of British Infantry of the Line: not a battalion of Foot Guards or a glittering cavalry regiment, or kilted Highlanders, accompanied by the skirl of the pipes, valiant as their contribution had been. The proud titles of 'Saviours of the British Expeditionary Force', or of Great Britain, or even of the British Empire, were bestowed upon a run-of-the-mill regiment of 'Feet'.

The Worcesters had never been what used to be known as a 'fashionable regiment' (in the British Army today, only the Brigade of Guards and cavalry regiments are labelled 'fashionable', in addition to being strictly functional, as events in Northern Ireland grimly prove).

But prior to 1914 and between the two World Wars, the term 'fashionable regiment' had a very real meaning from the viewpoint of the officers.

As stated earlier, officers of the Household Brigade were forbidden to travel on public transport, carry cigarettes in a packet, refer to London as 'town' or the telephone as the 'phone'! They were therefore expected to be rich, and nearly always were. Occasionally an officer of the Brigade of Guards came down in the world, and either resigned his commission or sought banishment and social extinction in what was sometimes scathingly called 'a bum line regiment'.

Officers of the cavalry and Royal Horse Artillery also had to be well provided with worldly goods, for they were expected as a matter of course to play polo and ride in steeplechases; cavalrymen and gunners were bound together by the horse, and one could not be well mounted without money and big money at that.

The Infantry of the Line—the sometimes despised 'Line' or 'Feet'—were sub-divided into still more social and financial compartments.

The Rifle regiments, now universally known as 'Greenjackets', hardly counted as infantrymen: they wore green instead of scarlet, and their buttons were black (for which many a rifleman and soldier servant was profoundly thankful); they marched at a theatrical quickstep and spoke of bayonets as 'swords'; some of them could even ride a horse and play polo, and the majority of officers in the Rifle Brigade or the 60th Rifles were at least comfortably off; indeed, the 60th were sometimes irreverently referred to as the 'Rude Rich Rifles'.

Riflemen apart, let us start in Scotland. At the top, geographically and socially, were the kilted Highland regiments: Argylls, Camerons, Seaforths, Gordons and Black Watch. Full dress uniform alone cost a newly-joined subaltern something like four years' pay; the Highland regiments were exclusive and therefore wealthy.

From the purely social standpoint, Infantry of the Line regiments were divided into three financial categories: those that required their officers to have 'comfortable' private means; those that cautiously explained 'that one must have a little money of one's own'; and those claiming that, in theory at any rate, an officer could exist on his pay—there were few, if any, of the last category about which this was literally true.

Every regiment of the Line had its share of tradition and past glory; some carried it off with casual modesty, others with a degree of snobbery which to a visiting officer from a less illustrious regiment must have seemed insufferable. Possibly because poverty and unemployment were always more prevalent in the North than in the South, officers in the regiments of Yorkshire and Lancashire had to make their meagre pay go the farthest. In some regiments a private income of a thousand pounds a year was considered desirable; in others six hundred and fifty pounds permitted a degree of gracious living. In others, again, one could just manage on four hundred; officers with less were apt to find themselves in perpetual and painful debt.

There were many more expensive regiments than the Worcesters, smarter regiments and regiments less prone to insobriety and absence without leave. But if the Worcesters' officers were not rich in worldly goods, the regiment was rich in Battle Honours—on its colours were emblazoned Ramillies, Rolica, Vimiero, Corunna, Albuhera, Salamanca and a round dozen more. But the proudest one of all—and never in the history of the British Army was a Battle Honour more hardly won—is 'Gheluvelt'.

*

The 2nd Worcesters, as British infantry battalions went at that time, were comparatively affluent in manpower on the morning of October 31: they numbered some 387 officers and men, which meant that they could muster nearly half of a full-strength battalion—a most unusual phenomenon in the Ypres area.

The Worcesters had already been severely tested in battle: they had slogged every weary mile of the retreat from Mons; they had been in the Marne and Aisne battles. They had sailed from Southampton on August 13 at a strength of almost 1,000 officers and men.

At first sight they looked far from formidable: ten days of continuous fighting had left all ranks haggard, unshaven and unwashed; their uniforms had been soaked in the mud of the Langemarck trenches and torn by the brambles of Polygon Wood, and many of them were without puttees or caps. They looked, in the memorable words of Sergeant Frank Sutton, like 'wrecks of the bleedin' Hesperus'—in more contemporary language the 2nd Worcesters were a 'shower'.

But they were in infinitely better shape than any other infantry battalion of Haig's 1st Corps: their period in reserve had permitted them two nights of uninterrupted sleep; they had a good breakfast under their belts, their weapons were clean and in good order, and they had plenty of ammunition. They had met the Germans in close combat and well knew who were the better men. The motto of the Worcestershire Regiment is 'Firm', and they had lived up to it on every occasion. In a word, the 2nd Worcesters were ready for anything.

They were fortunate in having a very exceptional soldier in command. Major Edward Hankey, at the early age of thirty-six, had achieved all that he had ever asked of life—command of a battalion of his regiment in war. He had prematurely become commanding officer because his predecessor, Lieutenant-Colonel Westmacott, had been suddenly and unexpectedly promoted to brigadier-general.

There was a fine spirit in the 2nd Worcesters, and between officers and men existed that splendid quality prevalent in the British Army of the period, the mutual respect of the leaders and the led.

The men of the 2nd Worcesters had complete confidence in Major Hankey: the spirit of the leader was the spirit of the men, and the spirit of Edward Hankey was one, not so much of hope, but of certainty of ultimate victory; one of calm and confident self-reliance and firm belief in the worth of his men. Every non-commissioned officer and private felt that the eye of the major was upon him; that he was at his side; that he knew not only what the soldier did, but what he thought.

With such a man to command them, lead them, discipline them and fight for and with them, the 2nd Worcesters knew that they could not and would not be vanquished.

Major Hankey knew the 2nd Worcesters as an old married man knows his wife; he knew every man of the battalion by name; he also knew their alcoholic capacity, marital status and fitness for promotion. As he strode among them in their rest billets on the morning of October 31, he warned them that the period of rest would probably be of short duration.

It was considerably shorter than they had expected. Hour by hour the thunder of the guns grew more intense, and stragglers and wounded all told the same melancholy story—a great German attack was in progress and the enemy infantry were coming on in overwhelming numbers against the remnants of Queen's, Welch, 60th Rifles, South Wales Borderers and Royal Scots Fusiliers—five battalions whose numbers barely totalled the strength of one—which were still clinging to the trenches about the Menin Road.

Against this meagre force the Germans launched thirteen cheering and singing battalions, and it seemed that they had plenty to sing and cheer about.

The skeleton British force did not succumb easily: the controlled accuracy of the rifle fire had been beyond all praise since the beginning of the war, but it had rarely if ever been so deadly as at Gheluvelt, and for a full hour the Germans were held at bay. A German officer who was captured said that they were opposed by a large number of automatic weapons: 'Over every bush, hedge and fragment of wall floated a film of smoke, betraying a machine-gun rattling out bullets.' As the British force boasted, at most, two machine-guns, this was a remarkable testimony to British musketry.

Baulked of an easy conquest, the German infantry pulled back before this shattering resistance, leaving their dead piled in front of the British line. They then set about the liquidation of this stubborn force with their artillery. Two batteries of field guns, one firing shrapnel and the other high explosive, promptly opened up.

The enemy tactics were simple enough: with the defenders dazed into semi-consciousness by the inferno of shelling, they drove a dense mass of infantry into the gap which had been made.

The village of Gheluvelt had become a salient, cut off from the outside world by a curtain of fire. On all sides were tumbling masonry and houses in flames. The village had been turned into a smoking ruin; a mess of bricks and rubble; a shambles of dead men, wounded men, dying men and men so shattered and dazed that they were scarcely responsible for their actions. But as long as there were men left in Gheluvelt who could bring rifles to shoulder and ram a fresh clip of bullets into a magazine, the German advance was opposed.

The Queen's, Welch, 60th, South Wales Borderers and Royal Scots Fusiliers shot and shot until a man could hardly hold his burning rifle; the ground in front of their shallow trenches was littered with grey wounded and cluttered with grey dead.

But such a one-sided contest could have only one outcome: they were overwhelmed by the final rush and the bayonets made an end of all but their glory. Those who did not succumb to bayonets were clubbed down with rifle butts or trampled underfoot by the storming wave. Only a very few suffered themselves docilely to be made prisoners.

Meanwhile, the 2nd Worcesters had their orders. Through his glasses Major Hankey had seen a furiously galloping staff officer approaching the Worcesters' lines.

'Here comes trouble,' said Hankey grimly to his Adjutant, Captain Brian Senhouse-Clark. 'If a staff-wallah travels that fast, he can only be bringing bad news.' Major Hankey was not over-fond of staff officers.

The news was bad enough; indeed, it was as bad as any that had afflicted the British Army since its arrival in Flanders.

The Queen's and Royal Scots Fusiliers had fought to the last, and each battalion had been reduced, at best, to one full platoon's strength; the Welch and 60th Rifles had virtually ceased to exist; the right flank of the South Wales Borderers had been rolled back. Gheluvelt seemed to be irreparably lost, and a great gap had been broken in the sagging British line.

All this bad news and more was communicated to Major Hankey by Captain Augustus Thorne, Staff Captain of the 4th Guards Brigade, as he dismounted breathlessly from his foaming horse. An officer not normally given to melodramatics, he gave Hankey the whole grim story: it boiled down, quite simply, to the fact that if the 2nd Worcesters did not mount an immediate and annihilating counter-attack there and then, the war was lost. In no war, in the history of the British Army, had any regiment been charged with such devastating responsibility.

If a representative private of the 2nd Worcesters, probably a long service man, an unreflective character with a militant thirst for beer and probably speaking in the untuneful accent of Birmingham, had been told that he was a saviour of Great Britain, he would have spat literally and metaphorically and said 'Well, cor blimey' or something equally significant. He would then have lit a fag (if he'd got one, and scrounged one from his neighbour if he hadn't), applied a thin film of oil to the bolt of his rifle and worked it backwards and forwards a few times to ensure easy shooting, checked his pouches and ammunition, conjured up a brief picture of fish and chips and waited for orders. On this momentous day, October 31, 1914, the orders were not slow in coming.

The orders came from Brigadier-General Fitzclarence, V.C., who was in command of the front about the Menin Road. Fitzclarence had won his Victoria Cross in the South African War, and there were many officers and other ranks of the 4th Guards Brigade who affirmed that he had earned it yet again on the Menin Road.

Fitzclarence would have preferred Guardsmen for this job, but there was scarcely a battalion of Foot Guards which was not shattered beyond recovery; the Worcesters were comparatively affluent in manpower—at this stage of the campaign a

163

battalion numbering five hundred men represented something like luxury—and they were tried in battle. For better or worse, the 2nd Worcesters would have to do.

'What are your men like?' demanded Fitzclarence, without preamble, when Hankey reported to his Headquarters.

'First class,' said Hankey without hesitation. 'They'll do anything within reason'; for a moment he was thankful that Fitzclarence, a Guardsman to the bone, could not see the 2nd Worcesters—their bedraggled appearance scarcely measured up to the standard of turnout demanded in the Brigade of Guards.

'There's nothing reasonable about the order that you're getting now,' said Fitzclarence grimly. 'Your battalion are going to take Gheluvelt. You're all that I've got to throw in. If you don't get Gheluvelt back, then the war's lost.' This last statement, Fitzclarence well knew, must have sounded melodramatic—for all that, it was not so far from the literal truth.

The orders issued by Major Hankey were uncomplicated, and would not have helped him towards a nomination to the Staff College, even if he had wanted one. 'The 2nd Worcesters will take Gheluvelt' was the order, and to the grim-faced officers and men, who had already been to hell and back but were ready for a second visit, he added, 'We can and will do it. Good luck to you all.'

The Worcesters were ready for anything, and this soon became abundantly apparent. Extra ammunition was issued and, to help carry it, packs were abandoned; in these packs were all the domestic paraphernalia of the front line infantryman—mess tin, knife, fork and spoon, cigarettes (if they were lucky), a tin of bully beef and a few biscuits of tooth-breaking hardness. It did not occur to any of the men that they might never need these items again; they only knew that they were going into the attack, to kill, or be killed.

At 1 p.m. the Worcesters' cooks produced a reasonably palatable stew, and at 1.30 Major Hankey authorised an issue of rum from a meagre store. Thus fortified, they filed out of their billets at 2 p.m.

The Worcesters had food, rum and plenty of fire in their bellies, but at first sight the scene was far from reassuring.

They advanced south-eastward across clear and open ground, down to the little valley of the Reutelbeek and up to the bare ridge above Polderhoek. The open ground ahead of them was dotted with dead, wounded and dazed stragglers. Artillery batteries could be seen limbering up and moving to the rear; everywhere there were signs of disorderly retreat—all movement was relentlessly rearward, and the Worcesters felt understandably superior to the rest of the British Army, for they alone were advancing towards the enemy.

Beyond a little wood the battalion deployed, 'C' and 'D' Companies in front line, with 'B' Company in second line behind. In front of them rose the bare slope of the Polderhoek ridge. The ridge was littered with dead and wounded, and along its crest the enemy's shells were bursting in rapid succession.

The Polderhoek ridge hid from view the château of Gheluvelt, and the exact situation there was unknown; but farther to the right could be seen the church tower rising amid the smoke of the burning village.

The route to Gheluvelt was across a mile of open ground, without a stick of cover in sight, and the ground underfoot was rank grass or rough stubble. Major Hankey, in a mood of grim fatalism, surveyed that deadly stretch: if heavy fire were opened upon them, as undoubtedly it would be, no man would be able to lie down and take cover. It was easy enough for a commander to give the order 'Advance', but until a man has experienced the feeling of having to stand up, away from the safety of cover, and into the belt of fire, he can never realise the weight on his shoulders that keeps him pressed and praying to the ground. This, declared Hankey to his officers in a hastily assembled order group, was where leadership came in: the officers would *lead* their men in the most literal sense, for if fire became too heavy men might be forced on to their bellies and reluctant to rise again; furthermore, the officers would lead their men with swords drawn. Today an officer's sword is a ridiculous item of armament, used only for saluting on ceremonial parades, cutting cakes and forming an archway at weddings. But it had a very real meaning in October 1914, and every officer of the 2nd Worcesters felt a better man for having one in his scabbard, even though it was an encumbrance to walking and made running well-nigh impossible.

Major Hankey decided that there was only one way to attack Gheluvelt, and that was by a single long rush. The companies extended into line and advanced: they went forward at the steady, purposeful lope of the well-trained infantryman, their rifles, with bayonets fixed, in the position which the British Army knew as the 'high port'.

As the Worcesters breasted the Polderhoek Ridge and came in sight of Gheluvelt château, the German artillery got them in their sights and rained down a hail of high explosive on the charging line: men fell at every pace, and over a hundred of the battalion were killed or wounded.

But there was no stopping the gallant Worcesters: the speed of the rush increased on the downward slope as the troops came in sight of the château close in front. The platoons scrambled across the light railway, through some hedges and wire fences, and then in the grounds of the château they closed with the enemy.

Now the rifles and bayonets had come down from the 'high port' to 'on guard'. Now the enemy were in sight, and the Worcesters started to shout—yelling as men will, to keep the heart from jumping out of the mouth. There was no stopping them: they tore aside undergrowth to come to grips with the enemy, and they winkled Germans out of hedges and ditches like hungry hunt terriers; they fought in the street, on well-kept lawns, in ruined houses and farm buildings—anywhere where a German was to be found.

To the men of the 244th and 245th Reserve Regiments and the 16th Bavarian Reserve Regiment, the appearance of the Worcesters came as a shattering shock: they were scarcely the cream of the German Army—many of them were raw recruits with only a few months' service—and showed a marked disinclination to stand their ground; they had lost many of their officers in the earlier fighting, and thought that only demoralised and exhausted British troops opposed them; they very soon learned the untruth of this.

A few of the bolder hearts among the Bavarians stayed to fight it out, but their prowess with the bayonet was vastly inferior to that of the Worcesters, for the 36th had practised the art most thoroughly in Aldershot before the war, and had put their expertise to good use at Langemarck and Polygon Wood.

The 242nd Saxons, a redoubtable regiment with a fine fighting record, were considerably more belligerent than the Bavarians, but they too found their match in the Worcesters: British and German soldiers swung and swayed across the smooth lawns of Gheluvelt, driving bayonets through one another or firing into each other's bodies at a range of six feet or less. Major Hankey, a keen fox-hunting man in happier days, invariably carried a hunting horn; above the crash and clamour of battle, its evocative notes could be plainly heard.

The Worcesters, in fact, resembled nothing so much as a pack of hounds, ferociously intent on a kill.

The Saxons must have thought that they were opposed by devils, and the 2nd Worcesters were no bad substitute. Suddenly, they had had enough; they broke and fled, but the Worcesters had not yet done with them; they pursued them through the village—shouting, cheering, shooting, stabbing. The Worcesters, in truth, had gone fighting mad and it was as well for the rest of Haig's 1st Corps that they had. It was said of the 2nd Worcesters this day that every officer and man was a hero; certainly nothing in the whole history of the war surpassed their exploit at Gheluvelt.

Many officers and men were decorated for their part in this splendid action. One of them in particular, Sergeant Frank Sutton, was a one-man wave of destruction throughout. Sutton was the prototype regular sergeant. A deadly marksman—he had first qualified as a first-class shot before the outbreak of the South African War—Sergeant Sutton attacked a German machine-gun post single-handed; he shot three of the crew dead and the fourth man, well-nigh crazed with terror, as well he might be, suffered himself to be taken prisoner—he had no wish to put Sutton's prowess at bayonet fighting to the test; it was advertised all too clearly by the blood which stained the bayonet.

Sutton put the machine-gun out of action with a single round from his rifle and a well-aimed kick from his size-ten ammunition boots. He uttered dreadful threats to his prisoner, which included disembowelling, castration, decapitation and immersion in boiling oil; the Saxon understood not one word, but the dreadful menace in Sutton's voice caused him to cower in the mud, begging for mercy.

Meanwhile, Sutton exterminated a section of Saxons with six slow and deliberate shots. He then administered a kick to his prisoner's backside, set a match to a lethal-looking clay pipe and shouted 'Any more for the Worcesters?' It is small wonder that, opposed by Sergeant Sutton and men like him, the Germans fled from Gheluvelt in disorder.

The Worcesters were not in the mood to spare any German, and continued relentlessly to hunt those Saxons who still felt inclined to hold their ground; as the Worcesters charged on through the hedgerows, last-ditch riflemen continued to fire at them. But eventually the last opposition was swept aside at the point of the bayonet, and the Worcesters covered the last few hundred yards across the lawn of Gheluvelt château to come into line with the South Wales Borderers. They arrived in the nick of time, for the remnants of the Borderers were at their last gasp.

Lieutenant-Colonel Leach, Commanding Officer of the South Wales Borderers, and Major Hankey were old friends. Their greeting was a mixture of raw emotion and astonishment at each other's survival. 'Thank God you've come,' said Colonel Leach. Then, pooling their resources, which amounted to a total of three full-strength companies, the two commanding officers set about stabilising a line to deny the Germans any return to Gheluvelt.

The violent eviction of the Germans from Gheluvelt by the Worcesters had an immediate and galvanic effect on the shattered 1st and 2nd Divisions. Brigadier-General Herman Landon, who had succeeded to the command of the 1st Division when General Lomax was killed, displayed enormous personal gallantry in rallying the 1st Division.

Landon had seen the near annihilation of the 1st Corps for himself. He had certainly not fought the war over a telephone —this would not have been possible in any case, for almost all the telephone wires had been destroyed by shellfire—but from a prancing seventeen-hand charger; eye-witnesses said that Landon's survival among the bursting shells, as he galloped among his scattered units exhorting them to stand fast, was little short of a miracle.

Still more incredible was the result of this rally; men, who had almost begun to assume that the war was lost, found themselves not only standing fast, but turning about and counter-attacking; Coldstream and Scots Guards, Black Watch, Royal Sussex, Gloucesters, Loyals and Northamptons. It was this counter-attack which amazed the Germans most; by this time they had become accustomed to the stubborn resistance of the outnumbered British soldiers, but that men, in body and mind at their weakest from exhaustion, hunger and lack of sleep, could *attack* passed their comprehension. It all but passed Sir John French's comprehension as well.

At first Sir John registered extreme disbelief, for he had seen for himself the apparent rout of the 1st Corps. It could hardly be true.

But it was true, and the messages were coming in every half hour: the 1st and 2nd Divisions were attacking the German right; even the 7th Division, reduced to the strength of one very weak brigade, was attacking. At 3 p.m. on the afternoon of October 31, a staff officer galloped headlong to Haig's Headquarters where Sir John French, filled with the direst foreboding, waited for news. The staff officer carried the most dramatic message of the war to date. It was from Brigadier-General Fitzclarence and said simply: 'My line holds.'

There was no diminution of the German attacks as October gave way to November, a month which brought with it every conceivable manifestation of vile weather: icy rain, sleet and swirling snow. The men at Ypres stayed in their holes, for now there was nowhere else for them to go. Any further attack was out of the question, for an attack requires fresh, eager and well-fed battalions of infantry supported by pulverising artillery support—there were no such things at Ypres.

The Germans often broke into the British lines in that first week of November, but could never break through; there was always another force of desperate men to deny them passage to Ypres. These scattered groups—it may have been a score of Guardsmen, a dozen South Staffords and ten Lancers, thirty A.S.C. men, a handful of Queen's Own Hussars, two dozen remnants of Royal Warwicks and 60th Rifles, fifty men from four different battalions—were withdrawn from one position to another and flung forward into furious counter-attacks against a force double their number.

The flower of the German Army had failed to dislodge them. The realisation had come to the German generals that they were beating their heads against a brick wall; on the debit side they had crippling casualties, on the credit side nothing. The line still held; the burning question was, for how much longer?

CHAPTER EIGHT

Clearly, they had all been there far too long. This was at once apparent from the staring, red-rimmed eyes which told of an incredible number of days and nights on end without sleep; from the gaunt and wasted faces covered in thick and filthy stubble—the British soldier has always contrived to present a clean chin to his enemies whenever possible, but there was little enough water for drinking, let alone washing and shaving.

Their hands were thickly begrimed with mud and many of them trembled uncontrollably—hands which now had but one function, to ram a fresh clip of ammunition into a rifle magazine, to work the bolt and press the trigger. But even these actions, as automatic to the British regular soldier as cleaning teeth, lighting a cigarette or going to the latrine, had by now become a fearful effort. Rifles were choked with mud, and there was a shortage of rifle oil.

The slick, easy and rhythmic mechanism of the rifle bolt was music to the British rifleman: he fired a round, flicked the bolt with a dexterous twist of the hand, and emptied the magazine of its five rounds. Automatically—he could do it in his sleep and many 'Contemptibles' almost did so—his right hand went to a pouch; out came a clip of five rounds, and a steady, deep pressure of the right thumb sent the cartridges deep into the magazine.

Then it was 'mad minute fire' again, the bolt working with smooth precision, the bullets spitting from the muzzle at the rate of fifteen rounds per minute.

Bolts of rifles, so said Standing Orders, must be 'bright, clean and slightly oiled'; bright meant that they shone like burnished silver, clean meant the same thing (only more so), slightly oiled meant a thin film of oil over the whole length of the bolt—not too little, not too much, but just right.

But now shortage of rifle oil—after rum, beer, tea and water, the most precious liquid known to the British soldier—

was in dangerously short supply, and the physical act of pulling the bolt back and pushing it forward again could only be performed with fearful effort.

To add to their troubles, a supply of rifle ammunition had been issued in which the brass cartridge cases were slightly oversize. A sharp movement of the bolt would force the round into the breech of the rifle, but the empty case could not be extracted by the flick of the right wrist. With ammunition like this, the usual fifteen rounds per minute had been reduced to something like five, and Germans, who should by rights have been corpses, lived to fight another day.

After firing each shot, it was necessary to lower the butt to the thigh and tug the bolt back—a manœuvre never previously practised on the rifle range. When the breech became almost red-hot, or fragments of sand, mud or grit (or all three at once) became clogged in the moving parts behind it, the rifleman had to place the butt on the ground and kick down on the bolt lever with his boot. Small wonder that rifle oil had become a precious commodity.

In the butt-trap of every soldier's rifle reposed precious cleaning material, similar to and just as essential as the housewife's dust-pan, brush, scrubbing brush and duster: the 'pull-through', which was a length of strong thin rope with brass attachment; the oil bottle; and the strip of flannelette, four inches by two—'four by two', as the soldier called it.

'Four by two', like everything else, was scarce; barrels of rifles were so clogged with mud that the rope of pull-throughs broke. But in spite of all these defects, fire continued to pour from these rifles and every day saw an increase in the number of German corpses piled in front of the British trenches, if a stinking, unrevetted hole, three feet deep, often knee-deep in water and frequently tenanted by at least two corpses, could be called a trench.

British and German artillery regiments fought an incessant duel against one another, but it was always a hideously unequal one; the ammunition of the British field batteries was running out fast, whereas that for the German guns seemed to be unlimited—for every shell the British guns sent over, the Germans were replying with twenty, thirty, forty, fifty. . . .

It seemed that nothing could possibly live amid the deluge of shells which fell on the positions of the British infantry huddled in their holes in the ground, and to this hellish rain of death the infantry could make no reply: they could only swear, burrow deeper into their holes, go out of their minds or die. The British batteries could and did reply, as long as there were men to serve the guns. But the cost in officers, men and guns was appalling.

All along the line, amid the scream of shells and exploding shrapnel, the unemotional voices of gunner officers could be heard calling out ranges, angles of sight, angles of elevation: all phrases incomprehensible to the infantryman cowering in his hole—they didn't know a clinometer from a drag-rope—but everyday language to the men who devoutly served the guns:

'Shrapnel . . . four six hundred . . . at gunfire sweep five minutes from zero lines. . . .'

'Five rounds battery fire . . . one-oh seconds . . . stop . . . add fifty. . . .'

'Drop one hundred—five minutes more right. . . .'

'At battery fire, sweep one-five minutes. . . .'

So it went on for hours on end—hours of interminable noise which deafened men, stunned men, blinded men, wounded men, killed men and buried men alive.

An artillery duel so one-sided could only have one end, and in the attenuated ranks of the field batteries casualties were mounting at a terrifying rate: forward observation officers—they died like flies in two World Wars—spotted suicidally from crests and were blown to pieces as they indicated new targets; signallers were killed and wounded and gun position officers had to do their own telephoning.

Many of these guns were fired by an incongruous assortment of personnel, often august technicians who had done no gun drill for years and had confidently and thankfully thought that they never would again; armament artificers were pressed into service as loaders; saddler bombardiers (known as 'waxies' in the Royal Regiment of Artillery) became range setters; bewildered battery clerks, storemen and officers' grooms had to learn how to be gunlayers again. The spectacle of colonels acting as 'Number One' on a gun, majors hauling on dragropes and captains manhandling shells had become almost commonplace.

Let us take a quick look at a battery of Royal Field Artillery, still comparatively strong in manpower, guns and ammunition: the battery commander, a fanatical professional gunner of whom it was said that he ate, drank and slept gunnery, could see through his field glasses targets to set any gunner dreaming: hordes of grey infantry in tightly bunched masses.

As imperturbably as if he were on the artillery ranges at Okehampton, the battery commander gave his orders: 'All guns, one degree right . . . one and two, add a hundred . . . three and four, add fifty . . . angle of sight-zero . . . one round battery fire . . . gunfire . . . at gunfire sweep two degrees. . . .'

This, of course, was gunnery as it should be, with signallers calling 'shot-over!' on the telephone to regimental headquarters and signallers from headquarters checking back: 'Task Monkey Two. Batteries—all. Co-ordinates. . . .'

But, for many other batteries, there was no time for such elaborate preparations; they were firing over open sights, with fuses set at zero—a single round of gunfire was enough to obliterate a whole platoon.

Sometimes, when it seemed that German guns were furiously shelling without response from the British, the infantry swore long and bitterly at the gunners:

'Wot's up with them bleedin' gunners then?'

'Never there when they're bleedin' wanted . . .'

'Ain't fired a bleedin' shell for 'arf hour . . .'

'S'all right for them, sittin' on their arses five miles back . . .'

'The poor bleedin' infantry always gets all the shit.'

The infantrymen were not to know that a shortage of artillery ammunition, which had already become acute, was now desperate; the lack of shells for howitzers and eighteen-pounders was such that field guns were placed on a miserable daily ration of ten shells. Nor was the situation improved by a series of 'wild cat' strikes among British munition workers.

Some artillerymen, indeed, from the batteries whose guns had all been knocked out or which had no shells left, had ceased to be gunners at all.

CHAPTER NINE

In the attempt to capture Ypres, by this time an obsession with him, the Kaiser had flung in crack regiments of Bavarians, Saxons, *Landwehr* and *Landsturm*; sacrificing German soldiers at a staggering rate, he had used and lost recruits with as little as two months' service—many of them beardless youths, whose military service had so far consisted only of learning to do the goose-step, and had not included more than rudimentary instruction in musketry or trench warfare. The Prussian War Staff were notorious for their disregard for human life, but they must later have regretted that so much of the fine flower of German youth had been frittered away in these futile attacks at Ypres; in another six months these young men could have been trained to a fine pitch of efficiency and used advantageously in the grim fighting which was to come. In Germany the battle of Ypres became known as *Der Kindermord von Ypern*—the Massacre of the Innocents at Ypres.

Reservists, too, were flung into this holocaust: men nearing middle age, whose thought were far from war and glory but with their growing families. There were men even in the forty-to-fifty group—men who rightly considered that they had earned a bit of peace and quiet, and longed to be sitting by the fireside with their grand-children playing at their feet.

The infantrymen of the B.E.F. knew nothing of this and cared a great deal less: they only knew that waves of infantry were coming at them head-on every day and every night, and whether they were Saxons, Pomeranians, Bavarians, young, old, married or single, they must be shot down as long as they had a clip of cartridges in their pouches. They had no time to consider their own women and children, let alone those of the enemy.

Yet another Division was flung in—the 4th, composed of West Prussian and Pomeranians. The 4th did little to add lustre to the German Army, and displayed a marked distaste for the 'mad minute' rifle fire of the B.E.F. To the men of the

B.E.F., the German 4th Division did not seem to be worthy of their steel—all they had to do to send them scurrying rearwards was work the bolt, the magazine and the trigger. 'They didn't like it a bit,' said Sergeant Tom Fish of the Bedfords with laconic contempt, 'and never got within a hundred yards of our trenches.'

The Kaiser paid a surprise visit to the Headquarters of the 4th, where a cowering general and an apprehensive group of colonels winced under the lash of his tongue; the Kaiser was in particularly sulphurous mood that morning, because his flea-bitten grey had still not been replaced by a magnificent white horse; yet another senior medical officer had diagnosed a possible heart condition and he was not only afflicted by constipation but painful piles as well. It was a bad look-out for any German soldiers who failed to subdue the 'Contemptible Little Army'.

When he had finished with the 4th Division—two generals had been fired, six colonels demoted, fourteen majors given one last chance, and eight junior officers and 140 N.C.O.s and men arraigned on charges of cowardice in the face of the enemy—the Kaiser summoned to his presence one General Winckler, Commanding General of the Prussian Guard.

Winckler was the prototype Prussian general and a fanatical disciple of the Kaiser: like his master, he had fierce upswept moustaches; his face wore the same imperious expression. He was ambitious and ruthless; he listened to no excuses for failure, and if a subordinate officer let him down he only did so once. If the Prussian Guard was given an objective to capture, then they captured it, heedless of casualties. Having captured it, they held it and never gave an inch of ground away to the enemy.

The officers of the Prussian Guard closely resembled those of the British Brigade of Guards, except that by British standards they had no manners and no sense of humour. They were born of the most illustrious families of the Fatherland, and behaved in a manner becoming to their patrician upbringing; they cultivated switchback moustaches à la mode the Kaiser and 'Little Willie'; they wore unnecessary monocles; walked with an exaggerated swagger, and laid ruthless siege to gull lible young women and less young women who should have known better, rendering round-the-clock and unfailingly virile stud service to all of them.

Young Prussian gentlemen destined for the Guard (they were most emphatic that they were the Prussian *Guard*, never the Prussian *Guards*, a frequent solecism uttered by the unwary) were conditioned by the fiercest possible disciplinary system which made the Royal Military College and 'the Shop', St. Cyr and West Point look like seminaries for young ladies.

The other ranks of the Guard were cast in the same mould, all being over six feet tall; they were invincible and indestructible.

The Prussian Guard was the Kaiser's ace; the failure of the rest of the German army to hammer a hole in the thin British line left William the War Lord but one arrow in his quiver—the Guard.

General Winckler's interview with the Kaiser was brief and to the point. The Kaiser was not interested in tactics or strategy, both subjects about which he was profoundly ignorant; he did not wind up with the usual query 'Any questions?' Winckler knew, in any event, that there could be no questions —his orders were: 'Take Ypres.'

Prior to November 10 the Prussian Guard had not been committed to battle, but had been groomed for stardom in rear areas. Now, at last, their big moment was at hand.

Kaiser Wilhelm II, Emperor of Germany, to give him his full title, or Kaiser Bill as he was known to the British soldiers, was clearly in a foul temper when he established his Headquarters at La Tache, a few miles from Messines. He was furious at the continued failure of his soldiers to subdue the 'Contemptible Little Army'—'trash and feeble adversaries, unworthy of the steel of the German soldier', as he scathingly described the B.E.F.

The Kaiser's arrival in Flanders caused an icy wind of apprehension to blow among the promotion prospects of German generals, because his timetable had been grievously upset: by this time he had calculated that he would be riding in triumph through Paris, and with this in mind regiments had been paraded to practise a victory march at a feverish goose-step of one hundred and ten paces to the minute.

No one escaped the lash of the Imperial tongue, from the aide-de-camp who called him in the morning to General von Kluck. In between were army doctors who were reviled for diagnosing indigestion as a possible heart condition; transport officers because his car kept breaking down; veterinary officers for failing to produce serviceable horses; the Prussian Guard—serried ranks of immaculate military perfection—for their slovenly appearance; and his son the Crown Prince for not having yet won the war.

Inevitably, heads started to roll. Regimental commanders were sacked, given last chances and threatened with punishments ranging from banishment to obscure backwaters in Africa to death by firing squad; junior officers assured their seniors that they were ready and willing to die the sorest of deaths; brutal N.C.O.s became more brutal than ever; private soldiers, many of them able prophets, wrote home to relatives telling them that this would be the last letter.

'The breakthrough will be of decisive importance,' the Kaiser told his generals, 'we must and will conquer.' He was, apparently, totally unconcerned about the appalling casualties suffered in the past and still more to come. 'Take Ypres or die' was the new slogan.

The choler of the Kaiser at his armies' failure to break through the British line was understandable enough: a flowing torrent of men from a seemingly bottomless well of manpower, frequently relieved and refreshed by periods of rest and supported by overwhelming artillery, had been flung repeatedly at the thin line of defenders, and had achieved precisely nothing.

Winckler's Prussian Guard Division—the 1st, 2nd, 3rd and 4th Foot Guard Regiments and the 2nd and 4th Guard Grenadiers—was a very different proposition to the West Prussians and the Pomeranians, who had shown such a marked distaste for British rifle fire. The Kaiser had ordered Winckler to brush aside 'these feeble adversaries', and the Guard were fully confident of their ability to do so.

The Guard, some 17,500 strong, advanced north and south of the Menin Road in serried ranks—'by the right', as the

British Brigade of Guards drill book phrases it. Officers led the way with drawn swords, bellowing *'Vorwärts!'* at the full pitch of their lungs; the men, with fixed bayonets, advanced with giant strides, conscious only of their own invincibility—the Prussian Guard could not and would not fail.

British artillery pieces were few and short of ammunition; machine-guns, in spite of the plaintive cries from German commanders that every British soldier carried one, were in woefully short supply. But opposing the Prussian Guard were 7,850 filthy, verminous, starving and sleepless men with rifles, who had already proved that they did not know when they were beaten, and did not know it now: Scots and Coldstream Guards, Black Watch, Camerons, Gordons and Royal Scots Fusiliers, Highland Light Infantry, Gloucesters, Northamptons, Duke of Wellington's, Royal Irish, Royal Sussex, Northumberland Fusiliers, King's Liverpool Regiment.

The Prussian Guard did not waver as the first volleys ripped into their closely packed ranks—they had been warned to expect heavy casualties, and they died as bravely as soldiers of any race ever have; they still did not waver when only one hundred yards from the British lines—they came on in solid, square grey blocks.

The British rifleman of average competence could be sure of firing fifteen rounds from his rifle in one minute; the most expert could achieve anything up to thirty. The Lee-Enfield rifle, probably the most lethal weapon in the history of the British Army, had a flat trajectory up to six hundred yards. On this day of mass slaughter, men who had reduced platoon sergeants to near apoplexy on the practice ranges found that they were killing automatically and almost effortlessly; it was, in truth, scarcely possible to miss. As the leading files of closely packed Prussian Guard fell, those behind them pressed ever forward. Some broke into a run; others, until urged and frequently kicked forward by officers and N.C.O.s, crouched behind dead comrades and returned the fire; and still they continued to fall—some dead before they hit the ground, some who would assuredly die before nightfall, some maimed for life.

The Prussians came to fifty yards . . . forty . . . thirty . . . now it was time to exterminate this stubborn force with the bayonet, for they had been ordered to take no prisoners.

The final volleys of 'mad minute' rifle fire halted the Prussian Guard—it halted them and finally broke them: officers, brave men all, frantically waved their swords and shouted in an effort to rally them, and these officers were shot down, many of them within ten yards of British bayonets.

It seemed that it was the total rout and defeat of the Prussian Guard as they fled from this stricken field, stumbling over their own dead who, in the half light, were mistaken for a second line of attack. But one detachment of the 4th Guard Grenadiers were made of sterner stuff: about 1,000 men strong, they recovered from the shock of the recoil and pressed doggedly on; the 4th had never known and never could know retreat. Death, yes, but not retirement—they were going to almost certain death and they knew it.

Just to the north of the Menin Road this doomed host, by sheer weight of numbers, forced a way through the British line where it was particularly weak. The few British riflemen still on their feet, in many cases so thin on the ground that there was only one man to every ten yards of trench, were swept away. The 4th Guard Grenadiers continued their steamroller advance; although they did not know it, they were heading, by the most direct route, straight for Ypres.

The Guard Grenadiers pressed remorselessly on, turned aside into the shelter of the undefended Nonne Bosschen and burst from the western fringe of the wood.

But the skeleton British battalions did not succumb easily: the machine-gunners of the 1st Scots Guards and 1st Cameron Highlanders emptied their few remaining belts at point-blank range before the crews went under; two companies of the 1st Black Watch—their strength was of about two platoons—obeyed the order 'hold on to the last man and the last round' quite literally and were completely annihilated; their commanding officer, Second Lieutenant Malcolm McNaught, just nineteen years old and six months out of Sandhurst, was last seen standing on the parapet and emptying his revolver into the Prussians; the combined Headquarters of the Black Watch and the Camerons—the two battalions could muster approximately one company—was defended by the two commanding officers, Lieutenant-Colonel Charles Stewart and Lieutenant-Colonel David McEwan, Sergeant Redpath, signal sergeant of the Black Watch, two batmen and an orderly room clerk.

The Prussian Guard got very short shrift from the 60th Rifles, and the prime architect of destruction was Lieutenant John Dimmer, the battalion machine-gun officer.

Dimmer was far from being the prototype regular officer of the King's Royal Rifle Corps; in fact, he was what was termed 'a ranker officer', and his military service had started as a private in the South African War. Promotion to corporal followed in 1902, he was a lance-sergeant in 1906 and by 1908 he was commissioned second-lieutenant in the 60th Rifles at the comparatively elderly age of twenty-five. John Dimmer was educated at a school which pre-war officers of the 60th had almost certainly never heard of—Merton School, Surrey. If any officer of the 60th made disparaging remarks about 'ranker officers', 'the top drawer' or humble origin in relation to Dimmer, they never did so after November 1914.

The 60th—a comparatively strong battalion of some 200 —had been hurriedly rushed into the line to reinforce the battered and sadly depleted 4th Guards Brigade. They got there just in time to see the masses of the Prussian Guard coming at them head-on.

In common with every other infantry battalion, the 60th had only two machine-guns, although at this stage of the battle of Ypres many had none. Those of the 60th, however, were still intact and lost no time in coming into action: in the first minute Dimmer's guns contributed generously to the slaughter of the Prussian Guard.

One of the guns and its crew were blown to pieces by shell-fire, but Dimmer, firing the other himself, continued to pour bullets into the Guard. Then, with the enemy barely one hundred yards away, a wet ammunition belt caused the gun to jam. But the mechanism of the Vickers gun held no secrets for Dimmer; he climbed on to the emplacement, in full view of the Prussians, and repaired it with a large adjustable spanner. He got the gun firing again, but a rifle bullet struck him in the jaw. Ignoring the wound, Dimmer continued to fire, but while traversing in search of fresh targets, the gun stuck. Reaching up to remedy this stoppage Dimmer was hit yet again, this time in the right shoulder; then a shrapnel shell burst above him and three fragments lodged in the same shoulder.

Now the Guard were just fifty yards away—walking, tripping, stumbling over their own dead. Dimmer was hit once more—this time in the face; almost blinded with his own blood, his right arm practically paralysed, he continued to fire the gun. At the moment the Prussians finally broke and ran, John Dimmer collapsed unconscious over his gun, a new belt of ammunition in his left hand.

For, in the words of the official citation, 'extraordinary heroism', Lieutenant John Dimmer was awarded the Victoria Cross.[1]

The guns of the 2nd Division Artillery stood in line with intervals from Bellewarde to Polygon Wood. The gunners had been warned by the fury of bombardment that something tremendous was happening on their front; the bombardment was the only warning that they did get, because there was no communication with the forward observation officers—all telephonic communication had been severed. The casualty rate of F.O.O.s had been astronomical, and the officers attached to the infantry battalions were more than likely dead or wounded.

Major Boyd-Rochfort of the 41st Brigade, Royal Field Artillery, had an eerie experience. He had established a forward observation post close to Second-Lieutenant McNaught's detachment of Black Watch. When he realised that this position would very shortly become untenable, he decided that his place was back with his battery of guns.

Boyd-Rochfort actually came back with the Prussian Guard. He threw away his peaked cap, and as he was wearing an old-fashioned blue coat of curiously Teutonic cut he was un-

---

[1] John Dimmer miraculously recovered from his wounds and was soon in action again. He won the Military Cross in 1915, and was killed in action while in command of a battalion of the Royal Berkshire Regiment in January 1918, just three months after his wedding.

recognised by the Prussians, who continued to advance, no man looking to his right or left. By gradually side-stepping Boyd-Rochfort managed to work his way clear of the masses of Prussians and raced to warn the batteries. The news he gave was dire enough: 'They're coming on in their thousands; forget about shell rationing and be ready to fire over open sights. Shorten fuses to burst within three hundred yards. *Do this, or the war is lost.*' Battery commanders got the gist of this message at once, and the Royal Regiment of Artillery prepared for the grim work ahead.

Also in the vicinity were some 400 men of the Royal Engineers—men who, in normal circumstances, would have been repairing bridges, building roads, tunnelling, sapping, mining; they could do none of these things, but every sapper had a rifle, and now they were all infantrymen, whether they liked it or not. There were the remnants of a Connaught Rangers company, perhaps sixty men in all. There were cooks, who had no food to cook but rifles in their hands with which to fire; there were officers' servants, whose officers were either dead, wounded or looking after themselves quite capably; there were grooms, with no horses to groom; there were clerks, without pencils with which to write or paper on which to write; there were transport drivers, with no vehicles to drive, and A.S.C. men, whose province was the distribution of rations, who had no rations to distribute; there were sanitary orderlies who did not know where the nearest latrine was, medical orderlies who had always thought of themselves as non-combatants, and had received last-minute instructions in the use of the rifle from infantrymen who had better things to do; there were signalmen, whose telephones had been silent for the past twenty-four hours, and despatch riders whose motor cycles had been blown into small pieces.

There was a red-tabbed major of the staff, who belonged to the Adjutant-General's Branch which dealt with such diverse matters as courts-martial and honours and awards, who found himself in command of a bewildered but still belligerent force of Coldstream and Irish Guards, Gloucesters, King's Liverpool and about fifty remnants of Household Cavalry.

Meanwhile, the Prussian Guard, still advancing for all the

world as if France had been conquered and they were marching down the Champs-Elysées, came within the sights of the guns of the 2nd Division. They debouched from the wood, indomitable still, and firing steadily from the hip. The cry of '*Vorwärts*' from the officers could still be heard, but in rather more muted key, for many officers had fallen in this headlong advance.

For the Artillery of the 2nd Division there was clearly only one course of action open to them: fuses were shortened to burst within three hundred yards—all was set for the Thermopylæ of the Prussian Guard.

There was no time for ranging or angles of sight, or any other niceties of gunnery. Major John Clark, commanding the 16th Battery, had his guns ready to fire over open sights. When he saw the massed ranks of the Prussian Guard a mere three hundred yards distant, there was only one order to give and he gave it: 'FIRE!'

The layers at the guns sat tense and breech blocks clanged home on the shells. This promised to be good: firing over open sights at a target that they could see. Recently 16th Battery had been given little opportunity to shine, for they had only been in action at extreme range with severe rationing of shells. But with a target like this Major Clark merely told his gun position officers, 'Just blast 'em as long as you've got any shells.' And blast them they did.

With these first salvoes of shells the Prussian Guard practically ceased to exist. But the survivors, displaying fanatical bravery, still came on, almost to the very muzzles of the guns, only to run into a withering rifle fire.

This was the end of the Prussian Guard attack; human flesh and blood could stand no more. The Guard wavered, halted and finally turned and fled. Two battalions, the 1st Northamptons and 2nd Oxfordshire Light Infantry, lay in cunningly-sited ambush positions in the wood; the Oxfords and Northamptons were fresher and more affluent in manpower than most battalions and both were spoiling for a fight. The luckless Prussian Guard floundered helplessly about among the trees; the machine-guns got them, the rifles got them, the artillery got them, the bayonets of the Oxfords and Northamptons got them.

For the Prussian Guard it was total, humiliating defeat. The result of their attack was a gain of some 500 yards of ground which, from the military point of view, was completely useless and had cost the Kaiser the flower of his army.

True to their traditions, few of the Prussian Guard allowed themselves to be taken prisoner. One officer of the Guard who was captured had started the attack with fiercely switchback moustache of the 'Kaiser Bill' type and a monocle screwed firmly into his left eye. Now his moustache drooped forlornly, and his monocle had been trampled into small pieces. He surveyed the guns of the 2nd Division and the thin, ragged and filthy line of riflemen.

'Where are your reserves?' he asked Major Clark.

'There are no reserves.'

'But what is behind you?'

'Divisional Headquarters,' said Clark.

'And behind that?'

'The Channel Ports.'

'*Almighty God!*' said the Prussian.

CHAPTER TEN

The plight of one regiment differed little from another's in those first two weeks of November. The Germans continued to batter the meagre and indomitable line, forever seeking a vulnerable point. What little ground that they had won was only gained by prodigious expenditure of ammunition, followed by a reckless sacrifice of men. Much of this ground had almost literally to be wrested from the dead.

Let us examine the straits in which these British regiments found themselves.

The South Staffordshire Regiment had been in the thick of the fighting right from the start, and at one stage of the Ypres fighting the two regular battalions of the Regiment— the 1st and 2nd—found themselves billeted together as neighbours. There was a riotous get-together, with issue rum in mess tins and enamel mugs as essential fuel, and officers and other ranks compared life in South Africa with Aldershot: the officers of the 2nd envied those of the 1st because polo and shooting were plentiful and cheap in South Africa, but prohibitive in England unless you had an income of at least £500 per year (which very few officers of the South Staffords had); the soldiers of the 1st envied the 2nd because the beer in South Africa was bloody awful and bore no comparison with the heady, satisfying brew of Aldershot pubs, and they had to do route marches over miles of *veldt* while the 2nd had nothing to do except slope arms and form fours in Aldershot.

The reunion did not last for long, nor did the rum; for the South Staffordshire Regiment it was business as usual, and there was not a man in either battalion who was not fighting for his life every hour of every day and night.

From the very start of the Battle of Ypres the 2nd Battalion the South Staffordshire Regiment had been most continuously and bloodily engaged. They had stood fast against hordes of Germans, who outnumbered them by something like ten to one; they had been directly in the path of murderous shellfire that had torn great gaps in their ranks; they had marched incalculable distances and been flung into despairing counter-attacks which promised little save further crippling casualties.

Typical of these assaults was one carried out by 'B' Company, commanded by Captain John Dunlop. The objective was a farmhouse, clearly strongly held, from which a machine-gun spat bullets with deadly accuracy.

This farmhouse was typical of a hundred other objectives in the Ypres Salient. It never occurred to Dunlop that the farmhouse was of dubious, if any, tactical value; it was enough for him that he had been ordered to capture it. His orders to his two subalterns, Lieutenants Bartlett and Hume, were simple and unequivocal, and owed nothing to an extended military education at the Staff College at Camberley: 'We're going in ninth wicket down with a sprung bat, but that farmhouse will be the property of the South Staffords half an hour from now.'

And it was. Bayonets were fixed and, with Dunlop at their head, 'B' Company—just forty-strong—charged across one hundred yards of bullet-swept mud.

It was unfortunate for the Germans that Captain Dunlop was one of the most universally beloved officers of the Battalion—'one of the bravest was our Captain,' said Private John Jones, 'and as good as a father to all his men'. The company commander, still cheering and waving his men on, was shot clean through the heart, just twenty yards short of the farmhouse.

Fortunate indeed was the officer of the British Army who could inspire such near idolisation in the men under his command, and unlucky the Germans who came up against these men after they had killed such an officer. When the men of 'B' Company saw Captain Dunlop fall, they became fighting mad and tore into the Germans with bayonets and clubbed rifles.

The German machine-gun was put out of action, but not before it had killed fifteen Staffords in that charge across open ground. But the objective had been won: Lieutenant Hume, Sergeant King, one corporal, two lance-corporals and twenty privates surveyed their handiwork—thirty dead Germans and one captured machine-gun – with grim satisfaction, and many bayonets dripped with blood. 'This farmhouse is South Staffords' property,' said Lieutenant Hume, echoing his dead captain's words, 'and we stay here until we're relieved. Any man who can't stay in this position alive will stay in it dead. And those are the orders.'

And so the Staffords took up positions in trenches which had been hastily dug by God knew what regiment in the first place, lost to the Germans, recaptured at the point of the bayonet, lost again, speedily vacated and captured once more. Ownership of these trenches had never been certain for more than twelve hours at a time, but it was certain now: they belonged to the 2nd South Staffords.

Cunningly and insidiously the German gunners sought out these trenches, and soon the shells were coming over: the Staffords burrowed deeper into the soft mud as the hail of death poured down upon them.

The first salvo of shells was well over—'missed us by a bloody mile', remarked Sergeant King to no one in particular; the second fell short. But these German artillerymen knew their business, and the third concentration fell among the recumbent Staffords. When the smoke had cleared and the cries of the last wounded man were silent, Sergeant King surveyed his command.

A shell had killed Lieutenant Hume, who had taken a splinter neatly through the brain; fragments of men told what had happened to a lance-corporal and five privates.

'What are the orders now, sarge?' inquired a young private, who had joined the Battalion in sunny South Africa and fervently wished himself back there.

'The same as the late Mr. Hume gave,' said Sergeant King uncompromisingly. 'Now, shut your trap and watch your front.'

So they shut their traps—there seemed nothing to talk about—and watched their front. And on this front, monstrous grey masses of German infantry came looming through the rain over the slight crest half a mile in front.

Now there was no time for Sergeant King to give any

further orders; there was no time for scientific fire control. Every man of the platoon had but one duty to perform—to seize his rifle and fire as rapidly as he could at the advancing lines. Hands had only one function: to press the trigger, to work the bolt, to ram another clip of ammunition into the magazine.

And so the Staffords shot on, at the regulation speed of fifteen rounds to the minute, and swathes of grey dead piled up in front of the trenches. But the Germans seemed to have a bottomless well of manpower, and as one mass came on, was shot down and shredded away, there were more to take their place.

The German commanding officer was losing patience: this stubborn pocket of resistance, whose numbers he estimated to be at least one hundred plus two machine-guns, should have been liquidated long since. He therefore ordered a further concentration of artillery fire; after this the infantry would assault again and this would be the last time.

The final rain of shells put an end to this gallant little detachment; when the grey masses finally charged into the trenches, there were only seven South Staffords still on their feet and German bayonets extinguished all but their glory.

While this battle was being fought, the rest of the 2nd South Staffords were equally bloodily engaged: cowering in their shallow trenches under a rain of shells and beating off incessant German attacks.

The work of the Commanding Officer, Lieutenant-Colonel Davidson, resembled that of a man trying to keep in repair a dam which is being undermined. He had to be here, there and everywhere; ammunition had to be distributed and gathered from the pouches of the dead—and they numbered over one hundred; patrols had to be sent out to guard against a surprise night attack; wounded had to be got back to the Regimental Aid Post, a noisome place of healing in a shell hole, where the medical officer strove to save life by the feeble glimmerings of an electric torch with an almost defunct battery.

But while all this was going on, at least one third of Colonel Davidson's mind was occupied with 'B' Company, who were totally cut off from the rest of the Battalion and without any form of communication. During a brief lull in the fighting the Colonel despatched a subaltern and four men to find out what had happened to Captain Dunlop's 'B' Company.

They found only bodies—grey corpses, something like two hundred of them, in front of the trenches and others, khaki and grey, inside them. Two of them were in a particularly grotesque attitude: they had bayoneted one another and were skewered as neatly as two joints of meat in a butcher's shop.

There were only twenty khaki bodies and fragments of bodies—the entire detachment, and all that was left of 'B' Company. But one of these bodies stirred and spoke: it was the young private who had questioned Sergeant King's orders. To the subaltern he said: 'The line was held as ordered, sir'; then he gave a little fluttering sigh like a child in final abandonment of a jigsaw puzzle, and died. But the line had been held as ordered. . . .

And when the Staffords were in the line, it always was held as ordered, whether by the 1st Battalion (the old 38th) or the 2nd Battalion (the old 80th).

The South Staffords, like the magnificent Worcesters, were not a 'fashionable regiment'; the Regiment's soldiers came from that somewhat bleak and inhospitable part of Britain known as the Potteries—from towns like Burton-on-Trent, Wolverhampton, Walsall, Dudley and Smethwick, none of them a 'must' on an American tourist's list of places to be visited. But in the Ypres fighting they were rich in heroes, and from the 38th came the greatest South Stafford of them all.

Captain John Vallentin was the British regimental officer *par excellence*. He had fought in the South African War and braved Pathan bullets on the North-West Frontier of India. He had been wounded in the earlier fighting near Gheluvelt, but had refused to be evacuated; it was only when he lost consciousness that his company sergeant-major halted a passing ambulance and placed him in it.

When John Vallentin was first admitted to the officers' ward in the hospital at Ypres, it was comparatively sparsely populated, but not for long: as the battle gathered fury, they started to come in by the score—officers on stretchers, officers painfully hobbling, officers dying, officers already dead.

By November 6 his wound was the least of Vallentin's troubles—he had also developed dysentery and a high fever; the medical orderly, who had taken his temperature that morning, morosely confided that it was 102. Propped up on his pillows, his face gaunt and wasted, John Vallentin viewed the proximity of death with a calm appraisal. And if death was coming to him, which seemed very likely, then he would seek and find it with his father, mother, wife and child—the old 38th.

Vallentin searched the incoming wounded officers for a sign of the Staffordshire knot on a tunic collar or cap: he very soon spotted one, for the South Staffords had 'caught it' at Krusiek and had lost thirteen officers and 440 men in two days.

'Where will I find the battalion?' he asked one of these officers, who had both legs broken by machine-gun fire.

'Probably you won't,' returned the other pessimistically, 'there's damned little left of it.'

A medical orderly remonstrated with Vallentin and was consigned to hell for his pains; a medical officer was summoned and issued with similar instructions. John Vallentin was weak and shaking with fever, and his wound throbbed painfully. But his sword was in its frog, and he was once more ready for battle. He walked out of the hospital, hailed a passing ambulance and was driven back to the front. Vallentin returned to the 1st South Staffords, and was greeted by the survivors, some eighty in number, with vociferous enthusiasm; as pleased to see him as anyone was Second-Lieutenant Foster—proud as he was to be in command, he considered that command of a battalion should devolve on an officer somewhat senior to a nineteen-year-old subaltern just six months out of Sandhurst.

Vallentin, in fact, was not in command of one battalion but four: remnants of the Queen's, Royal Warwicks and Royal Welch Fusiliers had attached themselves to the Staffords. Some of the heart had gone out of these men—they had been told that relief was on the way, but there was no sign of it and it seemed that there never would be—but John Vallentin put it back. Drawing on some incredible reserve of strength, he seemed to be everywhere at once. He derided the faint-hearted, and saw to it that they did not remain faint-hearted for long; he directed the wickedly accurate fire which brought half a dozen German attacks to a stand-still and littered the ground in front of the position with dead; he led three bayonet charges. It was in the third of these charges, at the head of his men with his sword drawn, that he was hit by six machine-gun bullets: when he could no longer walk he crawled, and when he could no longer cheer his men on he whispered. In this manner Captain John Vallentin won the posthumous award of the Victoria Cross.

Sixty years later the story of the Angels of Mons must be considered to be apocryphal, although a few of the more vintage Old Contemptibles swear that they saw them; no one will deny them this little fiction, if fiction it be, because they are fully entitled to a little flight into fantasy if they feel like one.

The story goes that some soldiers of the 4th Royal Fusiliers, during a brief halt in the Retreat, had collapsed in a state of utter exhaustion by the side of the road. Waking suddenly from a drugged sleep; they saw angels standing over them: young women of startling and ethereal beauty, clothed in spotless white, and accoutred with actual wings. To the soldiers they spoke words of a wondrous comfort; God was with them on this fearful march and would see them through safely.

'So help me, Fred,' said a hundred-per-cent secular soldier of the Royal Fusiliers, who normally only worshipped God when his name appeared on church parade detail, and then unwillingly, 'I'll go to church more regular when we get back to Aldershot.'

'So will I,' said another fusilier, 'you saw 'em, didn't you, Fred?'

'I saw 'em all right,' said Fred with conviction, 'all dressed up in white—wings and all.'

'You never saw nothing,' said a third fusilier sourly; he had slept through this beauteous vision and believed in only what he saw, and then only when strictly sober. 'You was drunk.'

'Drunk on what?' said the first fusilier indignantly. 'I tell you, I saw angels.'

'And so did I,' said Fred doggedly.

There was nothing ethereal or angelic about the voice of the company sergeant-major which roared out of the darkness: 'On your feet, you lot, and get moving', but the story of the Angels of Mons had been born, and it has been a long time dying.

Major Arthur Roberts of the 2nd Queen's has another story to tell about angels, and this one is not apocryphal.

The 2nd Queen's was one of the battalions launched into the desperate counter-attacks after the recapture of Gheluvelt by the 2nd Worcesters, and they suffered fearful casualties. At the head of his company, Roberts was shot clean through the pelvis. He was left lying in the thick, gelatinous mud of a ploughed field, and the shocked exclamation of the stretcher bearer who found him—'Christ, sir, you're shot to bits'—was not reassuring.

In a red haze of pain, Roberts was borne back to the hospital from which John Vallentin had just discharged himself, and drugged to the limit of the medical resources available at the time. As the pain eased, Roberts slipped into a semi-coma and concluded, without dramatics, that this was death. Only a few days before he had been consigned to hell by a harassed and irascible senior staff officer in divisional headquarters, but he had obviously graduated to the alternative habitat, for by his bedside were two undoubted angels.

They were both dressed in white, although Roberts could not see that their raiment was liberally spattered with blood. Their faces were of startling beauty. While one dabbed his forehead with a cold compress, the other spoon-fed him apricots of a delicious succulence.

Arthur Roberts can be excused for thinking that they were angels. There were no angels in the hospital at Ypres, but they were the next best thing: they were Flemish nuns from the nearby convent.

What does the regimental band do in war? In peacetime as everyone knows, they produce music of exemplary perfection —on church parade, in the officers' mess on guest nights, at cricket week and athletic meetings, at tattoos at Aldershot,

Tidworth and Edinburgh; they play at village fêtes, Armistice Day parades and recruiting drives in market towns. If they are commercially minded, and their music is good enough, they find themselves at the 'top of the charts', as did the band of the Royal Scots Dragoon Guards in the enlightened year of 1973.

There were many bandsmen—trumpets, clarinets, trombones, euphoniums, fifes and flutes cast aside in favour of rifles—manning the front line trenches at Ypres. But in some infantry battalions, still comparatively strong in numbers (this meant that they could muster two weak companies), the men of the band were used in their traditional role, which was that of stretcher-bearers. Musicians forgot about music and concentrated on the succouring of the wounded.

One bandsman had already won the Victoria Cross—the redoubtable Drummer Kenny of the 2nd Gordon Highlanders, following in the footsteps of the legendary Piper Findlater, who had piped the Gordons up the Tirah heights in 1898. In the latter stages of the First Battle of Ypres two more men of the regimental band were to win the supreme award for valour.

Bandsman Thomas Rendle of the 1st Duke of Cornwall's Light Infantry had blown down a trombone in the regimental band since 1902; he had contributed to martial music, developing a man-sized thirst in the process, in South Africa, Crownhill and on the Curragh. It could fairly be said that in his formative years the trombone was Thomas Rendle's life, and in twelve years his conduct sheet had only once been defaced, for 'playing his instrument in a discordant fashion' at Wynberg, Cape Colony, in 1906.

Near Wulverghem, in late November, as every 'Contemptible' knows, the trenches were shallow and waterlogged; the 1st D.C.L.I. were shelled and attacked without cessation.

The role of the stretcher-bearer at Wulverghem, or anywhere else in the Ypres Salient, was every bit as dangerous as that of the front line infantryman and frequently more so; it was often said that nothing demanded a higher type of courage than stretcher-bearing. To carry a wounded man steadily over rough ground under fire, when a stumble or jar might be fatal, was all in the day's work for the stretcher-bearers and rarely came under the heading of 'conspicuous bravery'—their work was largely unseen and unsung, and officers were usually far too busy to write citations for gallantry awards for men who, in their own phrase, were simply doing a job of work.

During eight days of furious fighting in the trenches at Wulverghem, which were occupied by the 1st D.C.L.I., Thomas Rendle seemed to be motivated by an almost divine mission—to succour the wounded without thought for his own safety.

The German artillery had the range of the D.C.L.I. trenches and the shells from their howitzers were blowing in the parapets—killing men, wounding men and burying men alive. Any attempt to get out of a trench was to risk certain death, for the Germans swept the D.C.L.I. position with machine-guns and rifle fire.

Just how many men owed their lives to Rendle was never calculated: a man of tremendous physical strength, he heaved wounded men from the trenches as if they were sacks of coal —in civilian life, at the tender age of seventeen, he had served an exacting apprenticeship as a coalheaver, and this training stood him in good stead.

One officer in particular owed his life to Bandsman Rendle. Lieutenant Colebrooke had been hit in an artery of his thigh, from which the blood was spurting like water out of a reservoir. Rendle ran out to him under a hail of bullets, bandaged the wound and stopped the bleeding; and then, with the officer on his back, he crawled back to the Regimental Aid Post. For this, and many other acts of rescue of wounded, Bandsman Rendle was awarded the Victoria Cross. When he was on sick leave in Exeter a persistent, 'foot-in-the-door' newspaperman sought an interview; Thomas Rendle, like many another 'Contemptible', was unpromising material—the newshound had to be content with the statement, 'I was just doing my job, that's all.'

Another member of a regimental band won the supreme award for valour at about the same time, but Drummer John Spencer Bent of the 1st East Lancashires, unlike Bandsman Rendle, won his Victoria Cross as a hundred-per-cent combatant.

No one looked for qualities of leadership in Drummer Bent.

He was issued with a rifle and fifty rounds of ammunition and told by an uncompromising platoon sergeant: 'You can play with your drum some other time, me lad. Meanwhile, you're a rifleman—got it?' John Spencer Bent got it immediately, and together with the sergeant and twelve other men—all that was left of Number Four Platoon of 'B' Company—he fired his rifle into the oncoming hordes until it was too hot to hold.

On the night of November 1 to 2 Drummer Bent had a singularly eerie experience. He had lain down in a dug-out to snatch half an hour's badly needed sleep and woke up suddenly to find himself alone in the trench; thirty minutes earlier there had been thirty-five men in the trench, now there was only one—himself.

Bent assumed that, as he slept, orders had been received to retire to the second line of trenches behind their position. But who had given the order? There was no means of finding out: it seemed that he, Drummer John Spencer Bent, was all that was left of 'B' Company, 1st East Lancashires, and he could hardly be expected to hold back the whole German army by himself.

There was only one thing for it, Bent decided, and that was to get out of it himself. But at that moment a figure came round the traverse, and Bent pushed forward the safety catch of his rifle. Might as well take one Jerry with me before I hook it, he thought.

But it wasn't a Jerry, it was Sergeant Jelks, the platoon sergeant, and Sergeant Jelks was clearly out of temper; he had been forward to company headquarters and had been told that there would be no retirement. So he had come back and, instead of finding thirty-five men in the firing line, there was one half-baked bloody drummer who seemed intent on murdering him.

'Who's that?' demanded Sergeant Jelks.

'Drummer Bent, sarge,' said Bent, recognising the Sergeant's voice with the faint sinking feeling in his stomach which sergeants' voices always seemed to induce in him.

'Where are the rest of 'em?'

'Dunno, sarge—hooked it, I reckon.'

'What the 'ell d'you mean, hooked it? What are you doing here?'

Whatever else he charges me with, thought Bent, it won't be deserting my post because I'm the only bloke here. 'I was having half-hour's kip, sarge, and when I woke up there was the rest of 'em gone.'

'Well, go and get the buggers back here,' said Sergeant Jelks testily. 'Orders say no retiring, so get 'em back here at the double—got it?'

'Got it, sarge,' said Drummer Bent, and set off into the darkness.

Bent found the remnants of 'B' Company in another trench, just fifty yards behind their original position. It seemed that someone—no one knew who—had heard the order 'retire', and obeying some herd instinct (there were no officers or senior N.C.O.s left in 'B' Company) they had gone back. In the grey words of the Army Act they were all guilty of 'shamefully abandoning their posts', but there was no time to think of that: another crushing German infantry attack was imminent, and every man was needed.

If anyone had told Drummer Bent before the war that he would ever command anything, he would have spat (literally or metaphorically) and uttered a rude word. But to his own amazement he found that he had qualities of leadership; his voice brooked no disobedience, and only one man queried Bent's order, 'We're going back.'

'Who says so?' asked a Private McNulty, who disliked drummers on principle.

'I say so,' said Bent. 'Come on, move yourselves.' And they did.

They got back just in time. Sergeant Jelks just had time to say 'Good lad' to Drummer Bent before he took a bullet through the brain.

At this stage of the First Battle of Ypres second-lieutenants in command of battalions, sergeant-majors in command of squadrons and lance-corporals in command of platoons had become comparatively commonplace. But surely in only one infantry battalion—the 1st East Lancashires—was a rifle company commanded by a drummer.

'Command doth make actors of us all' — if there were near-farcical elements about Drummer Bent's early tenure of command there was nothing farcical about his handling of the remnants of 'B' Company in the fighting that followed. The other privates of 'B' Company were happy enough to leave the command to Drummer Bent; clearly, here was a good man to die with, as many of them did.

He even found time to save the life of a wounded man. Private McNulty, who had earlier seen fit to question Bent's authority, was hit in both legs and left lying in open ground. Bent crawled out to McNulty, hooked his legs under his armpits and in this position crawled back to safety. Afterwards McNulty said to Bent: 'I take back what I said about drummers.'

'Any bloody fool can be a rifleman,' said Bent modestly. 'It takes time to make a drummer.'

The Highland Light Infantry, although their conduct was not invariably perfect in peacetime stations, had a fighting record since they arrived in France which was nothing less than splendid. Their Divisional Commander, Major-General Monro, paid them an extravagant compliment: 'This battalion has never failed in any situation which it has been called upon to face. There is no position which the Highland Light Infantry cannot capture.'

This adulation was fully justified near Becelaere on November 10. In shallow trenches reposed Sergeant MacInnes and thirty men of the 2nd Highland Light Infantry—all that was left of 'B' Company. Supporting them was the battalion's machine-gun section, commanded by Captain Walter Brodie.

Thirty yards in front of them was a trench, infinitely superior to the one they now occupied. During a more peaceful phase of the battle the men of 'B' Company had dug this trench, and rightly regarded it as their property.

This particular trench had changed hands three times: the H.L.I. were driven out of it by a German attack; in a furious counter-attack they won it back, with Corporal 'Sixty' Smith very prominent, only to be driven out yet again. The H.L.I. were often known as 'the regiment that never lost a trench'—now they had lost one, but not for long.

Their present trenches were scratchy, the weather was vile and for the past two days the Germans had delivered infantry attacks without cessation. The men of 'B' Company did not like it at all, the permanent defensive into which they were forced. It did not suit their temperament.

In 'B' Company was one Private MacFie: it was said of MacFie that he had eyes like a cat, and prior to his enlistment he was reputed to have earned a precarious living as a burglar in Glasgow. On this day MacFie's 'watery een', as Sergeant MacInnes described them, were to be used with devastating effect.

Only MacFie saw the shadowy shapes advancing on the forward trench. A private is not normally empowered to issue orders to the machine-gun section, but MacFie's yell of 'Jerries! Let 'em have it!' caused the machine-gunners to pour a fusillade of bullets into the gloom.

Nor did British Army officers normally go into action armed with rifle and bayonet, but Captain Brodie confessed to being a poor shot with a revolver and to date had only used his sword as part of an archway outside a church at a brother officer's wedding. He therefore ordered the machine-gunners to keep up the fire and positioned himself at the head of 'B' Company.

'This is where we get our trench back,' he declared. 'Follow me!'

The H.L.I. went into those Germans like a knife into butter. It was a charge in the best H.L.I. tradition, and although, as a regiment, they were not famed for the number of prisoners they took, on this occasion seventy Germans surrendered; the rest were killed, mostly with the bayonet, for the loss of eight killed and twenty wounded. Brodie himself was credited with having killed eight, and for his courage and leadership was awarded the Victoria Cross.

These were some of the deeds which won their doers the Victoria Cross, although in the First Battle of Ypres it was said and written, accurately enough, that for every V.C. won twenty more were deserved.

Quite different is the simple little saga of a soldier of the 1st Northamptons who won no gallantry award and was mentioned in no despatches. It concerns The Man With The Tea.

A battery commander of field artillery emerged from behind a hedge where his guns were sited. But these guns were now silent and useless, because every shell had been fired and there was no possibility of getting any more.

The battery commander was tottering with fatigue, for he had not slept for three days and nights; his ears were ringing and he had, he suspected, a perforated eardrum. He positioned his gunners in holes and ditches and instructed them to sell their lives dearly, for there could be no going back. Then he surveyed the scene in front of him.

The meadow ahead showed a positive tornado of bursting shells with earth spouting up from the edges of huge craters. The noise was stupendous: the tearing-linen rip of shrapnel and the express-train roar of howitzer shell. To the battery commander it seemed that nothing could possibly live in such an inferno. Then he saw The Man With The Tea.

He was a smallish man with slightly bow legs, and he stumped along through the mud, singing tunelessly, 'She was poor but she was honest'. To the battery commander, a keen racing man in happier days, he looked exactly like a jockey entering the paddock before a race. In each hand he clutched a large metal container.

The battery commander said, 'Hey, you! Where the hell d'you think you're going?'

The soldier stood to attention and jerked his head over his shoulder. 'Northamptons, sir,' he said, 'got their tea.'

The battery commander gazed across the fiery inferno ahead. 'Are you going out there?'

'Don't like the idea much, sir, but if I don't the blokes won't get their tea. Counting on me, they are.'

'A damned unhealthy spot,' said the battery commander.

'Don't I know it, sir. Permission to carry on, sir, please?'

'Carry on. Er. . . .'

The Man With The Tea anticipated the battery commander's thoughts. He produced a chipped and battered enamel mug from his pack, dipped it into one of the dixies and handed it to the officer. 'Have a cup yourself, sir,' he invited, 'but if you don't mind, sir, I'd like the mug back when I get back. I'll be off now, sir.'

The battery commander found that he had difficulty in speaking. 'Thank you,' he said, 'and good luck.'

In peacetime the battery commander was an officer who appreciated the good things of life: he was equally at home with dry sherry, gin and angostura, gin and vermouth; Bollinger and claret; cognac and vintage port. On this day he desired nothing more than that potent brew, often called the 'staff of life', which was known as 'gunfire'.

The battery commander rose to command a brigade of field artillery before the war's end and became a major-general. He did not acquire many souvenirs from the Great War: the D.S.O., the M.C., six pieces of shrapnel in various parts of his body—and one enamel mug, for The Man With The Tea did not come back. . . .

On November 6 the British Army lost an officer who would have undoubtedly attained the very highest rank, Sir John French lost an irreplaceable member of his staff, and the 2nd Life Guards lost their commanding officer: they were one and the same man—Major Hugh Dawnay.

Although it was always within sound, and frequently range, of the enemy guns, the atmosphere at Sir John French's Headquarters closely resembled that of an Edwardian house party. French was on Christian name terms with all his staff officers, many of whom had served with him in the South African War, and he had a paternal way with all of them. For their part, each vied with the other in his devoted loyalty to 'the Chief', as Sir John was invariably called.

Like a boys' schoolmaster who has his favourites French had his, although no staff officer would ever have thought so. One of his 'favourites' was Major Hugh Dawnay of the 2nd Life Guards.

French regarded Dawnay as one of his undoubted stars—a very up-and-coming young officer who, if he lived, would undoubtedly achieve the highest rank in the British Army. Dawnay was French's liaison officer with the 1st Corps, a job of tremendous responsibility, and without him French would have felt partially crippled, as at the loss of some of his fingers: hard-working, courageous, tactful and one hundred per cent trustworthy, Hugh Dawnay was a gem indeed.

It was painfully clear to French, however, that Dawnay's heart was not in his work.

In no way was it outwardly apparent but French, who knew soldiers (particularly cavalry officers) better than most men, sensed it at once: Hugh Dawnay's heart was not in General Headquarters, it was with his regiment, the 2nd Life Guards.

There were other staff officers of the same mind; others, again, were appreciative enough of the fortunes of war which had put them in appointments where they could eat and drink well every day, ride a horse and sleep between sheets at night. It came as no great surprise to Sir John when Dawnay approached him and asked to be allowed to return to his regiment. The 2nd Life Guards had taken a fearful pounding and officer casualties had been particularly heavy.

As in every regiment of the Household Brigade, the casualty list read like the guests at a London society wedding: Major Lord John Cavendish, Captain the Honourable R. Wyndham, Captain Lord Hugh Grosvenor, Captain the Marquis of Tweeddale, Captain the Earl of Caledon, Lieutenant the Honourable Alastair O'Neill.

Sir John French listened to Hugh Dawnay's request with sympathy as one cavalryman to another, but told him that it was his duty to stay where he was. He reminded Dawnay of the highly important work he was doing so well and that it would be most difficult to replace him in his appointment. With this Dawnay had to be content; he knew better than to question an order given by 'the Chief'.

But next day Dawnay repeated his request with great earnestness. He told French that he could never be happy or contented in his mind if at this juncture he did not take his place in his old regiment. He was, in fact, finding it increasingly difficult to live with himself.

French gave way, although he afterwards admitted to weakness. But it would have been impossible for any soldier to refuse such a request, or fail to understand and enter into Dawnay's feelings.

The last day of Major Hugh Dawnay's life was also one of the happiest.

He had been speeded on his way with a warm handshake from Sir John French, and a number of other senior staff officers at G.H.Q., all of whom had the uncomfortable feeling that they were seeing Hugh Dawnay for the last time. They were mostly men of few words, but they all knew in their innermost hearts that French had done the right thing. As a result of Sir John's firm directive that no more Guards officers would return to their regiments, officers thus affected kept their feelings to themselves: if officers of the Household Brigade had to keep on dying at the present rate, then that was what they drew their pay for. Such was the uncomplicated reasoning of Guards officers.

A morose-looking groom who, before the war, had worked for an exclusive livery stable, trotted out a horse for Dawnay's onward despatch to the 2nd Life Guards. ' 'E ain't much to look at, sir,' he said to Dawnay apologetically, 'but 'e's a 'andy little 'orse.'

'I don't doubt it,' said Dawnay, as he swung himself into the saddle; at this moment he would have ridden a mule, a camel, a bicycle, or walked.

The groom watched their progress sadly: he would dearly have liked to have given Major Dawnay a better mount than this melancholy steed, which ambled sedately out of the yard and down the road. But before he had gone fifty yards the horse's head had come up a little and he was walking more collectedly, looking as if he had regained the spring of former days. For on his back was a man who was born and bred to horses and their ways.

Hugh Dawnay returned to the 2nd Life Guards and was accorded a rapturous reception from both officers and men. He could not have arrived at a better moment from his own point of view, for the 2nd Life Guards and the Royal Horse Guards were hurled into one of those counter-attacks which amazed both the Germans and Sir John French. Major Hugh

Dawnay was killed, leading the 2nd Horse Guards in a bayonet charge, just four hours after assuming command of the Regiment.

The 1st Battalion the Connaught Rangers had been in the forefront of battle since the commencement of the war, and still were in the First Battle of Ypres: they would have felt grievously insulted had it been otherwise.

Like the Highland Light Infantry, the Connaught Rangers sometimes caused garrison commanders and military policemen to blanch when they appeared in a peacetime station. They were universally known as 'The Devil's Own', not less for their prowess in battle, and the terror with which they struck the enemy, than for the reputation which the Rangers acquired with men of more sedate units of the British Army. As an officer of the Regiment neatly phrased it, 'The Rangers always put in some very plucky work with the elbow in the wet canteen.'

There is good reason to believe that it was of the Connaught Rangers that their fellow-Irishman, the Duke of Wellington, made his famous and oft-quoted remark, 'I don't know what effect they'll have on the enemy, but by God, they frighten me!' For all that, 'the Iron Duke' never hesitated to call upon the 88th when a situation looked desperate, and the regiment never failed to justify his confidence. And the reputation won in the Peninsula was maintained and enhanced in the murderous engagements of the First World War.

November 7 found the Connaught Rangers holding trenches in Polygon Wood. Like the Highland Light Infantry, the Rangers did not take kindly to the permanent defensive position into which they were forced. They wanted a generous issue of rum and then to be launched into a bayonet attack. There seemed little prospect of either.

The weather was vile and the German attacks came in without cessation; the trenches were scratchy and inadequate, and in one of these reposed the large bulk of Private Patrick Grogan. His presence there requires some explanation.

The Connaught Rangers were what is known as 'a tough mob':

whenever they found themselves in peacetime stations these belligerent 'neutrals', with none of Britain's enemies to fight, fought other regiments—preferably Scottish ones or, in the absence of Scots, cavalry.

'There was a row in Silver Street,' Rudyard Kipling has told us in his barrack-room ballad economically titled 'Belts', 'that's near to Dublin Quay, between an Irish regiment an' English cavalree.' Clearly it was no ordinary brawl for it 'started at revelly and it lasted on till dark; the first man dropped at Harrison's, that last forinst the Park'. Although 'Belts' is a work of pure fiction, there is almost certainly a germ of truth in the theory that the Irish regiment involved in this gory punch-up was the Connaught Rangers.

On a glorious morning in June 1914 Lieutenant-Colonel Abercrombie read a charge sheet in his orderly-room which looked depressingly familiar: it stated that Private Patrick Grogan was charged with being absent from roll call on the 21st until 0330 hours on the 22nd, a period of five hours and thirty minutes; with being drunk; with assaulting an N.C.O. in the execution of his duty.

The evidence was uninteresting, as such evidence usually is. But a little light relief was provided by the sergeant of the guard on the night of the 21st who gave his evidence with an eye of positively indigo hue. This, then, was the sergeant who had been assaulted in the execution of his duty.

The Colonel perused the conduct sheet in front of him—a monumental document, liberally embellished with red ink—and sighed inwardly: in spite of himself, he had a sneaking affection for Private Grogan and if the Connaught Rangers went to war he would be an undoubted asset. But in the meantime N.C.O.s and the public houses of Aldershot must be protected.

Private Grogan departed from the orderly room, headed for a period of durance vile where there was little to eat, nothing to drink and scant sympathy: he had had his 'fifth drunk', and was faced with the prospect of being discharged as 'incorrigible and worthless', as the grim words of the Army Act described a soldier of his calibre.

But the war came just in time, and the 1st Connaught

Rangers, with the very considerable addition of Private Grogan (who was on strict probation and officially barred from any rum issue) sailed for France: there was no discharge in a war, incorrigible and worthless or not.

An order to retire did not immediately reach the 1st Connaught Rangers and would have been universally unpopular if it had for the Rangers were shooting down the Germans in heaps and had every intention of continuing to do so.

During lulls in the attacks, which were few and far between, Private Grogan, even without benefit of alcohol, treated the world to an impromptu concert. He had a resounding bass voice, and in peace stations (when he was not in the guard-room) he was much in demand at regimental concerts: it is even recorded in Connaught Rangers' lore that he was actually released for an hour and, flanked by two escorts, performed in front of the Colonel-in-Chief of the Regiment himself.

The attacks on the Connaught Rangers became more savage and annihilating every minute on the afternoon of November 7 and they could only have one end: shells rained down upon them and they were raked with machine-gun fire from one end of the slender line to the other.

In the early evening, as dusk was falling—a favourite time for German attacks—a burst of firing along the line proclaimed an all-out assault, intended to liquidate this stubborn pocket of resistance once and for all. The Germans reached the Rangers' trenches and got into them, and though they were twice driven out the battalion was forced to retire. Grogan's trench was more or less unconnected with the others, and the Germans passed it by. But the sergeant in charge rightly realised that it could only be a question of minutes before it became untenable.

'Get out of here,' the sergeant ordered Grogan and the other two Rangers, 'and join up with the battalion in the trenches behind.'

The other two men obeyed with alacrity; whatever it was like farther back it would not be any worse than their present position. Grogan, however, did not move; with his bayonet fixed to a rifle which was almost too hot to hold, he was watching a traverse of trench round which the attacking Germans must come.

'Are you coming back?' demanded the sergeant.

'I am not,' said Grogan, 'not if the King himself ordered me.'

The sergeant left it at that and departed; at the outbreak of war he was nearing the end of his service and looked forward to a hard-won civilian life. Life was dear and pension was near; if Grogan wanted to be a dead hero then there was very little that he could do about it.

No sooner had the other men departed when a German rounded the traverse, and with a howl of pure joy Grogan hit him with the butt of his rifle. From that moment he went berserk: he hurled himself over the traverse and found himself surrounded by Germans. Roaring like a bull and twisting his rifle round his head like a cane, Grogan fell on them.

It was only when he had killed seven—three brained with his rifle butt and four more with the bayonet—that Private Grogan deigned to rejoin his section. He had a gash across his forehead, four teeth missing and his bayonet dripped.

'Where the hell have you been, Grogan?' demanded the sergeant aggrievedly. 'There were Germans in that trench a few minutes ago.'

'So there were, sergeant dear,' said Grogan composedly, 'but they were not liking it, so they went. . . .'

CHAPTER ELEVEN

They bore little resemblance to a victorious army; indeed, they scarcely resembled an army at all.

They had lived in the same trenches for three weeks on end, fighting off continual attacks, subjected to murderous shell-fire round the clock, and every day—indeed, every hour—saw fewer men in the trenches.

Many of the infantry positions were dug above natural springs, with the result that the trenches were frequently knee-, sometimes thigh- and even waist-deep in water, and un-drainable. Dead men lay, and often floated, in these trenches, and between the dead and the living there was no sharp dividing line. Wounded men often waited for as long as eight hours before they could be evacuated, and of these many, on their arrival in hospitals, were tersely categorised as 'dead on arrival'.

Of all the categories of casualty, that of 'died of wounds' has always been the cruellest and saddest. 'Killed in action' was often comparatively quick—the quick bullet through the heart or brain or total obliteration by a shell; 'wounded in action' could mean anything from the amputation of both legs to a self-inflicted bullet through the big toe or a cursory peppering of shrapnel. But 'died of wounds' usually applied to a casualty who, if speedily evacuated and treated, might have lived.

It was impossible to keep warm; they were all frozen to the bone and could not make a fire (even if there had been sufficient firewood or matches) because it would have drawn the enemy guns. Hot meals or drinks were out of the question: they drank the stagnant water in their trenches and ate biscuits and minute portions of bully beef if they were lucky and nothing if they were not.

Their stomachs were shrunk and straining for food; they were begrimed with vermin which throve on filth; the smell of them blended vilely with the stench of corpses in front of their positions; they would have bartered their souls for a single luxuriant draw at a cigarette, but there were none—for many soldiers, in both World Wars, this was worse than being hungry and thirsty. All right, they said, so there's no tea and precious little grub. But some fags would come in handy.

In places the line was so thin that there was one man, a hollow-eyed ghost of a man, for every seven yards of front; in others there was a line of shallow pits, each containing two similar-looking ghosts, at intervals of fifteen yards. Here and there were gaps of thirty, forty or fifty yards, and into these gaps were flung infantrymen, cavalrymen, gunners, sappers, A.S.C. men; fit men—if there was such a thing—sick men and wounded men. Even dead men had their uses, and many of them had to wait a long time for burial: when there was no time and probably no tools with which to dig graves, a corpse, whether it were that of a man or a horse, provided a rampart from which to fire. Some officers and N.C.O.s, emulating the fictional and sadistic Colour-Sergeant Lejeune in *Beau Geste*, propped dead men, their rifles at the ready, against the parapet to give the impression of greater strength.

There were no war correspondents at Ypres, but Frederic Coleman, an American, was the next best thing. Finding himself in England at the outbreak of war he had volunteered, together with a score of members of the Royal Automobile Club, to take his car to France. He was by no means a typical American of the period, for the United States did not demonstrate a marked interest in a war which seemed to be no direct concern of theirs. Coleman, however, took a more exalted view and in this respect he closely resembled another great American, Quentin Reynolds, who sweated out the Blitz in London in 1940. 'I am an American,' said Coleman simply, 'and I have believed from the commencement of the war that the Allies' cause was just.'

Coleman saw the men of Ypres and described them thus: 'They were a terrible crew; they were like fierce, wild beasts.'

'Like fierce wild beasts'—it was no bad description: a cornered or wounded animal—tiger, leopard, panther or wild pig—is sullen or fierce, according to its temperament. There were sullen and fierce men in the front line at Ypres, and both were equally to be dreaded as fighting units. Whether they killed with a lustful joy, half-wildly or with the deadly matter-of-fact calm of desperate determination, killing had become the one paramount business, and never ceased for long.

There were a few men, but only a very few, who had succumbed to the frightful physical strain and were broken past all recovery: when the very skies seemed to rend apart with flame and pour down a deluge of thunderbolts, as the ground below rocked and heaved to endless concussion, so did exhausted nature snap and break and men went mad with the shock and horror of it. But not even these few — some cursed and raved, some giggled idiotically, some just stared fixedly in front of them — left their trenches, because there was nowhere else to go. And mentally unhinged as some of them were, they would not have left anyway — not as long as they had a rifle, ten rounds of ammo and 'one up the spout . . .'

The root cause of the stand at Ypres was that unpopular word of the 1970s — 'discipline'. 'Go on,' growled a vintage sergeant of the Coldstream Guards to a grumbling young Guardsman, 'moan about old-fashioned bull and baloney and Guards discipline if you like. But that's what kept us there. An' put that bloody 'at on straight . . .'

Asked a nervous young Scots Guardsman of his sergeant, as the shells rained down and the sections to right and left of him were buried alive, 'What'll we do, sarge?' To which the sergeant replied uncompromisingly, 'Look to your front and stop talking.'

And the young Grenadier, peering mesmerised at a wall of field grey which seemed almost on top of them, said: 'Getting 'orrible close, ain't they? When do we fire?'

'When you're told,' said the sergeant tonelessly.

The German failure to break through to the Channel Ports is not easy to account for. They had everything in their favour: overwhelming superiority in numbers of men and guns; ample space in which to manœuvre these vast forces; the opportunity to replace tired men with fresh ones. To keep up continuous and unremitting attacks against a stubborn enemy requires a crushing preponderance of artillery, followed up by fresh, well-fed and eager battalions of assault infantry; the Germans had all of these things. The British had nothing save guns and the old-fashioned discipline which told them to hold on without support or hope of relief; not the discipline of fear as practised in the German Army, but the discipline of respect for a system; the respect of the led for the leaders—the high proportion of officer casualties in the B.E.F. bore out this hypothesis over and over again.

By present-day standards, discipline in the old British Army was severe, if not occasionally actually brutal. True, the soldier no longer feared the lash, the normal deterrent prior to 1881, when flogging was abolished. But dirty cavalrymen were forcibly scrubbed in horse troughs in icy water with hand scrubbers; idle drummer boys ran the risk of six of the best from the drum-major on the bare rump; misdemeanours were sometimes corrected by senior N.C.O.s without any reference to company office; soldiers sentenced to a spell in detention barracks rarely went back to sample it a second time. There was the possibility of Field Punishment Number One—the malefactor was tied by hands and feet to a gunwheel in an attitude of crucifixion—and even the firing squad for cowardice or desertion in the face of the enemy.

In the First Battle of Ypres, however, there were certain signs, not quickly discernible to the private in his hole in the ground, that this discipline was, in its outward form at any rate, becoming slightly relaxed: platoon and company commanders lived in holes in the ground as well—battalion headquarters sometimes enjoyed the luxury of a strip of tarpaulin. Small human incidents here and there bore out this theory, although not a single soldier of the B.E.F. would have admitted it, and it served only to strengthen the basic discipline which brought victory to the Contemptibles at Ypres.

Between officer and man in the peacetime British Army there was a wide social gulf: the officers, according to their financial means, rode, hunted, shot, fished and played polo; the other ranks, again according to their current monetary status, smoked, gambled, pursued women (with or without matrimonial intent—usually without) and drank beer—they would not have had it otherwise and felt no envy for their officers.

Officers met the other ranks on parade, on manœuvres and

in the company office—the meetings in the last-named venue were invariably of a brief and chastening nature. They met on the football, rugby-football and cricket fields—an officer who did not play games with his men was immediately suspect and was considered to be spending his off-duty hours unwisely (as he probably was). They ran against one another at athletic meetings and hammered each other to pulp in the boxing ring.

They met convivially on Christmas Day, when the officers had pressed upon them drinks of at least ninety per cent alcoholic content. They had, however, never got together in filth and misery until the First Battle at Ypres.

First Ypres was a great social leveller. Brigadier-General Sidney Lawford, a man accustomed to doing himself well whenever possible, never enjoyed a drink more than the enamel mug full of issue rum which he shared with a corporal in his headquarters; Lieutenant-Colonel Louis Bols, Commanding Officer of the 1st Dorsets, had a weakness for Oxo— he found a cube of this precious commodity and personally prepared hot drinks for the men in battalion headquarters; Captain Dorrington of the Royal Dragoon Guards discovered a fortuitous slab of chocolate and walked from one muddy hole to another, giving a piece to every man of his troop; incredibly a large fruit cake appeared in the mail for Captain Victor Fortune of the Black Watch, and in the absence of any pay he held a 'cake parade' for the seventeen men left in his company.

At Ypres the officers and men became more *gentle,* although gentle was not an adjective normally applied to the British soldier of 1914. It was at First Ypres that the word 'chum'—a word lightly used in 1974, but never among Old Contemptibles—first acquired its real meaning. In the Old Contemptibles Association, still a live body sixty years later, every member, whether field-marshal or private, carries the appellation 'chum' before his name.[1] On all sides in the stinking holes which went by the name 'trenches' could be heard the comfortable words of the 'Contemptibles' and the word 'chum' was the most comfortable of all:

[1] Including Field-Marshal Montgomery.

'Lean on me, chum . . .'

'Have a swig from my bottle, chum . . .'

'Want a draw off my fag, chum?'

'Won't be long now, chum . . .'

On burial details there were very few chaplains to read the funeral service; graves were dug—the regulation 'six feet of earth'—and as often as not the body was tipped in without ceremony, with the accompanying farewell, 'In you go, chum —God bless.' Many a soldier has had a worse epitaph.

But these bedraggled scarecrows, who stank so vilely and seemed to be scarcely human, *were* the victors—let no one make any mistake about that: they had, by sheer guts and brilliant musketry, humbled the flower of the German Army —Saxons, Bavarians, Pomeranians, Brandenburg Grenadiers, Westphalians and the redoubtable Prussian Guard.

As November 18 dawned, the defenders of Ypres stretched their cramped limbs, scratched themselves, swore roundly, searched morosely and largely fruitlessly for fag ends, speculated bitterly on the non-arrival of tea. Then they charged their magazines (with one up the spout) and waited for the normal morning hate—the inevitable deluge of shells which had heralded each dawn since the Battle of Ypres had started. Then would follow the infantry attacks—the Prussian Guard had surely not given in this easily. It was the beginning of another ordinary day at Ypres, a humdrum day of horror.

But something seemed to have gone wrong this morning: no shells came over, only the depressingly familiar stench of German corpses which the wind wafted into the trenches. Some of the more pessimistic soldiers theorised that the enemy no longer thought it worth wasting shells to soften up the defenders; they would push the infantry straight in and finish the job once and for all.

In the waterlogged trenches, all along the line of the 1st Corps, speculation ran riot:

'What the hell are they up to?'

'Think they've packed it in?'

'Not bloody likely; the bastards'll be coming again soon.'

Yet, amazing to relate, no German infantry attacks materialised on that day or the next, although the smell from the bloated

213

and blackened German dead became worse hourly. The B.E.F. were, by this time, immune to any sort of foul smell and gave themselves up to the blissful knowledge that they were neither being shelled nor attacked. But this was unnatural: the attacks *must* come in again. A sullen, brooding silence hung over the entire front.

Soon rumours were circulating among the men that the Jerries really had had enough at last—rumours which were heavily discounted by officers and sergeants, who insisted on a greater than ever alertness to repel fresh attacks. Of course, it couldn't be true....

But it *was* true, and on the morning of the third day, November 20—the day which marked the end of the First Battle of Ypres—some men of the 1st Highland Light Infantry (always one of the B.E.F.'s more optimistic battalions) essayed a cautious cheer; there had been nothing to cheer about in the past month, and two days' freedom from shelling and infantry attacks seemed good and sufficient reason.

The cheering was taken up by the 1st Northamptons, 2nd Oxfords and 1st King's: all three battalions were in jubilant mood, for their musketry had contributed generously to the slaughter of the Prussian Guard; the Green Howards struck up a good Yorkshire song, and the Camerons, not to be outdone, gave a rendering of 'Loch Lomond'. The cheering gradually spread along the entire length of the line in a roaring crescendo of sound.

For now there could not be any room for doubt: exhausted, filthy, verminous but indomitable, the 'Contemptible Little Army' had beaten the mighty German Army.

The battle had been won, but at a hideously high price. Excluding the Indian Corps, whose casualties in British officers and Indian soldiers were mounting fast, there were eighty-four battalions of infantry in the B.E.F.

Let us examine the state of some of the Infantry battalions. As in almost every war, the Brigade of Guards were hardest hit of all: the 1st and 2nd Grenadier Guards could barely muster two companies, and weak ones at that; the 1st Scots Guards had Captain Stracey and sixty-nine men; the Coldstream Guards had all three regular battalions at the front—

the 1st numbered 150 other ranks, but not a single officer; the 2nd and 3rd fared slightly better but, like the Grenadiers, they could barely find two weak companies; at first sight the 1st Irish Guards seemed comparatively well manned with eight officers and 390 other ranks, but they had been virtually wiped out, rebuilt and almost wiped out again. The 1st and 2nd Life Guards and the Royal Horse Guards consisted of approximately the strength of one squadron still on their feet.

The kilted Highland regiments were easily recognisable, but there were tragically few kilts to be seen. The 1st Gordons had little opportunity to add further battle honours to the Regiment's superb record, for they had tragically taken a wrong turning in the early fighting round Mons in August and were captured practically *en masse*; the 2nd fared better, but on November 20 they numbered barely 300 of all ranks.

The 2nd Argylls had suffered 500 casualties—about half the original battalion strength; the 1st Black Watch consisted of Captain Victor Fortune and 109 men; the 1st Camerons had their commanding officer, Lieutenant-Colonel McEwen, one company commander, Captain Ernest Craig-Brown, and 140 men.

A look at the County regiments revealed the same melancholy story: here was a company of the 1st Loyals, reduced to a subaltern and eight privates; the 2nd Welch had one of their companies slashed from 130 to sixteen in half an hour of murderous shelling. The 2nd Queen's, 2nd Royal Warwicks, 1st South Staffords and 1st Royal Welch Fusiliers had been formed into a single battalion.

Every battalion's nominal roll was an appalling document, but none more so than that of the 1st Queen's: this battalion had been wherever the fighting was most deadly from the very start—at Mons, on the Marne and Aisne and in the Retreat. Battalions reduced to companies, companies to platoons, platoons to sections—these were commonplace situations throughout the 1st Corps, but the 1st Queen's were in a special category of misfortune.

The 1st Queen's had started the Battle of Ypres with only 150 effectives; these included Captain Aldworth and ninety-five men, the battalion's *sixth* detail of reinforcements—all the previous drafts were dead, wounded or prisoners.

The Commanding Officer, Lieutenant-Colonel Beauchamp Pell, desperately wounded, died in German hands; no officer of the rank of major or captain remained; the theory, to be put forward later in the Great War, that the life expectation of a front-line subaltern was a fortnight had, in the case of the 1st Queen's, worked out hideously well. It was left to Lieutenant John Boyd to take command of the battalion and, accompanied by the transport sergeant as second-in-command, he called the roll.

It did not take long. Battalion Headquarters posed no problems because it had received a direct hit from incendiary shells which killed or wounded every man in it. Boyd found that his command totalled thirty-two, and was made up as follows: 'A' Company—two corporals, two lance-corporals, twenty privates; 'B' Company—four privates; 'C' Company —two privates; 'D' Company—one lance-corporal, one private.

The melancholy round-up of infantry battalion strength at the conclusion of the Battle of Ypres read as follows: excluding the Indian Corps, there were eighty-four battalions in the B.E.F. Of these nine could muster between 300 and 450 all ranks; twenty-six could raise 200 or 300; thirty-one numbered between 100 and 200; eighteen were almost literally decimated, and less than 100 answered their names at roll call.

The endless quotation of casualty figures can represent an embarrassment to a commander, an unnecessary application of salt to wounds of the bereaved, and a downright bore to a reader sixty years later. But the figures must be set down here as a testimony to Haig's 1st Corps in the First Battle of Ypres. Haig was not universally popular in Great Britain in the later stages of the war—his conduct of the Somme battles was described by one of the more colourful military historians as the 'blood-letting of a mad military surgeon'—but everyone, soldier and layman alike, gave him honour for First Ypres.

Killed (including died of wounds and death from other causes): 127 officers and 1,666 other ranks; wounded: 316 officers and 7,669 other ranks; missing (including prisoners): 74 officers and 3,663 other ranks; total: 517 officers and

12,998 other ranks. Reduced to their simplest terms these figures indicate that the 1st Corps had lost rather more than half of their original effectives. German casualties at this stage of the war—the best and most practical tribute to our fighting men—were never published in reliable form, but the estimate of a quarter of a million can be taken as a fair one and, if anything, an understatement.

As Winston Churchill said in the Second World War, it was not the beginning of the end but it was the end of the beginning. The battered and exhausted remnants of the B.E.F. were relieved by the French and went into rest billets. They posed few problems for billeting officers, for their numbers were so very few.

Just why the Germans did not press home their advantage has never been, and probably never will be, satisfactorily explained: it seemed that they only had to brush aside the last thin line of khaki, march on the Channel Ports and mount an invasion of Great Britain. They did not do so because men like Stewart Hawkins and Paddy Smythe stood in their way.

They were both out there right from the beginning, Hawkins with the 2nd Life Guards and Smythe with the 3rd Coldstream. They went out in August 1914 and were still out there in November 1918. Between them they acquired five bullets, a dozen pieces of assorted shrapnel and about half a cylinder of poison gas. In the Second World War the British Army was only outdone by the Americans in the prodigal issue of medal ribbons: Africa Star, Italy Star, Burma Star, Pacific Star, Atlantic Star, Air Crew Europe Star, Defence Medal, Victory Medal. The Americans had medals for joining up at all, crossing the Atlantic Ocean to Great Britain, the Purple Heart for being wounded; Occupation Medal (Germany and Japan); European Theater of Operations, Asiatic-Pacific Theater of Operations, Air Medal, Soldier's Medal, National Defense Service Medal and so on and so forth. A well-travelled British or American serviceman, without necessarily ever hearing a shot fired in anger, could sport a chest like the High Priest's breastplate.

Hawkins and Smythe received just three medals each: 'Pip, Squeak and Wilfred', as the 'old sweats' style the 1914–15

Star, the General Service Medal and the Victory Medal; the last two, awarded to the later arrivals to the slaughter, were known colloquially as 'Mutt and Jeff'. These were the only outward and visible signs on the left breasts of men who survived a four-year holocaust in France, Italy, Egypt, Palestine, German East Africa and Mesopotamia.

To be entitled to 'Pip'—and the ranks of the holders of this medal are thinning every year—a man must be at least seventy-seven years of age in the year 1974. 'Pip' is a very special medal; across the red, white and blue watered ribbon is a thin silver bar, bearing the inscription 'August 5th–November 22nd, 1914'.

'The Mons Star', as it is universally known, is rarely to be seen on a uniform today only on the left breasts of a very few of the more vintage members of that peerless host, The Corps of Commissionaires, hall porters and club servants of great antiquity, who are on the inventory of the premises where they work. A sharp eye will discern on the ribbon of the 1914 medal a small silver rosette, similar in size and design to the gold rosette on the 1939–45 Star of the Second World War which was awarded only to the pilots who fought in the Battle of Britain. The similarity is appropriate enough, for they saved Great Britain at the beginning of two World Wars.

'Stew' Hawkins and Paddy Smythe, Mons Star men both, are in their eightieth year. Paddy Smythe recently went into somewhat fractious retirement from the post of 'Lollipop Man' as a busy children's crossing in Aldershot. Motorists learned to give meticulous hand signals on approaching this particular crossing and slow down to an apologetic crawl; for Paddy Smythe—every inch and indeed every foot a Coldstreamer—in his white coat and dark-blue peaked cap tended to favour motorists with a baleful, parade ground stare. With his 'Lollipop' labelled 'STOP' he was as resolute and immovable as he had been at Ypres sixty years before. The children all called him Paddy and knew that there were always packets of sweets in the pockets of his long white coat.

'Stew' Hawkins recently retired from his civilian trade as a house painter. Ten years ago he was apt to be a little cantankerous at times and given to explosive utterances about the modern generation; he looks a little like Alf Garnett, and sometimes sounds like him too. In his local pub one night one of his targets, looking straight at 'Stew', said, 'Hitler was a house painter, and look where it got him.' Stew's rejoinder was of such all-embracing violence—and he looked and sounded more like Alf Garnett than ever—that two middle-aged ladies precipitately left the bar. The landlord told Stew that if he made any more remarks like that in the presence of ladies he would be barred from the pub. But "Stew" is benign and mellow in the year 1974, a year in which income tax at forty-one pence in the pound, shoulder-length hair on males, £20 a week for private soldiers, three-day working weeks, Social Security and the Pill are supposed, separately and collectively, to make sense.

Ask Paddy Smythe and "Stew" Hawkins about First 'Wipers' and they will shrug their massive shoulders, produce wry grins, and say, 'We just done what we was told, that's all.'

Perhaps, after all, it was as simple as that. . . .

BIBLIOGRAPHY

Frederic Coleman: From Mons to Ypres.
Field-Marshal Viscount French of Ypres: 1914.
Ernest Hamilton: The First Seven Divisions.
Robert Blake: The Private Papers of Douglas Haig.
Beatrix Brice: The Battle Book of Ypres.
C. S. Forester: The General.
A. Corbett-Smith: The Retreat from Mons.
A. Corbett-Smith: The Marne—and After.
'Sapper' (the late Lt.-Col. H. C. McNeile): The Lieutenant. And Others.
Field Marshal Lord Wavell: Allenby.
Gilbert Frankau: Three Englishmen.
Gilbert Frankau: Royal Regiment.
Ian Hay: The First Hundred Thousand.
The Times History Of The War.
H. W. Wilson and J. A. Hammerton: The Great War.
P. C. Wren: The Man Of A Ghost.
John Masters: Bugles And A Tiger.
John Terraine: Mons.
The Old Contemptible—Official Organ of The Old Contemptibles' Association.
Lieutenant-General Sir James Willcocks: With The Indians In France.
Anthony Farrar-Hockley: Death Of An Army.
Peter Verney: The Micks.
A. J. Smithers: The Man Who Disobeyed.
Bruce Marshall: Only Fade Away.
Mr. Punch's History of the Great War.
Histories of Every Regiment of the British Army (1914–1918).
John Giles: The Ypres Salient.

VOYAGE OF THE DAMNED

GORDON THOMAS AND MAX MORGAN-WITTS

On 13th May 1939, the luxury liner *St Louis* sailed from Hamburg, one of the last ships to leave Nazi Germany before World War II erupted. Aboard were 937 Jews – some had already been in concentration camps – who believed they had bought visas to enter Cuba. The voyage of the damned had begun.

Before the *St Louis* was halfway across the Atlantic a power struggle had developed between the corrupt Cuban Immigration Minister who had issued the visas and his superior, President Bru. The outcome: the refugees would not be allowed to land. In America the Brown Shirts were holding Nazi rallies in New York, and Father Coughlin was making impassioned, anti-Semitic speeches to an audience of fifteen million. In Europe, the final solution was about to be implemented.

And aboard the *St Louis*, 937 refugees awaited the decision that would determine their fate.

'Gripping and compulsively readable'   *Sunday Express*

CORONET BOOKS

A BRIDGE TOO FAR

CORNELIUS RYAN

To follow THE LONGEST DAY and THE LAST BATTLE here is the best of Cornelius Ryan's three books about World War II – the story of one of the most fascinating yet terrible battles of all time.

'Unquestionably the most brilliant account of a battle which I have ever read'

Lt. General Sir Brian Horrocks, *The Spectator*

'The whole book is a remarkable performance by a master craftsman. He has written popular history in the best sense of the term, a narrative that is sure to captivate a huge audience of readers'

The New York Times

'Presented with absolute mastery of the situation. Magnificent'

A. J. P. Taylor, *The Observer*

CORONET BOOKS

THE SERGEANT ESCAPERS

JOHN DOMINY

One of the most courageous and dedicated of the British POW escapers during the Second World War was Warrant Officer George Grimson, who, with his fellow NCOs of the Royal Air Force, was imprisoned at the notorious camp at Heydekrug on the Baltic. Here, fired by a determination to defy the Germans, the NCOs gave their captors no peace. From the foolhardy and disastrous escapes of their early imprisonment their plans developed in sophistication and ingenuity. The inspiration behind their attempts was George Grimson. Grimson himself finally succeeded in the most daring escape of all – and went on to create an escape route through enemy country with safe houses from Heydekrug to Danzig.

The author, himself a POW and an eye-witness to the Grimson escape drama, has written an unforgettable tribute to those remarkable and heroic days.

CORONET BOOKS

AVAILABLE FROM CORONET BOOKS

All these books are available at your local bookshop or newsagent, o
can be ordered direct from the publisher. Just tick the titles you wan
and fill in the form below.

Prices and availability subject to change without notice.

....

CORONET BOOKS, P.O. Box 11, Falmouth, Cornwall.

Please send cheque or postal order, and allow the following fo
postage and packing:

U.K. – One book 19p plus 9p per copy for each additional bool
ordered, up to a maximum of 73p.

B.F.P.O. and EIRE – 19p for the first book plus 9p per copy for the
next 6 books, thereafter 3p per book.

OTHER OVERSEAS CUSTOMERS – 20p for the first book and 10
per copy for each additional book.

Name...

Address..

....